the sailing
misadventures
of two

Innocents
at Sea

Praise for Innocents at Sea

"[When] Jim McCracken and his wife, Betty, went to sea for the first time, they knew nothing about sailing. The errors they committed, sailing from Maine to Long Island Sound, are hilariously highlighted by the author. Neither he nor his wife seems to give a hoot that the joke was on them."

—HOLGER LUNDBERGH, *Yachting*

"This is by all odds one of the most enjoyable and delightful things I have read in many a day. It is simply wonderful."

—THE REV. DR. NORMAN VINCENT PEALE

"Although I've journeyed by dog-team, sampan, oxcart, and with camels, yaks and elephants, rarely have I travelled with more delight, and more trepidation too, than when I went voyaging with Betty and Jim McCracken in their Innocents at Sea."

—LOWELL THOMAS, *CBS Radio Newscaster and Adventurer*

"A thoroughly enjoyable, unpretentious story of day sailing on the Long Island Sound and along the New England coast. McCracken makes no false claims for his seamanship and is quick to admit and illustrate his errors. Many weekend captains will be able to identify with McCracken's book."

—SAUL J. AMDURSKY, *Library Journal*

"This is a delightful book. Even if you are not a boating enthusiast, you will find these reminiscences of a man and his wife and their sailing weekends and vacations—on Long Island Sound, off the coast of Maine and waters in between—humorous, exciting, warm, gentle, and bruising."

—JAK MINER, *The Christian Science Monitor*

the sailing
misadventures
of two

Innocents
at Sea

by James A. McCracken

Custom Communications
Saco, Maine

about the author

Jim McCracken was born in Sewickley, Pa.; his wife, Betty, in New York City. They met during their undergraduate days at Allegheny College and went to sea shortly thereafter. Fortunately, the sailor was also an author who was able to turn the radio adventures of *Boston Blackie* and the *Cisco Kid*, for which he wrote 600 scripts, into down payments on his yachts. He was also a senior editor at *Reader's Digest* for 25 years, and originated the concept for a series of articles on the human body, *I Am Joe's Body*, which proved to be one of the most successful series of articles in magazine history.

Published by Custom Communications, 7 Paul Avenue, Saco, ME 04072
(207) 286–9295. E-mail: custom@desktoppub.com.
Web site: http://www.desktoppub.com

Printed in the United States of America. This is a revised edition of "Innocents at Sea" © 1976 by James A. McCracken.

Library of Congress Cataloging-in-Publication Data
McCracken, James A.
  Innocents at sea : the sailing misadventures of two at sea / by James A. McCracken—Rev. ed.
    p. cm.
  ISBN 1-892168-09-X
1. Atlantic Coast (U.S.)—Description and travel. 2. Yachting—Atlantic Coast (U.S.)
3 Sailing—Atlantic Coast (U.S.) 4. McCracken, James A.—Journeys—Atlantic Coast (U.S.)
5. McCracken, Betty—Journeys—Atlantic Coast (U.S.) I. Title.
  F106 .M26 2003
  910'.9163'4–dc21   2002155829

Design, Typography, and Setup: Custom Communications

Photo Credits: Front and back covers, pp. iii, vii, 27, 49, 90, 130, 174, 203, courtesy of Carol McCracken; p. v, courtesy of Sue Killebrew Jenkins; pp. x, 8, courtesy of Ann Riley, pp. 169, 171, courtesy of Richard Howison; p. 173, courtesy of Mark Rowe

10 9 8 7 6 5 4 3 2 1

Sterling Killebrew

To Sterling,
who now sails seas
unknown to me.

foreword

a few changes

It is with joy that "Innocents at Sea," my father's legacy, is reprinted in paperback for the first time ever. Originally printed in hard-cover 27 years ago, the book quickly sold out and was never reprinted. I don't know why. The only change to this edition is the inclusion of photographs from our family album.

Rereading "Innocents" from time to time as I have over the intervening years has been bittersweet. I laugh all over again at my father's funny tales as though hearing them for the first time. I wince as I remember some of my parents' more dangerous misadventures. They sailed the New England coast just as fiberglass boats became available and before sophisticated ship-to-shore communication systems had come on the market. They couldn't have afforded such luxuries even if they had wanted them.

There have been a few changes since the book's publication in 1976. After his retirement from *Reader's Digest* in 1975, Dad wrote human interest stories for the magazine. That is also when he seriously began work on "Innocents." In writing this book, he relied on my mother's detailed diaries, in which she had recorded tides, winds, the course they followed, and other pertinent information.

My parents retired to Damariscotta, Maine, in 1980. Although Mom was born in New York City in 1914, she had strong roots in Maine. Her mother and older sister were Portland natives. As long as there was a good golf course nearby and he could follow the Pittsburgh Steelers, Dad was relatively

Jim and Carol McCracken, motoring into Mamaroneck Harbor, New York

content. He died in December 1987 in Damariscotta, and Mom followed in August 1999 in Portland.

I always admired my father's writing talent greatly. That will never change. I always was in awe of my mother's courage and strength under duress. That will never change either.

I hope you enjoy this book as much as I have.

> — *Carol McCracken,*
> *Portland, Maine,*
> *Spring 2003*

acknowledgments

To Edward W. Ziegler, for discovering it; to Bruce Lee, for encouraging it; to Andrew W. Williamson, for examining it with a mariner's sharp eye, the author expresses his sincere gratitude.

in praise of susan gold

When in the spring of 2002, I decided to reprint "Innocents at Sea," I knew the person I wanted to do it; Susan Gold, owner of Custom Communications. The book speaks for itself better than I ever could.

More than ten years ago, I first met Sue when she was editing a community newspaper here in Portland. Writing intrigued me and so I joined the staff as a volunteer writer and eventually became photographer as well. During the course of a few years, I developed a high degree of respect for Sue and for her skills.

She taught me about writing and photography and in such a diplomatic manner that I never felt judged or inferior because of my inexperience. She played no favorites. This went a long way toward eliminating conflicts and kept the monthly production of the paper humming along smoothly. She backed her writers and praised their work for articles especially well done. Sue knew her role, and she performed it to perfection.

Praise for Sue comes easily and naturally. So it's no wonder she'd be my choice to reprint "Innocents." I wanted someone no less talented than she is to reprint my parents' legacy. Probably they are nodding their heads enthusiastically!

— Carol McCracken

contents

The Rileys and friends aboard their gaff-rigged boat, the vessel used to rescue the McCrackens in their first of many misadventures

one

step to the music

Why do people sail? What makes all the labor, expense, concern, fear, frustrations—all these and more—worthwhile? Each person has his own answer, consciously or unconsciously arrived at. One man sails because "it gives me the only escape from pressures and crowds"; another because "in my boat, the demands on me are made by the elements. Those I can meet head on." Also, "a boat beats owning a cottage, with grass to mow and gardens to tend." And at the other extreme, there's the sheer risk of it. Despite all his precautions, a man's vessel may betray him. And the most meticulous care cannot fend off the unknown. Sailing not only provides citified man with a chance to pit his wit and nerve against nature, it may at any moment force him to. Under his keel lie things he fears, and out of the sky come other things he fears. So what is the sense of it? Where the irresistible attraction?

The man sits at the tiller, his body moving easily with the roll and pitch of his ship, the tan of his hands and arms and torso whitened by a flash of salt spray. The jib luffs and he brings the bow a bit off the wind. Now the jib is asleep again and his eyes flick through the doors of the companionway, down to his cabin, which glistens with brown mahogany and white paint, to the row of books on the shelf above his bunk. His eyes stop at a particular book. His mind opens it to a page and there is the answer. Thoreau said it. Henry D. Thoreau of Walden Pond. He lived beside a little pond, not the vast ocean, but he knew freedom. "If a man does not keep pace with his companions, perhaps it is because he hears a different drummer. Let him step to the music he hears, however measured or far away."

The man on the boat smiles a satisfied smile and settles back against the combing. The music is here; it is not distant at all, for its tune and its cadence are heard in the slap of waves against the sides of his ship, the creak of a block and the tap of reef points on the sail above his head. This is the music he hears; it is the only music he wants to hear.

As nearly as can be determined, it was in the fifth century A.D., that the story of the three princes of Serendip was born. These three princes, sons of the ruler of Serendip, a country now known as Ceylon, were sent out into the broad world by their father to find a secret formula, one which the king believed would rid the seas around them of frightful dragons that snatched sailors off the decks of their ships. The brothers ventured forth to search foreign lands for the magic formula, and strange and wonderful experiences which they could not have imagined and did not seek came to them. Hence the word "serendipity," which Webster's defines as "the gift of finding valuable or agreeable things not sought for."

Unlike the three princes who took to ships, my wife, Betty, and I took a cottage one summer and, serendipitously, found ships.

The place was Mere Point, a small peninsula deep in Maine's Casco Bay. Betty had cousins in Maine and we had spent brief periods there on the oceanfront, but that was to be our first protracted stay and the prospect was an exciting one. The cottage, large enough for Betty and me and our two children, was situated on a low bluff not more than 50 feet from the blue waters of the bay.

"White Plains, New York, was never like this," Betty sighed, as she gazed out over the grandeur of the water and the distant islands shimmering in a purple-blue haze. We could hear the faint hum of an outboard motor; a sail spotted the water, like a small white moth on a blue curtain. A fresh breeze blew in our faces off the sea, and white-capped rollers dashed themselves to destruction on the beach below. Two or three hundred feet from shore a small sailboat tossed its mast to and fro as it tugged at its mooring tether. Betty and I held hands, enchanted by the beauty of it all, and even our children paused in their busyness. It was all we could have hoped for.

"Oh, there you are," a woman's voice hailed us from the open door of the cottage at our backs. "I thought I'd better come out from town to show you around." The owner of the voice turned out to be the owner of the cottage, and in a brisk five-minute tour she showed us the kitchen, utensils, tools, bathroom, bedrooms, pumphouse, storage space for linens and blankets, gave us the name of the plumber and the telephone number of the fire department.

"There's a good vegetable stand just down the road and the stores in Brunswick can supply you with anything you might have a need for. I'm going traveling this summer so I won't be around, but I understand you've met the Rileys, three houses down, and Tim and his wife can give you any help you might need."

We thanked her, and then, as she turned to go, she added,

"That little sloop moored out there. She's a Snipe. If you've a mind to do any sailing, the sails are in a bag in the shed. She'll take you out and she'll bring you back—*if* you're a hand at sailing a boat."

She turned and was gone.

A week or so later Tim and Ann Riley dropped by for a visit.

"Have you taken the Snipe out yet?" Tim asked.

"Snipe? What's a—oh, that little boat. No, we haven't even given it a thought," I confessed.

"Should think you'd enjoy it," Tim said. "I've got a cat-boat an' I take her sailin' every chance I get."

In a moment we had pencil and paper out and Tim was busy diagramming and explaining the rudiments of a sloop, the function of a centerboard, and how to put the sails on. With arrows indicating wind directions, he explained how a sailing vessel moves upwind and down. Betty displayed her keen interest in all this by discussing children, menus, and dress shops with Ann. Any sailing instincts she might have inherited from Maine ancestors were so far well concealed.

"Just one thing I might add," Tim said. "When you do go out for the first few times, I'd advise not goin' out in a northwest breeze. She's on the puffy side an' you might just end up in the bay."

I was engaged in writing radio scripts in those days, and I usually knocked off in midafternoon to go swimming, mow the lawn, or just idle around with Betty and the kids. But Tim's enthusiasm for sailing had had its effect. Two or three times I rowed a little pram out to the Snipe, sat in her cockpit, and studied her. Sure, why not? Nothing complicated about it. If I could drive a car, I could sail a boat.

Now, instead of being content to gaze out at other boats sailing in fine breezes on the bay, I gazed at "our" boat out there tugging at her mooring line, beckoning, beckoning us to be up and gone. The wide, blue Atlantic was out there. Columbus, Magellan, Sir Thomas Lipton. Shades and spirits of the Vikings and John Masefield and the China clippers and the great whaling ships. "Venture forth!" voices seemed to call. "Shed your earth shackles. Down to the sea in ships!"

And, of course, the day came.

It was one of those beautiful "Maine days." Square-rigged clouds sailed the cerulean skies, the sun shone, the sea sparkled, whitecapped rollers raced.

"Great sailing day, Betty."

No answer.

"How about going out?"

"Wel-l-l—"

"Nothing can happen. I know I can handle it—Tim showed me."

"Can you keep it from tipping over?"

"Of course. Anyway, just take a look at that boat sailing around on the bay. It's a beautiful sight. We can be out there doing the same thing, instead of just sitting here."

"Okay, but if I drown, my blood will be on your hands."

"People who drown don't bleed. They just—"

"Stop! I'll go."

At roughly three-thirty we cast off. It wasn't quite so easy as I had thought. We backed and filled and fell off and rounded up. Ropes, as I called them then, got tangled with the anchor line and wrapped around our legs. But at last a blast of wind struck the little boat and off we scudded, on our beam ends and terrified.

"Take me home," Betty urged.

"I can't. We're headed in the wrong direction—toward Spain."

Suddenly there was a lull. The wind became soft and

gentle. The Snipe righted herself and once again it was a silver-white-and-blue day with the sun winking in and out behind pillow-soft cumulus clouds.

"Boy, this is really it," I exulted.

"Maybe, but it seems to me we're getting pretty far from shore. Do you know how to turn around, or back up?"

"Sure. All I have to do is push on the tiller, the boat will come around into the wind and then head back home."

"Well then, why don't you just do that? It's getting along toward suppertime and the kids don't know we're out here."

"Okay, just watch." There was time for no more. We were sitting ducks. The wind struck. Suddenly we were gasping for air in the frigid waters of Casco Bay and blinking at the barnacled bottom of our capsized Snipe.

"You were saying something about the tiller?"

At least I think that's what she said. My mouth and ears and nose and eyes were full of water. "Just hold onto the bottom of the boat," I managed to sputter.

"That sweater I'd just about finished for you—I brought it along to work on—it's gone. The sneakers I just bought—gone. *And I'm freezing to death!*"

We held on for dear life. How long could we stay alive in this water? Suddenly I was aware of a brown face, with warm, liquid eyes staring at us.

"Shark!" No—cocker spaniel. No cocker spaniel in his right mind would be swimming around out here. "Look—a s-seal!"

"I've already seen two of them," Betty answered. "We're in a sea of seals!" And it seemed like it. They would rise, one or two at a time, stare, then disappear.

Where? Do seals eat people? Do they bite and slash like sharks? I wanted to take Betty in my arms and tell her I loved her, adored her, that she was too good for me, that I was a rat to have brought her out here. I thought of our children—our beautiful children, about to become orphans. What a way to go, freeze to death in the middle of a summer vacation!

"Hey—a boat!" Betty pointed behind me.

I turned. Sure enough, a beautiful white sail was looming up, scarcely a hundred yards away. Quickly the boat closed on us, and 30 or 40 feet away her bow swung around and up into the wind beside us.

"Ann," the man at the tiller said, "give me a hand here and we'll haul Betty aboard."

"T-Tim—Tim R-Riley!" I chattered.

Quickly they got Betty into the cockpit and threw a blanket around her shaking shoulders.

He turned back to me. "You ever hear about a northwest wind?"

"A northwest—holy smokes, we—we're out in a northwest wind?"

"Godfrey Mighty," he said disgustedly, "you don't even know one when it comes right up and knocks you down!"

Failure went to my head. The idea of sailing became an obsession. All the while my body stayed ashore my mind was going sailing. Where once it had taken an hour to mow the grass, now it took two. One hour to mow, one hour to gaze at the Snipe and dream.

The first practical step was to determine the origin and direction of a northwest wind. So. The sun rises out there, out in the ocean. I was sure of that, for Michael and I had observed it once, rising out of the sea. It was a memorable moment.

Standing together one morning with wisps of mist drifting off the water like smoke from a spent campfire, we had watched the great red globe move with awesome majesty from the depths of the mid-Atlantic Ocean. First there was a slash of fire, like a woman's lip. The pewter surface of the sea picked up droplets of vermilion. God needs no roar of engines, no

Ann and Tim Riley in 1987 at Tim's retirement party

clash of gears to shift his world around. A bird twittered. The
sound died in its throat. The sun rose quickly, to a fanfare of
pink and purple clouds. My son and I stood hand in hand. This
moment, I knew, would be forever.

"Dad?"

I bent down to the sturdy figure at my side.

We were suspended in a moment of gold. "Yes, my son," I
replied softly.

"Dad, if water can put a fire out, why doesn't the ocean put
the sun out?"

"What! Oh, I—"

A crow cawed. The engine of a fishing boat coughed,

cleared its throat, sighed, and rumbled into life. The lid of a rubbish can clattered. My son had brought the world back to earth.

So I knew where east was. And the sun would set back there, somewhere around Minnesota. North was up that way. A northwest wind would blow from about where that tall pine tree is. I explained this momentous discovery to Betty one evening as we sat on the bank looking out over Casco Bay. "So we just wouldn't go sailing when the wind is blowing from the direction of that pine tree," I finished.

"Okay," she answered reasonably. "But what if the wind is blowing from, say, the grocery store over there when we start out. And what if it then shifts to the pine tree when we're about a mile offshore?"

She had me. If the wind shifted around to that damn pine tree when we were out sailing, we'd just have to hope that Tim Riley was nearby.

But we did venture out again. And again. As the summer wore on we became proficient not so much in sailing as in capsizing and righting the Snipe. And when the early September morning arrived that saw us taking leave of the cottage on Mere Point—and the Snipe—we knew we would go sailing again. In a boat of our own.

two

new world, new lingo

In our career afloat, we were to own four boats and to sail them at every opportunity. There were week-day evening sails that, on hot nights, lasted sometimes until one or two o'clock in the morning. Of course, we were tired the next morning, and getting up and going to work was a chore, but those quiet, enchanting nights on Long Island Sound more than compensated for it. We sailed not out of Casco Bay, but out of Mamaroneck, a town 20 miles north of New York City. Sometimes the two of us sailed alone.

We would leave the steaming land at six o'clock or so, power out the channel, hoist sail, and move into the Sound. If there was no breeze, we had a swim, then a picnic supper, and ran on the engine. If there was a breeze, we crossed the Sound to Cold Spring Harbor, Hempstead, or Oyster Bay, munching on chicken or cucumber-and-lettuce sandwiches and making it all a bit tastier with a can of ice-cold beer.

Our first boat was a mistake. Instead of asking the advice of someone with boating experience, we made the choice ourselves. It was a 16-foot bucket that wouldn't go to windward at all and wouldn't sail off the wind very well, either. Her mainsail was old canvas stretched so badly out of shape it looked little different hoisted or in its sail bag. We didn't know about such things as poor sails, leaky seams, or dry rot, but we found out. Each time we went out it was the same question: "Do you want to bail while I sail, or do you want to sail and I'll bail?"

Innocents that we were, when we joined the Orienta Yacht Club in Mamaroneck, we not only did not know how to buy a boat or sail one, we couldn't even speak the language.

Every sport has its special names or designations for things, names with which the participants are entirely familiar, the general public less so. Baseball has its squeeze plays, hit-and-run plays. Football has its flair passes, split T, I formations, button hooks, down-and-out or down-and-in passes. But a football is still a football, sidelines are sidelines, goalposts are still goalposts. Bases are bases, the infield is the infield. *Ad infinitum.*

In boating, though, it's quite different. The rear end is not the rear end. The front end is not the front end. The floor is not the floor. Some people learn the lingo one way, some another. I began learning it my way. The hard way.

In our club we had a lean, dignified gentleman, elderly but agile. I called him "Commodore." He liked that. He encouraged it, in fact. He had been Commodore of the Club at one time. Again, in yacht clubs the head guy is not the president or the chairman (chairperson today). He is the Commodore. And it doesn't matter whether he has ever been in the Navy, the Coast Guard, or the Sea Scouts. He is the Commodore until the next guy comes along. Then the next guy's It.

Well, one day shortly after we got our very first boat, I happened to be fussing around the yacht club doing nothing of any consequence when the Commodore came along. He was going sailing. He invited me to go with him. Well! I assented, eagerly. When does a neophyte, a landlubber get to go sailing with such as he?

His boat was out in the harbor someplace, so he slung a sail bag or two at me (I think I ended up carrying all the sail bags) and we headed down to the float where he said his "dink" was tied up. A "dink," I was about to learn, is nautical for dinghy, the little boat that you row out to your big boat. So I slung (that's sort of nautical, too) the bags full of sails into the back end of the boat and crawled into the front end. The front end went pretty far down into the water, but I thought nothing of that. My companion ordered me out of "the bow" and into the "stern." So I moved all the sail bags into the front end, or bow, and sat myself down in the back, or stern. The Commodore sat on the middle board. He rowed, as was his right. He was captain of this ship.

"This is one nice little rowboat," I said. To make conversation.

He looked at me. "This is not a rowboat. This is a dinghy."

I wondered if all boats that you row around a yacht club are dinghies.

I didn't particularly care for my position in the stern. The Commodore would reach the oars 'way up toward the front in order to get a good grip with them in the water for the next stroke. But when he did so, he had to lean in my direction so that his face was within a foot of mine. I sat there and watched the wart on his nose come forward, then go back. Forward to me, then back, with each stroke. I never would have noticed that wart if we hadn't been so close.

And it was getting embarrassing, sitting there staring eyeball to eyeball. His eyes were brown. They had little red veins running through them. And they kept staring at me. No, it was more of a glare. It *was* embarrassing.

"We're here," the Commodore announced gruffly.

And we were. We came up beside his boat. I stood up. "Sit down! You'll have us in the water." I sat. He had a strong New England accent. People told me that the accent got worse, or stronger, as each year passed.

He got up on his boat and then I stood up. The dink was tippy unless you stood right in the middle of it. I handed him the sail bags and other things. I scrambled up onto his boat. I didn't do it as gracefully as he did. He took the dinghy around to the rear and tied it onto something there. Then he moved things around downstairs and finally came up to where I waited.

"Now we'll bend on the sails," the Commodore announced.

Bend them? I hadn't seen the sails yet. They were still in the bags. But sails were soft. Maybe his were stiff with salt from years of sailing and needed to be bent, twisted.

"What?" I asked.

"We'll bend the—oh, Lord. Just give me a hand here while I *attach* the sails to this stick here. This is the boom. You see that thing that stands up in the air? That's the mast!"

Well, I knew *that*. He seemed to be getting huffy.

"We have to attach the sail, this one here, to the stick that is horizontal. That's the boom. Then we have to attach it to the stick sticking up. The mast."

Okay, okay. I could help with that. I didn't help much, actually. I seemed to spend most of my time *under* the sail trying to fight my way out of it. But we did all those things. Then he tied the sails down, so they wouldn't blow away.

"If I had a good hand aboard, we'd sail out of the harbor. But with you..." He left it unfinished. This wasn't turning out quite the way I thought it would. Or like he thought it would, either.

"Now then, sir," he said, with a sigh, "do you know how to weigh anchor?"

I stared. The Annapolis midshipmen sang "Anchors Aweigh." Sure, I knew. They—but what *did* they do? They did not actually *weigh* anchors.

"When you weigh anchor, you haul it up," the Commodore was saying. "You go forward there—" (ah, forward) "—and take hold of that line. See that rope there? That's a line. A rope is always a line on a boat. *It is never called a rope.* Well, haul on that line and pull up the anchor. It will have mud on it. *Don't haul it aboard with the mud on it.* Dash it up and down in the water until it is clean and *then* bring it aboard." He said things so slowly. Distinctly. As though he were talking to a school kid. "While you're at that, I'll be getting the engine started." He turned away, but I thought I heard something about its being humiliating to have to "power" out of the harbor.

We got out of the harbor. He hauled the sails up to the top of the mast, then stopped the engine, and we started to sail. The wind was good and it was nice and cool. The boat bounced around a bit and it occurred to me I shouldn't have drunk all that milk at lunchtime.

"Are we going to sail up that way—to the left?" I asked eagerly.

"I am going to pa't, eventually," he answered.

What did *that* have to do with anything? This was one strange man. "Oh no, you won't," I forced a laugh. "Never!"

He *wheeled* on me. He spun around. Even with sneakers on.

"What!" It was a roar. It seemed to explode out of him. If he didn't watch out he would lose his dignity. "Do *you* mean *you* can prevent me from going to pa't?"

"No, no," I stammered. "I don't mean *I* can. *You* can." I didn't know where *I* was in this conversation, much less where he was.

The Commodore threw up his hands in despair. "Explain

yourself, sir. Will you try to do that? Will you go slowly now and explain yourself to me?"

"Yes—yes. I'll try." I wanted to put this as clearly as possible. "You said you were going to pot, eventually. I can't prevent you from doing that. But *you* can. By exercising, taking care of yourself you—"

"Good Lord." The Commodore sank to a cushion. He let go of the tiller and put his head in his hands. The sails began to shake. Sails, he might have told me, don't "shake." Finally he brought his face out of his hands. He didn't have a very good color. Stroke? Even his hands seemed to be "luffing." "Please. Now listen, I said pa't. P-O-R-T." They could have heard him in Mamaroneck. On the main street. With all the traffic. It was that accent of his that had fouled things up.

We messed around for a while. I tried to make conversation, but he didn't want to talk. He'd never met such a damn fool in his life. He didn't say it, but he didn't have to. Left is port. Right is starboard. You didn't just pull up the anchor. You weighed it. That sounds stupid. Even today. A rope is a line on a boat. Why? I don't know, but it is.

To top it all off, I got seasick. The only time I ever got seasick. And it was on the Commodore's boat. I hung over the side and tossed my cookies. But you can bet I didn't land them on the side of his boat. I nearly fell overboard being careful.

Later, I hustled down to the library in White Plains and got a book. I learned that the things that haul sails up and down aren't called "ropes" or "lines." They're called "halyards"! On a boat you don't go downstairs; you go below. Stairs in boats are ladders even when they lead *below*, not up. A little flag at the top of the mast isn't a flag. That would be too easy. It's a burgee. The bottom of the inside of a boat isn't the bottom; it's the bilge. "Bottom" sounds better. But don't call it that. If there is water in the boat, you've got water in the bilge. And the floor in the cabin, downstairs? It's not the floor. It's the cabin sole. If you want to know where the bathroom is, you ask for the "head." When a boat rocks back and forth, from bow to stern, it is pitching. When it goes from side to side—that's what made me seasick—it is rolling.

There are lighthouses and whistle buoys and all kinds of signals and things the Coast Guard maintains to keep you from running up on rocks or reefs or sandbars in a fog. But the ones you see most often are the buoys around harbors. The two most common types are those which are painted red and those painted black. The red ones are sort of conical. The black ones are like big trash cans. The red ones are called "nuns." I don't know why. I've never seen a red nun. Maybe they have some in Russia. Communists are called Reds, sometimes. But then nuns wouldn't be Communists. I just don't know about that. Black ones are called "cans." That makes sense. They actually look like cans.

Red buoys line one side of the channel of a harbor, black ones are on the other. And there is a good reason for that. You stay between those two lines. If you don't, you'll hit a rock. And do you know how to tell where the channel is? Where to stay so you won't run into a rock? There's something to remember. Keep the red ones on your left—port—when you're leaving a harbor, and the black ones on the starboard side. That may be confusing, so you can remember it this way: "Red right return." When you are coming into a harbor, keep the red ones on the right—starboard, damn it! Going out, red on the port.

Memorize that "red right return" business. A newspaper reporter, I believe he was, was once riding with the captain of a great oceanliner when the captain was bringing the liner into the harbor. The liner was the *Queen Mary* or some such. Anyway, the captain was steering, and he kept mumbling something, over and over. Finally, the reporter couldn't stand it any longer. If this man was talking to himself, maybe he wasn't quite the man to be doing this job.

"What in the world are you mumbling to yourself?" the reporter finally asked, with some concern.

"Eh? Oh—" The captain seemed a bit embarrassed. "I—I was saying 'red right return, red right return.' Funny, I've been sailing oceangoing vessels for 40 years and I'll be damned if I can remember which side of the channel the red ones are on.

Betty and I didn't learn all these things in a week, or a year. It took time, and a little embarrassment, to say "below" when we meant downstairs. And sometimes, in a particularly exciting time, we got mixed up, even after years of sailing. Like the time we were sailing into York Harbor, Maine, among the lobster traps. But that was my fault.

We never did say we were going to weigh anchor. We always just pulled it up. That is, when it didn't get fouled in a cable or an old automobile on the bottom. And we could never bring ourselves to "top off the tanks." That means filling the water tank or the gas tank. That's what they say. We always just "got some gas" or "got some water."

three

enter merrimac

So little did we think of that first boat of ours that we never bothered to put a name to her. She served us well, however. She taught us our finger exercises. She took us out on the water. We could smell the salt, feel the breeze, and watch the stars. She introduced us to the Sound, and her bow pointed out such exotic harbors beyond the horizon as Stamford, Bridgeport, and Port Jefferson. She never took us to those faraway places, for we never were foolish enough to ask her to. But we knew they were there, and the next year, with a larger, safer craft and more experience, we would go—and we did.

Those were the days of great hope and little money. We sold old no-name for what we could get for her and then began to haunt the boatyards. When the weekends came, it was never a question of what to do today. The only question was, Where shall we go to look? We could not possibly have described to each other precisely the boat we wanted, but somehow we were confident we would know when we found her.

It was a cold day in January. We had looked for a month and had come up with nothing; nothing, that is, that $800 would buy. It was a blustery Saturday afternoon and we were in the Orienta Point Boatyard, bundled to the teeth. A bone-chilling wind blew over the packed ice of Mamaroneck's West Basin. There were three or four inches of new snow on the ground and it whispered around the cradles of the huddled boats. We were the only souls in the yard that day, and some-how it was as though we were walking through a graveyard. The boat covers were shrouds and where the frames were not properly constructed, the covers sagged and the pockets were filled with snow. They looked like hulking, shapeless monu-ments—monuments to bright days of summer now dead and gone. Here and there where a line had parted or had not been properly secured a corner of a cover flapped dismally in the biting wind.

I don't recall which of us saw her, but down close to the edge of the ice was cradled a small white sloop. We walked closer and there, *nailed*, mind you, to her topsides was a "For Sale" sign. I guessed she was 22 feet or so (she turned out to be 23). Even on that gray day we could see that she had a flair to her and a sheer that was delight to the eye. We took in all of her lines at a glance, for this little boat stood alone at the ice's edge. She must have been the last boat hauled, probably as an afterthought, and nobody had bothered to put a cover over her shoulders.

We found a short ladder and climbed the three or four steps to her snow-covered deck. Not even the hatch cover had been closed properly. Well over a foot of ice and snow lay in her bilges. The companionway doors were closed by a hasp, but not locked, so we opened them and descended the two steps to her cabin. The doghouse afforded headroom of about four feet. Forward of the doghouse, it was only three feet. The cabin sole—three boards—had been pulled up and set aside, but one could see nothing of her rib ends, the keelson or keel bolts, hidden as they were by the snow and ice. One final touch of ignominy was a pair of worn-out work shoes that were frozen tight in the bilge ice.

Her power was an ancient one-cylinder engine. The head was amidships directly aft of the mast step. Two bunks were forward on either side. They weren't bunks, of course, simply panels of plywood sawed to a rough fit and set on frames. On either side of the cabin amidships were shelves covered with dirty and torn oilcloth. We gazed about us in silent dismay. The appalling slovenliness of some human beings.

Betty shivered in the damp cold.

"Like what you see?" I asked.

"Well, I like what I think she might be," she answered.

"Then let's go up to the office and find out what we can get her for, and if we can afford it, we'll get Sterling to look her over."

"Let's go," Betty answered. "I'm frozen."

The price was right. Well, it really wasn't right, but by emptying our meager bank account, preempting the few pennies in our young son Michael's piggy bank and assaying a loan from the kindly neighborhood banker, we figured we could swing the purchase—*if* Sterling approved of the boat.

Sterling Killebrew was a friend. He was a tinkerer and a putterer and a genius with wood or metal. Moreover, he was a top sales engineer for a large New York-based industrial organization. The Killebrews, Sterling, his wife, Connie, and their three children, lived in a large, comfortable, and rambling white clapboard house with lots of shade trees and lawn. But lawn, flowers, and shade trees were not Sterling's primary interests. His family came first; but then came his workshop. He always seemed to smile in his workshop. No matter how vexing or perplexing the problem, that little half-smile never completely disappeared, and from that cluttered, sawdust-*cum*-shavings-littered room emerged works of beauty and efficiency. He made tables, lamps, kitchen cabinets, picture frames, a veritable plethora of doodads and dohickies that were always beautiful to behold but sometimes of dubious use. Which didn't matter to Sterling; his joy was in the making.

Would Sterling come to the yard and look at "our" boat? Sterling would. One of the most useful and used tools in Sterling's workshop was an icepick, and, with this in his pocket, he and Betty and I arrived at the yard the next Saturday morning.

Beginning at the stem and working aft, he jabbed and picked and stabbed. So intent was he that at one point Betty murmured, "This boat may have floated last summer, but I sure don't want to be aboard when it's launched this spring."

At last he was finished. Mahogany planking on oak ribs. Sound as a dollar. (This wasn't yesterday.) What more can you ask? In the cabin Sterling gazed at the one-lunger of an engine, patted it on the cylinder head, and stated that he just knew *it* wouldn't give us any trouble. (It gave me a hernia.)

Long before winter ended our work began. Someone had made a clumsy attempt at fiber-glassing the outside of the doghouse and had failed. So Sterling, with me running errands, handing him tools, and paying out money at a terrifying rate, sheathed it all, and the sides of the trunk cabin as well, with mahogany plywood. We recanvassed the deck, fashioned a new bowsprit to replace the old one which had a touch of dry rot, and practically rebuilt the inside of the cabin. We took pains with that boat. We took them to the boat and took them home with us, pains and aches and cuts and bruises, abrasions and lacerations. But we were happy; worked like dogs, ate like horses, and most of the time looked like pigs in a hog wallow.

Spring came, and Betty and I turned to with sander,

caulking material, paint, and varnish. Winter covers began to be peeled off wooden frames of other boats and, like the Biblical voice of the turtle, sanders came to life and whined all through the yard. It was the season at last, and boating people were alive and stirring.

Late one Saturday afternoon Betty and I were totally absorbed in laying a piece of linoleum on a small counter-top in the cabin. It was painstaking work for us and we weren't aware of the lateness of the hour until the rays of the setting sun slanted into the cabin. I crawled out of the cabin, into the cockpit and stood up.

"Betty," I gasped. "They've launched us!"

A body catapulted into the cockpit. "What do you mean?" She stared in utter amazement. Our boat was almost afloat in fully three feet of water. Only the fact that the boat was suspended a full foot above ground by the cradle prevented us from going to sea. We learned later that this was a "spring" tide, an oddity that seems to occur only when the moon rises as the sun sets, a condition that only God and other experts seem to understand. Water had already risen into the yard 50 feet beyond us, and as we observed bottles, empty paint cans, seaweed, kelp, and a miscellany of sodden cardboard cartons float by us, it was apparent that the tide was still rising. The yard was quiet; we were the sole survivors in a darkening and watery world.

"How deep is it?"

"Well, there are five rungs on the ladder and only two are showing, so it must be three feet."

"And this morning I noticed ice chunks floating around—." Betty's voice trailed off.

Silence.

"Freezing, filthy water, and three feet would come up to about here—ugh!" She shuddered. "So let's gather things up and go." And then added, "But it sure isn't what I had in mind a while ago when I was thinking about a bath."

Early in the spring we had become aware of two young fellows in their late twenties, we guessed, working on an old hulk that was close to 40 feet long. They were hard at work every Saturday and Sunday morning when we arrived and were still at it when we left. As it turned out, they came up from New York City by train every Friday evening, set up a camp of sorts in the cabin, and stayed there until they left late Sunday evening.

One day I walked over and introduced myself. After the usual amenities—weather, comments about my boat and theirs—they told me they'd bought her cheap. I believed them. I've seen trees that had lain on the forest floor for ten years in better shape. They allowed as how she had some rot in her, but they'd cut that out eventually. But right now they were fiber-glassing the bottom. That would keep her dry. They intended to do only the essential work on her in the yard, get her launched, and then as the season wore on they would get into the cabin, the rot, and other jobs. Meanwhile, they'd be sailing.

To fiber-glass the hull of a boat that size was an imposing job, but they labored mightily at it. She was a schooner, with two solid spruce masts which they stripped down to bare wood, then varnished. At last the fiber-glassing was done, her topsides glistened with a new dress of white paint, and *Wanderer*, as she was named, slipped down the railway and into the Sound. The whole yardful of people gathered to watch her go overboard, for all of us had taken *Wanderer* and her two stalwart owners to heart.

Our tasks that spring were nothing compared to theirs. We were happy for them, but somehow, apprehensive too, for we knew about the rot and we knew that the old boat's seams were so badly sprung that, if the fiber-glassing was not perfect, she'd fill up and make McMichael's dockside her permanent resting place. But she didn't. She drifted away, then a small launch put a line on her and brought her back to the dock. We were all there, waiting, talking in low voices, waiting for word from the two owners, who were below. At last came a whoop of delight. "She's dry! Dry as a bone. We're going sailing!"

There were cheers and handclapping. Grins wreathed every face. The dock was bright with laughter and chatter. They'd done their job well. And no one dared think beyond today. Gradually, then, people began to drift back to their own boats, but the successful launching made for a happy day.

When we arrived at the yard the following Saturday, *Wanderer*'s spars had been stepped, she'd been rigged and sails bent on. The two young men spent the day loading gear and supplies aboard, taking on gas, chatting happily with us, tuning the engine, and getting ready to sail. Late that afternoon with the turn of the tide, they took their schooner down the channel and out into the Sound.

A short while later Betty and I packed up and went home. It had turned chilly and a strong breeze had come up. That night we thought of *Wanderer* and her masters and wondered where they were and how they were faring. They'd worked hard. They deserved every bit of pleasure their old ship would give them.

Unhappily, their pleasure was short-lived. The next day, Sunday, the word came back to us. They'd sailed across the Sound and anchored. But the wind was strong, and during the night while they slept she'd dragged her anchor. *Wanderer*'s days of wandering were over. She had fetched up on a boulder, the rotten hull had collapsed under the fiberglass, and she'd gone down. The two young men got out safe and unharmed, but we never saw them again.

One day in the latter part of May the yard foreman walked over as I was putting the finishing touches to the first coat of copper paint on the bottom.

"Ready to go overboard?" he asked.

For a moment I gaped at him. The moment! But then—is the work all done? Aren't there a hundred things still to do? "Why—why, sure."

"Sometime next week, then," he answered, and started away.

"No," Betty said, "Please, not during the week."

The foreman stopped and came back. "Why not?"

"We couldn't be here. Our children couldn't be here, or Sterling. Can't you launch her next Saturday? Please?"

The man paused. "Well, I guess so. 'Bout noon, then. The tide'll be right 'bout noontime."

We had bought the first boat in the water, so this would be our first launching. Only those who have experienced the first launching of their own boat can truly appreciate the pride, the tension, the boiling excitement of the momentous occasion. The men at NASA have nothing on us. A week of beautiful weather crept by. Sunlit days, starlit nights. We gave the topsides their finishing touches, gave the mast and boom a last coat of white paint, bought and rove new halyards, and painted a name, *Merrimac*, on the transom. Sterling came over one evening to give the Palmer engine one final checkout.

"She won't give you any trouble at all," he pronounced. During the spring while Betty and I worked on other projects Sterling had gone over every inch of the engine with loving care and attention: "One thing you'll have to get used to, though, is the fact that you can't reverse her."

I'd forgotten. Would that mean problems?

"It could. A reverse gear would be helpful in lots of situations, but this baby just ain't got one."

Then came Saturday. "It's raining," Betty said from her side of the bed. "It's a horrible day." The sky was a sullen, sodden, dripping gray blanket. "I'd so wanted the children to go for the first ride, but they'd catch their deaths of cold."

Sterling and I went over early. There were a few last-minute things I wanted to do, including putting another coat of copper paint on the bottom, and Sterling wanted to fiddle with the engine. Something about the magneto, he said. Shortly before noon Betty arrived, with a marvelous picnic lunch. Then the foreman and hand arrived. No one said much, for the day discouraged talk. It was raining harder than ever. The men hitched an old Ford truck to the cradle and dragged it and *Merrimac* over greased timbers to the railway. Once there, we hopped aboard, and gently the cradle and boat were eased into the water. The tide was coming up and the rain was coming down, but this moment was ours, and when *Merrimac* floated out of the cradle and rode by the dock at the end of her tether, we lived an unforgettable moment.

Merrimac took some water, as all plank boats do until they swell and the seams close. By midafternoon the leaks had almost stopped and the foreman said it was safe to take her away. We had a mooring space in the East Basin, but the big mushroom anchor we'd ordered had not arrived yet, so the foreman suggested that we find a space on the land side of the channel and lay our old anchor up on the shore. That would hold her until the mushroom arrived. The mast would not be stepped for another few days.

It was a distance of less than a quarter of a mile down the channel of the West Basin to the point where it meets the channel that leads up into the East Basin. We'd be going down the west channel with the tide and against it going up the east. No problem.

Sterling had had the engine running in the morning, so

Betty at the tiller of Merrimac

now it was time to start it up again. I took the starter rope, secured the knotted end in a notch in the flywheel, took a couple of turns around the wheel, and awaited the word. Sterling fiddled with something in the cockpit, then called down to me in the engine space beneath: "Pull!"

I pulled, and the flywheel spun clockwise to a compression point, stopped, and flung itself back in the opposite direction. The wooden handle of the rope yanked itself out of my hand with force enough to dislocate a shoulder.

"Pull again," Sterling commanded. I did. Same thing.

"Again!" Pull. Nothing. "Pull!" Nothing. "Pull, damn it!" Nothing, damn it. Shifted rope to left hand. Right shoulder giving out. "Pull!" Sterling tinkered with something. Pull. This time the handle whipped out of the left hand. Two sore shoulders. Betty pumped water out of the bilges. Sterling tinkered. I

pulled and muttered dark curses. At last the engine sputtered.
"Pull harder!"

"Listen, Sterling! While you're up there yelling 'Pull,' I'm
down here crippling myself for life. If this — — — doesn't
start soon, I'm going to..."

"Come on, Jim! Pull!" One more time. It spat, sputtered,
coughed, shot exhaust fumes at my face, and caught!

We were off. I was certain I could never raise my arms
again, so Sterling took the tiller and we chugged down the
channel. With the tide *Merrimac* fairly sped along to the junction. Then we turned left, and suddenly our speed was
reduced to a crawl. This was going to be something else.
Against the tide our land speed was barely perceptible. The
rain pelted down, the engine chugged, I brooded over how I
could perform certain functions with both arms in a cast, and
Betty gazed anxiously at the shore.

"Let's see," she mused. "The foreman said our space is
about a hundred and fifty yards up the channel. I figure we're
moving about a foot an hour, so at that rate..."

"The children will be grown and married by the time we
get anchored," I finished for her.

"Naw," Sterling laughed. "We'll be there in about five minutes."

And we were. We'd gotten fenders out and hung them
over the sides, because we were bound to scrape against other
boats already there.

"Jim," Sterling said. "Why don't you take the screwdriver,
hop down, and cut the engine when we start turning in to the
shore. Something's wrong with the accelerator, and I can't
reduce speed. When we turn across the current, she'll pick up
and we'll ram the bank."

"Screwdriver? What do I do with that?"

"Oh. Hold the shaft of it against the sparkplug and the

point of it on the engine. That'll short it out." I stared at him. "Got to put some kind of a switch on it so we don't have to do that in the future," he added.

I "hopped" down the ladder, got in position, located the sparkplug, and waited. I could feel the change in direction. We were heading for the bank.

"Now!" Sterling ordered.

I jammed the screwdriver against the plug, aimed the point at the engine and BLAM! I catapulted across the cabin and landed on my back in a bunk. I lay there in shock. Where'd that horse come from?

Betty peered down at me. "Why are you lying down? Shouldn't you be up here helping?"

Sterling stared. "You had hold of the metal part of the screwdriver?"

No answer.

"The engine bit him," he addressed Betty. "He got shocked by the plug, and—hey, we're not going to make it! We cut the engine too soon and we're still ten feet from shore. Jim."

I struggled up.

"Jim, start the engine!"

Oh, no. I grabbed the starter rope, wound, and pulled. Nothing. Pull. Nothing. Pull.

"No use," Sterling called. "She won't start now. Too hot."

"What'll we do?" This from Betty.

"I'll grab the anchor and jump ashore." That from Sterling.

"You can't jump ten feet with an anchor in your arms." Already Sterling was running along the deck. "No" he called back, "maybe not, but the water can't be more than a couple of feet deep!"

"But you'll get soaked and muddy, and Connie—"

Splash. I started up the ladder.

"Sterling jumped—and he's out of sight."

We ran forward. Right. No Sterling. I kicked off my shoes. He had to be *someplace*, and that someplace was straight down.

Suddenly there was a splash, and under our gaze Sterling rose to the surface, sputtering and coughing.

"By God," he croaked, "if you ever want to go down fast in ten feet of water, carry an anchor!" With that he turned and swam toward shore, leaving us doubled up on the deck. Laugh? We thought we'd die.

The Orienta Yacht Club is located adjacent to the shipyard of one of America's finest yacht builders. One day we brought our new boat in to the club float to pick up a few items of gear. We had barely tied up when the builder himself, whose finest attributes do not include tact or a quiet, gentle manner, boomed out, "Where in hell did you get *that* thing?"

Our lovely new boat "*that* thing"? He strolled out to the end of one of his finger-piers, laughing and pointing.

"Dear," Betty said, urgently, "that wrench in your hand. Please put it down."

"What? Oh, yeah. He's 40 feet away. I couldn't throw it that far with any accuracy anyway."

The man continued to stare and laugh. "That—that's the damnedest thing I've ever seen!"

"Just what is the 'damnedest thing' you've ever seen, you big jerk?" I demanded quietly, in a voice which Betty later said could have been heard in Port Jefferson.

"Why, that's the first boat I ever built," he roared. "I built her when I was a kid in my old man's cellar. Built her and then had to take her apart to get her out through the door."

"You—you did?" Somehow, my opinion of him was changing.

"Sure. An' I've never built a better one since. She'll take

you to the Maritime Provinces or across the Atlantic, for that matter. That is," he added, "if you're man enough to get her there."

He turned to go, then came back. "Tell you what. I'll give you a hundred bucks for her as she sits."

"A hundred bucks! Why, you—she, we've—"

"Honey, that wrench."

Well, he was right. She was a fine little boat, and she did take us wherever we wanted to sail, and as it turned out, we sailed into just about every harbor in western Long Island Sound. She had just one fault: the deck leaked. If someone so much as spit in the next town, that deck would leak. We got to the point of dreading rain. We even dreaded a heavy dew. And try as I might—and Sterling, too—I could never find all the places where water found its way in. We wore out three suits of foul-weather gear *in the cabin*.

On cruises (it always seemed to rain on our cruises) the first thing to get wet was our bedding. Next came the changes of clothing Betty had so carefully laundered, pressed, and stowed away. After that, mildew would set in. It got so bad in a few days of cruising that you couldn't tell a sneaker from a loaf of bread. Everything turned green.

And, of course, the engine. No matter how much Sterling fiddled and patted and praised it as "one fine little engine," it failed to start—or stop—at crucial times. The switch he installed was not the success we had hoped for, and so in times of trial I'd plunge madly down the companionway ladder, screwdriver in hand, and either stop the motor or electrocute myself. On some cruises I had so much electricity in my system my hair stood on end for hours.

One hot mid-July Sunday Betty, Carol, Michael, and I went for a sail, and we took along with us a friend of Michael's named Tennessee. Tennessee was a big kid, not only big, but fat. Feeding that boy was like stoking a Bessemer converter. There must have been a raging fire inside him that consumed food the way a furnace burns coal. There was a breeze that fine, sunny Sunday, and we hoisted sail and made our way across the Sound. In anticipation of Tennessee's presence, Betty had made lunch for eight—one each for the four of us and the rest for him. We anchored, ate, watched Tennessee feed, lolled around for a while, then went swimming.

About two o'clock our guest announced that maybe we'd better be heading home because his mother was having a huge steak dinner that night and she was serving it at six o'clock. And at about that time someone noticed that the breeze had died. Well, okay, we'd head back on the motor.

I opened the petcock on the gas line, choked the engine a bit, and pulled. I pulled again. After half an hour or so I decided that something was wrong. Sterling had always insisted that one had to be patient with a balky engine. No kicking it, no cursing it, no clanking a hammer on its head. Patience. So I checked the gas line. I checked the sediment bowl under the carburetor and I removed the sparkplug to look it over. Everything smiled at me. We're all clean, Daddy. The gas line is clean, the plug is clean and pure. I sighed, replaced the plug, connected the wire to it and gave one more tired pull on the rope. Inexplicably the engine started up, coughed a time or two, and settled down to a steady chug, chug. It was getting late and we headed for home, hot and sun-burned.

There was not a breath of air stirring and the slow pace of *Merrimac* created little of its own. The long rollers that a steady breeze creates had subsided and in their place we had a disturbing chop, created by the hundreds of power boats that thundered or putt-putted around us. The chop jostled our small craft this way and that like a pedestrian on Madison

Avenue at high noon. Conversation died. Michael stretched out on the deck forward, a T-shirt covering his scarlet back. Carol lay on one cockpit seat, Betty on the other. Tennessee had gone below to save his fast-fading strength and I steered. All was quiet. For a moment.

Groan. Another groan followed by a sound suspiciously like that made by one who is about to lose some cookies. Betty sat up. Carol uncurled. I peered down into the dark interior of the cabin.

"Tennessee? Are you all right?"

Groan. Unpleasant sound. Betty dashed below. If Tennessee was going to throw up, he wasn't going to do it down there if she could help it. And in a moment he emerged, perspiring, trembling, and pale green.

Michael was alert. "You look sorta sick, Tennessee," he observed safely. "Want a cookie or something?"

GROAN. "Just lemme be." Whereupon he sagged to the deck and Betty turned his head over the side. A classic case of seasickness, induced by heat, lots of food, and the ungainly motion of the boat. There is no illness more devastating. One only wishes one could die, quickly.

"We can't go any faster?" Carol asked.

Nope. She's wide open, all one cylinder of her."

"Poor Tennessee." Groan and heave.

Steadily, but oh, so slowly we gained on the harbor, made it, and went directly to the clubhouse dock, where gentle hands eased the patient ashore.

"Feel like walking around a little bit, Tennessee?"

"Want a drink of water?"

"Maybe he just wants to sit there for a little while, and maybe that's what he should do," Betty observed. Everyone trying to be helpful, nobody knowing quite what to do.

A small party was in progress a short distance away, with

tall glasses, canapes, and a hibachi filled with glowing coals. And even as I watched, a member of the party strolled over to a table beside the hibachi, removed some hamburgers from their wrappings, and placed them on the grill. We'd better get Tennessee moving somehow, I thought, because it was getting on toward dinnertime. There was a sizzling sound, and that oldest, loveliest perfume of all, the odor of meat cooking over an open fire, drifted in our direction. Tennessee was seated in a chair, his chin on his chest, but now slowly his head came up. His nose seemed to quiver, color flooded back into his face, and he turned to stare at the now-flaming food.

For a moment he hesitated, then flung himself from his chair.

"Man," he cried, "I've jes' got to get home real quick or I'm gonna go over there an' do those nice people out of their supper."

It was, without a doubt, the quickest recovery I've ever witnessed.

four

long island sound

To the millions of people who live in the towns, cities, villages, and harborsites that line its shores, Long Island Sound is their inland sea. Small in area when compared to the Great Lakes or the old Romans' Mare Nostrum, the Mediterranean, the Sound is at one hour a gentle, docile body of salt water. An hour later it can be a towering, glowering tyrant. Storms bearing high winds can get themselves up quickly and rage through the Sound. Those boaters who can make it scuttle for shore. Others too far from shore to seek shelter in some safe harbor batten down and hope for the best.

Long Island Sound is a hundred miles long. At its widest it is 20 miles from shore to shore. When one is out in the middle of those 20 miles riding out a sudden storm, it is sea enough. Like Lake Erie, the Sound is shallow. Unlike the open ocean, where heavy winds make long swells, the waves in the Sound are short and steep. The bow of a boat rises high to climb over a six-foot wave. Then falls down the other side. The Sound, though, gives the boat little chance to recover. In fact, while the bow is valiantly trying to rise again, the next wave will crash and wash the deck with creaming white water. It can be a treacherous body of water. More than one person who had thought it not has come to grief.

Tides rushing in from both ends, Throgs Neck at the west and a place called The Race, at the east, do what they can to flush the Sound. They do well, did well, rather, for thousands upon thousands of years. But now the effluvium of factories and cities and the detritus of millions of people who use its waters wage a war the tides cannot win.

Glaciers of the Ice Age helped form this inland sea, and favored the north, or mainland, shore with countless coves, inlets, and harbors. Islands, too. This northern shore is mainland, being occupied contiguously by New York State and Connecticut. Long Island bounds the Sound on the south. The north shore of Long Island is not so well favored with harbors. There are long stretches where a sailor anxious for haven can seek in vain. One stretch, from Eaton's Neck east to Port Jefferson, runs for 16 long miles with an unbroken shoreline. The next stretch, from Port Jefferson eastward to Mattituck, is 25 land miles. A person with a keel boat cannot simply haul it up on shore and wait for the blow to end. Power boats, too, would suffer almost irreparable damage to their undercarriages, propellers, and such if they were caught between pounding waves and sandy shores. The Sound is no place for unattended novices.

On a given fair Sunday in summer a million or more people will litter, and they *do*, the Sound's shores. And two or three hundred thousand more board boats to move about on its broad bosom. These figures give the impression the Sound is crowded. It is, particularly at the western end. At Mamaroneck, it is roughly five miles across and narrows down quickly as one proceeds west from there. Within these western confines, on a breezeless Saturday or Sunday in summer, the chops set up by thousands of power boats, from rowboats with outboards to palace-size yachts, is incredible. The water seems to tremble. Bow waves rush out only to meet other bow waves coming in. Boats with outboards dart here and there. Boats towing water skiers do the same. Chaos! Sails slat and shake. Blocks rattle and bang on decks. It is like ten thousand mixers buzzing in a huge bowl containing only water. The wise, or weary sailor will drop his sails and head for home. The only alternative is to stay out and add the churn of yet another propeller to all the others.

Of course, there are boat owners who endure none of this, people who buy boats so they can occupy a mooring in some crowded harbor. They are the people who occupy apartments or houses, who buy waterborn front porches. They read the paper or books, or listen to ball games on radios, gossip with neighbors on other boats, drink beer, sit back and take the sun. Occasionally they will take a run "outside," but it is generally of short duration. If the Sound is rough and choppy, they duck right back in. They want a place where they can see the sky, a patch of water, and other people. And be seen. These people are not oceangoing souls. They don't claim to be. And it is not of them that I write, though they have their own stake in Long Island Sound.

Let me not give the impression that the Sound is mainly a play pool for the toiling millions, rich and poor, who share its murky waters. It is first of all a broad, vast avenue of commerce. Squat, straining tugboats haul trains of barges east and west. The tugs and their battered barges are the queens of these waters. The most prestigious yacht clubs may be conducting the season's most important races; they dare not contest the right of way with these burdened vessels. The center of the Sound is theirs, and they take it.

See the waters of the Sound, particularly at the western end, on a hot, windless July day. You will not be impressed. Oil stains smear iridescence in long streaks. Despite noble efforts to clean it up, there is still the garbage that human beings have a compulsion to take along, only to discard. But see the Sound when a merciful wind comes to the aid of these victimized waters. Then it turns a blue that will match the heavens. And it casts up from its depths happy whitecaps that dance over the waves to whatever destination.

See the Sound on a day of storm. Even a boat of substantial size becomes a cockleshell. Or see the Sound at night. The land plucks stars from the heavens. Pearl strings of auto headlights bead her collar.

See the fickle, feckless Sound. She lies quiet. A summer haze creams her breast. Boring Sound, one is likely to say. Some years ago a friend of mine was out one Sunday afternoon, sailing. The breeze was light. His sloop ghosted along. He had his radio tuned to a baseball game at Yankee Stadium, just 30 miles away. All was calm, all was bright.

The pitcher was moistening the ball—trying to conceal his actions from the ump. The announcer was in the middle of a joke. Suddenly he broke off. "I don't know what's going on here," he said. "The air is filled with paper. Newspapers, cups, wrappers. Hey! Dirt at the pitcher's mound is rising in a spiral. The pitcher forgets the ball. His tongue is still hanging out. The wind is shrieking through this Babe Ruth monument."

My friend sat up quickly. No wind here. Only the slight, capricious trickles of breeze that sketched cat's-paws on the water. My friend was a knowledgeable man. He hastened to the cleats on the mast, released the halyards, and dropped his sails. That wind would come this way. West to east. It would be—it was here. Howling. A violent hand smote sails around him. Hundreds of boats were knocked flat. Confounded people shrieked through mouthfuls of water. Broken masts collapsed onto decks.

The wind passed as fast as it came. My friend powered about, picking up survivors, one here, one there. The surface of the Sound was as surprised as the people. It raised hardly a wave. That was fortunate.

The Sound can do that. It's a fair-weather friend, with a foul sense of humor. Derring-do, city man, is right on your doorstep.

See the Sound east of, say, Stamford. She widens out. On a weekday one might not see a sail at all. The Sound becomes a sea. One has the feeling of being at sea. The sails fill, the boat heels. The sailor sits on the windward side of the cockpit, feet braced. The land recedes. Smudges of land smoke take on the appearance of clouds. Gulls wheel. There is the smell of salt, the smell of ocean. The sailor's head rises to face the sun. Shades of Joshua Slocum, of Sir Francis Chichester. Our sailor and these others are one.

This, then, was our Sound. The Sound that *Merrimac*, Betty, and I were about to explore. And we would do that, too, eventually.

five

the great adventure

It was the evening of the first day of the first cruise. The weeks of anticipation were behind us. The anchor was down in a quiet little backwater of Lloyd Harbor on Long Island, and peace descended on *Merrimac* and Betty and me. What did it matter that the only place to stow clothing, gear, sails, food, and even pots and pans was on our bunks, and the only way to get into our bunks was to shift everything aft to the doghouse, and then in the morning to reverse the process? We were cruising, we were beginning The Great Adventure, three weeks of sailing the high seas.

Daylight had faded from the sky, a gentle evening breeze had come up bringing with it a cooling dampness that bathed the decks with dew. It is this same freshwater bath that conscientious sailors use early in the morning for mopping up decks and brightwork, washing away the salt deposits that play havoc with varnish.

I had made a great nautical discovery shortly after dark. It was phosphorescence, that strange, miraculous, Milky Way of light that leaps into being when plankton-filled sea water is disturbed. And now I was sitting amidships on the deck splashing the water with a paddle, staring with fascination at the results.

"Honey?" It was Betty's voice from below. At the same time I became aware of the fact that she was pumping out the head. A new note had been added to the sound, however, a metallic clanking I had not heard before.

"There's a rod or something here that's broken. At least, I *think* it's broken."

It was, of course. I examined the broken part with careful deliberation, even though I knew immediately there wasn't a damn thing I could do about it. Here we were, suddenly faced with disaster when only a few moments before I had been in a state of bliss.

"Is there something we can do about it?"

I scratched my head. It was a mannerism I'd seen Sterling use when perplexed. He'd scratch for a moment, then invariably come up with the solution. Unfortunately, it did not fool Betty. She knew that solutions to problems such as this were beyond my ken.

"What'll we do?" she asked.

"Well, this rod's busted and only a welder can fix it," I answered.

"But we can't go on a cruise without a toi—I mean, a head," she wailed.

"What do you suppose Columbus did?" I asked.

"Who?"

"Christopher Columbus. You don't suppose they had heads in those days, do you?"

She stared at me, disbelieving. "You know," my beautiful wife replied at last, "you'll have to forgive me, but it's just never occurred to me to wonder what Christopher Columbus used for a john."

"Yeah, well, in a way I can understand that, but once I read an article by Francis Herreshoff in which he said that boats shouldn't have heads. They're unsanitary and they're always breaking down."

"Well, since I didn't know what Columbus did and I don't know what Francis Herreshoff did when he had to go, what *did* he do, and you've got to realize that I don't have the necessary appointments to do what they did. *And this is a disgusting conversation anyway!*"

"Herreshoff used a bucket, a plain cedar bucket," I said, plaintively.

Silence. Glare.

"Ah, well—we don't want to go back now when we're just starting, do we, honey? We've got a perfectly good galvanized bucket aboard."

The conversation seemed to run down to a dead stop, like an automobile that had just developed engine problems. And that pretty well ended the starlit, breeze-swept, dew-bathed evening.

The next morning there was only a whisper of breeze from the south, but it was enough to keep the sails filled, and we drifted slowly out of Lloyd's and into the Sound. It was a lovely day and we imagined we had the whole earth to ourselves. Where only 24 hours before there were hundreds of boats, sail and power, milling and churning the water to a froth and a chop, boats that filled the air with whines from outboards or deep, pounding throbs from power plants of large yachts, now there was only peaceful silence about us. Gulls with searching eyes wheeled overhead and little waves tapped out their own Morse code against our planking.

Occasionally a tugboat with its burden of barges moved ponderously by. Other cruising boats, towing dinghies, as did we, appeared like spots of white china on the blue platter of the distant horizon, grew larger, passed and hailed, then diminished in the hazy reaches of their destinations. Betty and I talked a bit, then lapsed into long silences. We read, we dozed after relieving each other at the tiller, contemplated the distant horizon or speculated about what life lay beneath our keel. And thus the euphoric day passed.

"How about another drink?" Betty stuck her head out of the companionway. Sure, why not? It had been a fine day and this was a fine way to end it. We lay close by nun buoy number eight, anchored across the harbor from the Black Rock Yacht Club, just west of Bridgeport, Connecticut. Black Rock is an easy harbor to enter, but its exposure to the south makes it a somewhat uneasy anchorage in a south wind. Another drink seemed the perfect antidote to *Merrimac*'s ceaseless pitching and rolling. We were surrounded by a fleet of boats of sizes ranging from Snipes to luxurious yawls, and across the way we watched yacht-club members strolling the green expanse of lawn which lay between the lovely white clubhouse building and the waterfront. Nonstrollers lounged in lawn chairs and all were dressed in summer finery. We were in shorts, and Betty wore a halter. I did not. We were dirty and sticky from salt spray, which clung to our skins like a fine, white crust. I saw Betty watching the scene 300 yards away with considerable yearning.

"What do you say we get bathed, dressed up, and have dinner at the club?" It must have been the liquor speaking, because we didn't have the money to spend on such a luxury.

"We can't afford it," Betty replied, eyeing me with the open hope in her eyes that I'd say the hell we can't afford it, and I did.

First, overboard with soap that was supposed to cut salt water but didn't, then back aboard for a rinse with fresh water

from our 25-gallon tank, and then a dive into the cabin, where
we found our "dress" clothes neatly jammed away under sail-
bags, sails, canned goods, and the storm anchor.

"We might have another drink here," I suggested. "It's a lot
cheaper than buying one at the club."

"Don't you think we've had enough?" Betty replied. "I
know I have."

I'd had enough, too, but didn't know it, and had another. A
good chop was rolling into the harbor, and the dinghy seemed
unusually unstable, causing Betty to say, "Please! The idea is to
get the oar into the water and then pull. You're just swishing it
over the tops of the waves and getting me soaked." I looked
and, sure enough, she was right. She was soaked.

Getting hold of myself, I proceeded to row with decorum
toward a dock that seemed first to be over my right shoulder,
then left, then nowhere in sight.

"This is some damn boat ride, buster," Betty finally stated.

"Why? What's wrong now?" I panted.

"Wrong? If you make one more circle you'll wear a groove
in this water that won't come out for a month!" What's making
her so fussy? I wondered, but knew enough to refrain from
asking.

A launch boy was standing at the end of the elusive dock;
Betty handed him the dinghy painter and neatly stepped
ashore. Liquor has some advantages, they claim, but sharpen-
ing one's wits is not one of them. The bow of the boat was held
secure, but the stern was not and neither was I amidships;
what happened next went out with Snub Pollard and the Mack
Sennett comedies.

I proceeded to step ashore, and did so, with one foot. The
other was still afloat, and I was in between. Naturally, the stern
moved slowly, inexorably away. The attendant hauled mightily
on the painter, but the bow was not the end that was giving me

trouble. I flopped over, grasped the gunwale of the dinghy with one hand and clutched a ringbolt on the dock with the other, and it helped. But it did nothing to solve the problem. I could not bring the stern in. They say a drowning man sees his entire past before his eyes in those last few seconds. I didn't see my past, but I did see my wife, my faithful, loving wife, lying, literally lying on the dock, holding her stomach and laughing to the point that tears were streaming from her eyes. "Make a wish," I heard her gasp to the convulsed dock-hand. And that was the last I heard, except for the splash as I sank beneath the waves.

Later, back aboard *Merrimac* and concealed by the cover of merciful darkness from the mirthful stares of the yacht-club dandies, Betty said she was sorry she laughed, she was sorry the launch boy and all the spectators had laughed, but it was —her voice trembled a bit—the very funniest—hah, hah— fun-funniest, and off into gales of laughter she went once more. I don't recall if we had dinner that night. Certainly, we didn't have it at the Black Rock Yacht Club.

The southerly held all through the night, and *Merrimac*, with an overall length of only 23 feet and a waterline of 16 feet, tried nobly to rise to each incoming swell, with the result that she didn't pitch so much as she bounced over the waves. To vary this motion, when the tide changed, *Merrimac* turned herself broadside to the seas so that she commenced a frantic rolling, weaving, pitching set, and try as we might by wedging ourselves into our bunks with pillows and extra blankets, there was no sleep that night. Long before dawn we were up, break-fasted, and powering out the channel.

There was no other life as far as the eye could see—no boats, no lights, nothing but the heaving, rushing sea. Once outside, we hoisted the main, and since we were heading east, before the wind, we decided not to raise the jib. To the west and northwest, where night clung, the sky was dark and brooding. Overhead and eastward shreds of clouds looking like tatters of oily rags scurried along, driven by a wind that was now backing into the west. And at last the sun rose, red and bruised-looking, behind a veil of heavy, broken clouds.

"If ever there was a warning in a red sky at morning, this is it," Betty said quietly.

"Looks like we're going to be in for some trouble," I answered, scanning the heavens. It didn't do any good, but I scanned them, hoping for a break in the overcast. There wasn't any.

It was roughly a 20-mile sail to Branford, our next destination, and in a breeze like this it would take more than three hours to get there. Can we make it before the storm strikes, if it indeed will strike? Should we turn back to Black Rock? We both vetoed that idea. In all our years of sailing, decisions such as this were never made without both of us agreeing on a course of action. But if one or the other felt very strongly to go on or turn back, that was almost always the course we took.

We were now boiling along downwind and Penfield Reef Light was receding into the blackness behind. *Merrimac* rolled easily in the overtaking seas, and the shoreline curved away from us where it began to make in toward New Haven. It always seems to take longer to sail past New Haven than any other harbor along the East Coast. No doubt that is because one picks up the New Haven channel lights miles before the harbor itself is breasted. That day, though the sky threatened, the atmosphere had a clarity to it that enabled us to see for miles. We gazed at the lights of cottages along the shore and watched the wind snatch black smoke from cargo-ship funnels and shred it as they moved slowly in and about New Haven harbor.

Merrimac raced along as though she fully understood our

need for speed, but her best was only about six miles per hour. We should have waited at Black Rock for a radio weather report, or at least a careful look at the sky. But the sleepless night had stolen our judgment. We spoke very little. There was nothing, really, to say. Both of us were aware that either we would beat the storm to Branford or it would beat us. The wind, at about 20 knots, held just north of west, so I figured we would leave Cow and Calf rocks to port, then get the jib on and sail in, close-hauled. But we had to get there first.

We almost made it. With sighs of relief, we had left New Haven astern at last, and dared hope we'd make the four-mile run to Branford, when Betty pointed to the north. Fog? That would be all we needed. Fascinated, we watched a gray wall move down on us. Neither of us moved. Then we saw what it was—a white squall. I brought the boat around as quickly as possible into the wind and Betty leaped to the halyards. Down came the main, with the boom crashing on the doghouse roof. I sheeted it in as it lay, and we were engulfed. There was no lightning or thunder that we were aware of. Instead, the wind and the rain pounded on us with a fury we'd never before experienced, afloat or ashore. So bad was it, in fact, that we literally gasped for air as the wind-driven rain filled our eyes and mouths before we turned our backs to it. As we lay huddled on the floor of the cockpit I tried to recall what lay astern—rocks, another boat, a cargo ship? Well, there was nothing for it. Ashore, one is rarely helpless in a storm. There is always a house, a car, a building, some sort of shelter. There must have been a foot of water in the cockpit, even though both drains were functioning, and the rain pounded on our backs like a demon determined to swamp us and our boat. My arm pressed against Betty's side and it was ice cold, and her hair floated in the pool beneath us. We waited in shock for it to end.

How long the storm lasted neither of us could say. But suddenly the wind eased off a bit and in a few moments we could raise our heads. Then we stood up, and at that moment we witnessed the most awesome sight of our lives. The water suddenly boiled with life and out of it and all about us were leaping creatures. Porpoises! There must have been a school of 20 or 30 of them. They rocketed high into the air and splashed down again, not five feet away from us. It seemed as though they were leaping as high as the mast and we feared they might fall onto our deck. If the heavens had opened up and a chariot of gold had come to carry us into the sky, we could not have been more stunned.

The squall swept over us and deep into the Sound. Suddenly the wind died, the torrent became a gentle shower, and at that instant the porpoises disappeared. All we saw were a few gliding, rolling dark backs as they moved off, dived, and disappeared. I stared at Betty, and she, at me. Had each seen what the other had seen? We knew we had, but it was too much. She sat down, put her hands to her face, and cried.

After the squall the wind died completely, and the angry sky turned sullen. Where before there had been massive, churning, rolling black clouds, now nature shrouded the world in gray, and a steady, cold rain fell on us. And while the sea still heaved from the storm's fury, the chop and the whitecaps had been ironed flat. In the cabin every stitch of clothing we owned was soaked, as were utensils, mattresses, bedding. Surprisingly, the engine started on the first pull of the starter rope. We quickly made up the half mile or so we had lost to the wind and presently were entering Bran-ford channel. We passed Lovers Island (we wondered how it had gotten that name), between Big Mermaid and Little Mermaid rocks, thence into Branford River. Like Black Rock Harbor, Branford Harbor is exposed to the south, but by moving up the river, one

Carol and Betty aboard Merrimac

achieves some protection from the swell behind the land. The harbormaster at the dock directed us to tie up fore and aft to mooring stakes driven deep into the riverbed across the channel, which we did.

Suddenly we felt drained, cold, and weary. Oh, for a hot shower and a change into clean, dry clothes. But the deck leaked in a dozen places, and the shorts and sweaters we changed to were but little dryer than the clothing we shed.

It rained all that day, that night, the following day, and the following night. We lay in our bunks and read by the hour. We got up at times, Betty cooked, we ate and tried to stretch, but that was not easy to do in a cabin with only three feet of headroom and a doghouse with less than four. I had seen a plank being steam-bent and I wondered if Betty and I wouldn't be steam-bent into a permanent crouch.

In the afternoon of the next day, we trudged into Branford to purchase a few supplies, then Betty resolutely marched into the railroad station. Naturally, I thought it was to use the facilities, and that was just one of the reasons. The main reason for it was to get a timetable.

She picked one out of the rack and turned to me. "If it rains one more day, I'm going to get on a train and go right back to Mamaroneck. And when I get home, I'm going to climb into my nice, dry, warm bed and I'm not going to climb out until sailing season is over." With that, she marched into the ladies' room.

We walked back down to the harbor, got into the dinghy with our supplies. As I was rowing back to *Merrimac*, I glanced down the channel and saw a sloop, a large one, powering up the river. I turned away, then back again. There was something familiar about her.

Betty followed my glance. "It's the Arnolds!"

The Arnolds, Orville and his wife, were members of Orienta Yacht Club. We knew them. We hadn't gotten to know them well, but at this moment we loved them. They had a 42-foot fiber-glass sloop. Fiber-glass doesn't leak. Perhaps they would invite us aboard and we could sit in their cabin with them for a little while. We might not get dry, but it wouldn't be raining in there and we would *feel* dry.

We watched every move they made. They went over to the dock. The harbormaster greeted them, with a bit more warmth and deference than in greeting us, we thought. He pointed to stakes a hundred feet away from us. They motored over, tied up, and went below. We wanted to be considerate and give them time to do whatever they needed to do before we arrived. I am sure we waited fully 45 seconds. Then, like tigers pouncing on prey, we arrived.

The Arnolds, kind people that they were, did invite us

aboard. That cabin! That great, warm, dry cabin. I could stand up in it, straight up to my full five-foot-nine-inch height. We walked around in it, touching dry things, meanwhile dripping puddles of water onto the cabin sole wherever we stopped. We sat down, instead of crouching on bunks, and talked. They had been up to Essex for a few days and were on their way home. Later, Betty told me she was tempted to ask them if they couldn't use *Merrimac* as a dinghy, tow it home, and we would go by train.

Orville asked us if we would like a drink. Yes, we would, we said. He got out a bottle of rye and glasses, and then, wonder of wonders, he reached into a magic box, picked up an ice pick, and produced *ice!* With ice you could have cold drinks. With ice you could have meat on a boat, and vegetables and fresh milk—not the powdered kind we used—and fruit. The list is endless.

It was with considerable reluctance that we left their wonderful boat, their Taj Mahal, and it was with reluctance that they let us go, because they knew what we were going back to. Strangely, though, it wasn't so bad going back to *Merrimac*. We had lived for a while, and we had friends nearby.

Sometime during the night or early morning it stopped raining. We did not know it, of course, for by now the leaks were like dripping faucets that would never turn off. I believe we were the ones who introduced to medical science the warm wet-pack, and truly, I think we produced our own fog.

The next morning before coming fully awake I was conscious of a strange glow in the cabin. Fire? Fire! I sat up quickly, then fell back. That damned frame directly above my head. But that glow? This time I squirmed over onto my stomach and looked about. It was the sun! Betty, oh, Betty. Wake up! The sun is shining. I felt like Noah on Mount Ararat. The flood was over and we creatures could emerge from the Ark.

There was never a thought of spending another day in Branford Harbor. We have been back there since and have found it to be a delightful place, but at that time Branford meant storm and rain. It meant wet clothing and wet blankets and wet towels and wet mattresses, and all we wanted to do was to get away into a land of sunshine and blue skies. We did not know where this land lay, but we guessed it was east, and it proved to be so.

While Betty prepared breakfast on the alcohol stove, I hoisted the sails part way to let them start drying in the morning breeze. In the days before Dacron, wet or just damp sails of cotton mildewed quickly if left furled or packed away in sail bags for even a relatively short time. And irreparable damage can be done in sailing with them wet, for Egyptian cotton sails will stretch out of shape and lose their power and efficiency.

The smells of the sea, salt air, marshes, tidal flats, rope with sea salt in it, the bilge of a vessel, are all things that are stamped indelibly in the minds of those who have sailed. There is something unique about sea smells and I do not doubt that the love of them is acquired like a taste for Scotch whiskey. However, one of the most memorable of all odors aboard ship is that of bacon frying and coffee percolating. One sits in the cockpit and looks into the cabin where humanity's most time-honored ritual is being performed, the preparation of food. It is a symbol, of course, of domesticity, home, union. With both of our children in summer camps, this cruise on *Merrimac* was a reunion for us, a coming together again, a sharing, as life had been in the early years of marriage before the children.

Presently Betty handed out plates and cups and we had a leisurely breakfast, enjoying and savoring every morsel. What luxury to live again under a dry blue roof! How truly elemental are a couple's cruising needs. The craft must be sound, of course, but in addition to that, they need food and rest, some fair weather, a fair wind, and that is the sum of it.

We took on water at the dock and gasoline. We then powered over to the Arnolds' sloop, expressed our sincere gratitude, and turned downriver. Soon we were out in the Sound once more, out where the squall had battered us. But where just a few days ago the wind had roared and walls of water had driven their needle points into us, wavelets now danced in the sunshine, shimmering and seductive. The Sound was now a maiden who beckoned and we hoisted our sails in eager response.

We were tempted to make the Thimble Islands our next anchorage. But we were still unsure of ourselves, so we decided to sail to Clinton. We saved the Thimbles for later cruises and were to find what unforgettable spots they are.

The breeze was light and we were in no hurry. Betty was lying on the deck forward and I was sitting with a leg over the tiller, reading.

"Jim," Betty called suddenly. "A submarine!"

I looked up with a start. Sure enough, dead ahead lay a submarine, motionless on the surface. It was an exciting moment, and we studied her for a long time. What was it doing there? Obviously she was not under power, for the gap between us was being closed by our own speed alone. At last, suspicious, I left the tiller and went below for the glasses, and they revealed to us the real nature of the "ship." It was Falkner Island, which lies less than three miles offshore from Sachem Head. We were a bit embarrassed by our naïveté, but every time we have seen Falkner Island from a distance we have been struck again by the resemblance, with the island itself forming the hull and the lighthouse, the conning tower.

Since the tide was ebbing, we arrived off Clinton earlier than we had thought we would. The channel into the inner harbor is narrow and the tide runs considerably faster than *Merrimac* could move against it under power, so we sailed on east past the end of the breakwater and started to turn to port toward Duck Island Roads. Immediately we were caught in a strong rip tide, and *Merrimac* tossed and leaped in the boiling, swirling water. Pots and pans clattered off the bunks below as *Merrimac*'s bow swung hard to port and then starboard. Fortunately, the breeze was strong enough to sail us out of it and in a few minutes we were again in quiet water. This was our first experience with a rip tide. Our next, some cruises later, made Betty, to me, a heroine forever. By now the ebb had ended and in the slack water we sailed into the outer harbor, dropped the sails, and powered past Cedar Island on the port hand and came up to the dock on the mainland.

Clinton has its own small fleet of fishing boats, and after we had tied up, we gazed about us at the quaintness of this little harbor, the shape of which is roughly elliptical. The channel, running almost the length of the harbor close by the shore, was the only navigable part. The rest of it was safe for shoal-draft boats only, particularly at low tide.

In a few moments a small, wiry man of sixty or so came out on the dock to greet us. We asked where we might anchor or tie up and he pointed to stakes directly across the channel. This was our first sight of Mr. Petri, who owned the dock, supplied cruising boats as well as local boats and fishermen with gasoline and water. Additionally, Mr. Petri supplied us with some of the best Block Island swordfish we have ever eaten. During the ten days we stayed there on *Merrimac* and on many later occasions, Mr. Petri was a good friend, the warmth of his greeting one of the charms of Clinton.

Every day of that first visit was ideal. The sun shone, the air was clear, and the nights were sufficiently cool to permit us about ten hours of sleep. Often we would hop into the dinghy and row to Cedar Island, which, as the charts showed, was really not an island but a pencil-thin isthmus. On one side of the spit of land is the harbor and on its outer side the sound. We lay in the sun on the beach, hunted for seashells, walked, watched the waves, loafed.

For lunch we headed to a small stand close by Mr. Petri's dock where hotdogs were served that would send the most fastidious gourmet into transcendent ecstasy. Then as often as not we rowed back to *Merrimac* and changed into clothing presentable for our afternoon trip to town. It was a longish walk but good exercise and a pleasant diversion from our water world. The long street that led from the harbor into the heart of Clinton was lined with houses, some of them very old, all neat, tidy, cared for. One in particular we remember. It had a large living-room window, and the lady of this house was either a seamstress or she loved her hobby, for I do not believe we ever, that first year or in any subsequent stay there, passed that house that she wasn't seated at her sewing machine in the window. I hope she is still there, the lady in the window.

The days passed, ran into each other, fused into ever-darkening sunburns, long hours of reading or staring at the harbor sights, or sitting on the shore listening to the fishermen's stories.

On the tenth day we powered down the channel near the final hour of the ebb tide, at nine o'clock in the morning. The north wind was fairly light, but the tide changed to flood, which helped us move west. At this point, Long Island is roughly 20 miles from the Connecticut shore, and from the deck of our boat, about three feet above the water, the curvature of the earth tucked the island below our line of vision. Heretofore we had sailed at most only three miles or so offshore, and we had felt that, if an emergency should arise, we could get to safety fairly quickly. But now we set out on a

30-mile diagonal line south and west across the open Sound and, as the Connecticut coast receded, we felt as though we were really putting out to sea.

We were not out more than half an hour before we lost one of our most useful pieces of equipment, the flyswatter. It rolled overboard. Perhaps there is a perfectly valid, reasonable explanation why cruising boats accumulate flies, but if there is, I have not heard it. They do, by the hundreds, and those sea flies are much faster and more elusive than their shore-bound brethren. So it turned out that the loss of the swatter provided me with many hours of interesting pastime. I launched into the decimation of our fly population with gusto. I would catch one, plunge my hand deep into a bucket of water, and then release the fly. It would pop to the surface and swim—for a while. I occupied myself in this fashion for a considerable part of that day's sail, while Betty manned the tiller. This was a side of me she had never seen, the killer. At first she was somewhat distressed that I could spend an hour or so at a time thus absorbed, but she had learned in the early days of our union that there are some unfathomable, irresponsible quirks in my character.

We had not been aware during this period that we were being overhauled by another cruising boat, but such was the case and we were startled by a hail. We turned and saw a 30-foot sloop with a couple aboard coming down to leeward of us. They were laughing and the man shouted, "How many have you got?"

We were struck dumb. They had seen me at this moronic business. I smiled weakly. "We lost our flyswatter," I replied.

"See how I get 'em?" he called holding up a rubber band. "I shoot 'em! How many?"

The worst part of it all was that I *had* been counting them.

"I—I've got 68 in the bucket," I said.

"Hell, you're just beginning," the stranger replied, and I recall thinking that he was stranger than most strangers. "I've got a hundred and thirty-five in a pile here. And I shot 'em all with this rubber band."

"We've been cruising for five weeks," his lady companion called over, "and he's been shooting flies for three days now. I can't wait to get back home before maybe I start doing it, too."

At this, they put the tiller up, veered off from under our lee, and began to pull ahead. "Maybe I'll switch to your method," he shouted, and they sailed away.

"Boy, he really *is* nuts," I murmured.

"Why?" Betty asked. "Because he shoots 'em instead of drowning 'em?" It was a sobering question.

By this time we had negotiated the crossing of the Sound and were within sight of our destination on Long Island's North Shore.

I do not know if Mt. Sinai is open to yachting any more, for there was a period when it was closed due to shoaling conditions. But at the time of *Merrimac* it was open, and a turn to starboard just beyond the entrance led to a button of blue water surrounded on the Sound side by a sliver of land and on the other by a high sand hill. From the summit of this hill, the voyager looked down on his craft immediately below and beyond to the Sound. It was a delightful spot.

One of the many improvements Sterling had made on *Merrimac* was an engine cutoff switch which he placed on a small panel in the cockpit. But this day as we entered the tiny harbor the switch failed to function with the result that I gave the tiller to Betty so I could go below and ground the sparkplug. Later in the day I took the switch apart and found that corrosion had done its work to the point that the switch was useless. The only way to stop the engine until a permanent repair could be effected was to ground the plug. The engine was directly beneath the cockpit, and I had found that by throwing myself over the bridge deck, hanging head down and reaching under and back, I could kill the engine without going below. The perfect weather held and we were reluctant to leave such an idyllic anchorage. We stayed at Mt. Sinai until well into the afternoon the next day, when we sailed out destined for the Connecticut shore again. The breeze was light in the crossing so it was evening when we made our way into Milford Harbor. It became immediately apparent that not only were there no free moorings, but the harbor was so crowded with boats of all sizes there wasn't even room to swing to an anchor. We putt-putted around for some minutes until someone aboard a moored boat called to us that we should proceed up the Wepawaug River until we came to a wharf on the port hand. Our kind informant was quite sure we could tie up alongside either the wharf or one of the boats already lying there. We thanked him and in the darkening night we moved on. Presently, we saw ahead of us the wharf, but there was no space along its entire length. It was a solid line of boats. I strung fenders along *Merrimac*'s side, then picked up the screwdriver, Betty moved over to the tiller and steered for a handsome yacht. We would tie on to her. Then I assumed my position over the bridge deck to short out the motor. Below, all was Stygian darkness and I could hardly make out the outline of the engine much less locate the sparkplug atop it.

"You'd better stop the engine," Betty warned. "We're getting close."

"I can't find the damned sparkplug," I grunted.

"You'd better!"

"Circle around, then,"

"There's not enough room."

The urgency in her voice drove me to drastic action. I dropped the screwdriver and groped for the sparkplug with my bare hands. You may be sure I knew when I found it. The jolt almost set me back into the cockpit, but I did manage to knock the wire off it and the black demon below stopped. I was just beginning to pull myself up when we struck, not precisely head on, but near enough to plunge me headfirst down the companionway ladder. I sprawled on the cabin sole for a few moments, waiting for the volcano of voices that would surely erupt from the yacht. Instead, there was only Betty's voice. "What are you doing down there? We're floating the wrong direction, away from the wharf!"

I rushed up, saw that we were indeed drifting out into the river. We both lunged for the yacht, caught hold, and slowly pulled alongside. In another few moments we were secured, after a fashion, fore and aft.

I went below again, this time on foot, found a flashlight, and turned it on the topsides of the yawl to which we were secured. Fortunately, Betty had borne off at the last moment, and instead of crashing bowsprit on, we had brought our forward quarter into her amidships and then sheered off. Close scrutiny showed only a small mark on the yacht's rub rail. It was a rather humbling experience, for it demonstrated what little weight we had to throw around; *Merrimac* had bounced like a ball off a concrete wall. Obviously, no one was aboard our victim, so the next morning before we left we slipped a note into the cabin bearing my name and address and the information that our insurance company would indemnify them for what damage we had done. I doubt if the owner ever discovered the damage; at any rate, no action was ever taken.

Our last anchorage of the cruise was at Sheffield Island, the westernmost of the Norwalk Islands. One approaches Sheffield from the west, leaving Green's Ledge Lighthouse to starboard, then following the well-marked channel east to an area between Sheffield and Tavern Island. The holding ground is good and the anchorage is protected in all directions but south. We did not know at the time that Tavern Island was the summer retreat of then famous showman Billy Rose, but we were impressed by the handsome house situated in the island's center. A tall flagpole flew a huge white flag with a brilliant red rose as its decoration. We tried to guess what that represented, but it baffled us.

We were rowing back from an after-supper exploration of Sheffield when the dark peace of the evening was abruptly broken. Betty, seated in the stern of the dinghy, pointed past my shoulder. Her face was a picture of astonishment.

"What on earth?"

I turned. It was hardly an earthly sight, for the house on Tavern Island, dark a few moments earlier, was bathed in an eerie green light. Then it wasn't green; it was purple. Suddenly the house turned an orange color, then blue, yellow; in fact, every color of the spectrum. We could see now that the house, the terrace, the gardens, were lighted by concealed floodlights with filters placed before their rays to change the hues.

"Do you see what else I think I see?" Betty gasped.

"I see things, but I don't believe it."

"Would you believe—peacocks?"

"Ducks, geese, swans I'd believe, but peacocks? If you weren't seeing the same things, I'd think I'd been secretly drinking, even keeping it from myself."

But peacocks they were, strutting over the orange, green, blue, purple lawn, which swept from the house down to the water's edge. Arabian Nights on Long Island Sound. Ever so faintly we heard music, then the laughter and chatter of voices, and people walked through French doors, out to a patio, thence to the lawn. How long the spectacle lasted neither of us could say, but time passed, we sat spellbound, and at last the colors faded and only lights from the house continued to burn.

What happened to the peacocks? Perhaps some genie wafted them away. The orchestra continued to play for a moment. That, too, ended, as the guests returned to the house and the French doors were closed. We sat there in our dinghy transported, hoping that perhaps the display would be repeated. That was not to be. A good showman—and Billy Rose was the best of his time—never repeats a line or a trick.

We looked at each other and laughed. A show by Billy Rose was not something we could have dreamed up for the last night of our cruise.

The next night at home, Betty called to me from the basement where she was sorting clothes in front of the washing machine.

"Look at this," she said, and held up a sports shirt of mine.

"That's one I didn't wear," I answered.

"Right. And you never wore this one either," she said, picking up another shirt.

"Well, I didn't need to," I replied, somewhat defensively.

"No, and I didn't wear those two skirts over there, or those blouses," Betty said, pointing to two large stacks of wrinkled but clean shirts, blouses, slacks, skirts, shorts, socks.

"You know," she went on, "we carried enough clothing on that cruise to last six months. And just think what we could have done with the space all this occupied."

It was indeed something to think about. For three weeks we had crawled over, under, around, and through jackets, towels, pots, pans, sweaters, duffel bags, and myriad other odds and ends for which we had had no use. We wore the same few items of clothing day in and day out, for cleanliness is no problem in coastwise cruising. We went over the side every day, swam, and washed. Admittedly, it is not easy to bathe thoroughly in sea water, but knowing that, we had heated a pan of fresh water each day for washing ourselves and all items of apparel that could be handled in a dishpan. A plentiful supply of fresh water is no problem on anything but a long sea voyage. One can take on water at any dock or wharf, and for bulkier items of laundry, you are never nowadays far from a laundromat. And while we were eliminating useless things, high on our list were wool blankets. Even on the driest nights a dampness settles into the cabin of a boat and, blotter-like, wool blankets soak it up. The result is a heavy, soggy covering. So now we knew. On the next cruise, it would be nylon fitted sheets and Dacron blankets, and a change or two of clothes, all lightweight, warm, fast-drying synthetics. Never again would we clutter up our boat with nonessentials.

six

friends in need

To all intents and purposes, with the end of the cruise in early September, the sailing season was over. It was true the first year and it was true in all the years thereafter. The cruise was the climax of the season; the event we always saved and savored throughout the sailing year. It was not unlike the build-up to Christmas. The cruise was the apogee, the climax, and all weekend excursions to such places as Cold Spring Harbor, Lloyd's Neck, Sheffield Island, Oyster Bay, while enjoyable enough in themselves, were in a sense trial runs for the great occasion.

We did sail after our cruise that fall, but September ran down into October and October into November. The water held some of the heat of the summer sun, but the sheen, the patina, the keen pleasure were gone. Even though the winelike air of October is the clearest, the water and the sky the bluest of all the 12 months of the year, it held for us a melancholy aloneness. Autumn days are for football games, for leaf raking and bonfires, for parties, good fellowship. In the fall the tired sun runs off to bed early, dampness closes down, the decks are chill and wet. There are other weekending boats still about, but hatches and companionway doors are closed early, the voices of children are no longer heard, and cabin lights glow before the color is gone from the heavens. Geese in great ragged wedges fly over. The lone sailing man looks up, his attention drawn by the urgent honking he hears. The geese are heading south and the man thinks of the long, cold months ahead; he thinks of the shortness of the gray days, the snow, the ice. It will be a long time before the geese come back this way again. It is autumn, summer is gone, and one feels it is time to turn the last page.

I built a frame for *Merrimac* and covered her against winter with tarps newly purchased for the purpose. Christmas came and we exchanged presents we knew would be useful for next year's sailing. We had done so much work on *Merrimac* the previous spring that we felt there was little left to get her into condition for another summer. But all that was changed by one telephone call from Betty to me at the office. It was in April, if memory serves.

"I've just gotten a telegram from the boatyard," she announced. "There has been a fire in the spar shed."

"Was it bad?" I asked, postponing the inevitable question.

"The wire didn't say," she replied. "Can you leave early and go over?" There was no question about that. I stacked my work, put on my hat, and left. Betty was waiting for me when I arrived home.

"What about insurance?" she asked.

"I'll call and find out if we're covered," I replied apprehensively. Just a day before, I had canceled with one company and changed to another because an acquaintance had gone into the insurance business and we wanted to help him.

"I haven't had time to place the business with my company, Jim," our new broker replied to my query.

"We—we're not covered?" I asked.

"I'm sorry. You aren't covered," was the reply.

We sped to the boatyard. "It couldn't happen, it couldn't happen to us," we kept repeating, knowing all the while that it could. We had been meticulously careful about insurance, and because we had wanted to do someone a favor and help him get started in business, fate could not possibly be so brutal. Surely our spars would have been spared. They *had* to be. But they were not. Ours, along with those of 40 or 50 other boats, had gone up in flames.

We stood with other boat owners and stared at the still-smoldering remains. One man sobbed in rage and despair. He was the owner of a 40-foot ketch and he had lost everything, as we had. But his loss was worse, for where ours might amount to three or four hundred dollars, his would be thousands. He was a school teacher and his tragedy was that he could not afford to carry insurance. Now he would have to find a way to afford far more expense than years of insurance premiums would have cost.

Others were shocked but comparatively casual about it. Their only concern was to find boatyards that could start building spars. The rush to yards from New Jersey to Massachusetts started soon and cost was no object. People wanted *spars* and they had insurance companies to pay for them.

That evening I telephoned my staunch friend Sterling and told him the news. We could hardly afford the cost of a new mast and boom and all the fittings for them.

"We'll work something out," Sterling assured me. "I'll meet you in the morning and we'll go over." There was no question about taking time off from work. Sterling would do that, because I needed his help.

We met early the next day and drove to the yard. Except for a few questions and answers, we rode in silence. No matter how severe the problem, Sterling was always contemplative, calm, and optimistic. At the yard he surveyed the damage quietly, but his eyes roved over the charred ruins with care. Suddenly he turned and started walking away.

"Where are you going?" I asked, tagging along.

"I thought I'd speak to that man over there," he said, pointing to a man kicking at the unburned stub of a mast.

"You got caught, too." Sterling spoke pleasantly as we stopped beside the stranger.

"Sure," he replied. "This is all that remains of my 210 mast, but a yard down at City Island is going to build me one right away.

"Do you have any use for that butt?" Sterling asked.

"Hell no. Do you?"

"I could use it, if you don't want it," was the reply.

"It's yours, and good luck," the man replied.

I knew better than to speak up then, but walking back to the car, I asked Sterling why on earth he'd want six feet of mast.

"That's all we need for the start of a new one," he replied. "That 210 mast will fit your boat perfectly. It's hollow, and that'll be better than the solid stick you had. It will be lighter. Come on over to my house tonight and we'll start drawing plans."

"But who's going to build the new one?"

"We are," he answered, smiling.

"But you've never built a mast," I said.

"No, and I never had any experience raising children until we had them," he answered.

"Well, if you say you can build a mast, you'll do it," I said.

"We'll do it," he corrected.

The engineering problems in extending a six-foot stub into a 27-foot mast were far too complicated for me to grasp. It must be tapered, it must be inwardly braced, there must be interior backup sections where tangs and other fittings would be attached, it must be strong enough to take any strain, yet flexible enough to bend. The butt could not just be sawed off square and sections added, for that would present an insurmountable weak point. Thus one side was cut back to two feet, the next to three and a half, then five, and the last was six. In this way each side would be joined at a different point from the others, thus ensuring maximum possible strength, and these staggered joints were carried through the entire length of the mast.

I sat with Sterling in the evenings and listened as he puzzled out the problems involved. When at last the drawings were done to his satisfaction, I purchased long-grain spruce boards, waterproof glue and the odds and ends that would be needed. Sterling strung up lights in the driveway of his home, built supports which served as a 20-foot workbench, assembled the tools necessary for the job. We started to work. I sawed boards where I was told to, drilled holes where pencil marks plainly indicated that they should be drilled, handed things, carried things, picked things up where they had fallen on the driveway. In general I did the tasks usually assigned to the obtuse. Where scarfs were cut and the joints glued, clamps had to be used to hold the joints until the glue was set. The clamps we had were too few and too small. Sterling devised clamps from rubber strips cut from old innertubes, and they served admirably.

All this took much time and infinite patience, and the lights in the driveway burned many nights until midnight. A boom had to be made, and then spreaders. We went back to the spar shed and found some fittings that could be used; others I purchased. We had to be careful that the tensile strength of the fittings had not been destroyed by the heat; that was a matter Sterling somehow was able to judge, and judge correctly.

During this time Betty and I were caulking seams, sanding

and painting *Merrimac* on weekends. We had her in the water simultaneously with the completion of the spars. The sanding of the mast and the boom took endless hours, but at long last the task was done. We hauled them over to the yard. The mast was stepped, the new stainless standing rigging (the value of the old rigging had been destroyed by the heat of the fire) was rigged and taken up, and *Merrimac* once more was a bird with wings. To me it was a monumental accomplishment involving considerable engineering genius, time, patience, and skill. The only elements I contributed were time, effort, and a small amount of cash.

To top it all off, at the finish of the job I received a letter from an insurance company informing me that, although the insurance was not in effect at the time of the fire, their broker, my acquaintance, had asked them to reconsider. They had. Please find check for $400! Ah, life can truly be beautiful.

The miracle Sterling had wrought on *Merrimac* did not mark his last appearance as rescue squad that season. I had to call on him once more. The engine had become increasingly obstinate. It refused to start when I most needed it or, once started, it ran until we were abeam of a rock ledge in an adverse tide and then it stopped. We held our breath whenever we approached a rock or shoal water—and we got to know where every one of them was within miles of Mamaroneck. I began to suspect even our friends with power boats were avoiding us. Otherwise, it would mean coming alongside, taking our line, and pulling us off whatever we had gone on to, or else coming about just as they were setting off for some distant point and towing us back to our mooring. Those who know Long Island Sound know that the wind there is not always the most reliable method of propulsion.

One lovely day in July Sterling and his wife, Connie, and two of their three children were going to join us for a day's sail.

Betty and Connie made sandwiches, canapes, cookies, the works. Joyously, we descended on *Merrimac*, got the sails bent on, prepared to cast off, and start the engine for the trip out the channel. Nothing doing! We tinkered, we muttered curses and imprecations, we experimented.

"Well," Sterling said at last, sitting back on his haunches, "either this engine will have to have a complete overhaul or you'll have to buy another one."

"Another engine?" I asked, sinking onto the toolbox. "A new engine will cost more than the boat's worth."

"Not a new one, another one. I think I know a place down on Water Street where I can pick up a good used one, cheap."

"I like that last word better than any we've said yet," I answered, and we crawled out into the sunlight. Instead of the picnic lunch being a gay affair out on the Sound, the talk between Sterling and me was about getting the old engine out of the boat and the problems of installing another one. As I recall, Betty and Connie and the kids didn't have much of anything to say.

By the next weekend *Merrimac* had been hauled out of the water. The old engine, an ancient, rejected hunk of metal, was lying in a corner of the yard. During the following week Sterling, as good as his word, had located a seven-horsepower, air-cooled Briggs and Stratton engine and brought it out from New York in the trunk of his car. Another weekend of work saw it installed, brought into proper alignment with the propeller shaft. Operative. As usual, I handed Sterling the tools.

Before another sailing season arrived the Killebrews had moved away. It is true they did not go out of our lives, only to Greenwich, Connecticut, but there is a certain finality about crossing state lines. Perhaps Sterling feared that next time, if he stayed so handily close, he'd have to mold and bolt a new keel for *Merrimac*.

seven

slightly out of tune

We had one more cruise in *Merrimac*, and this time it was in the company of another boat. A business acquaintance of mine, Harry Carson, worked in a large advertising agency in New York and lived in New Jersey. Harry owned a 23-footer, too, and we used to regale—or bore—each other with tales of our sailing experiences. Harry was married, but he had to sail alone because his wife had a mortal fear of the water. Thus his experiences were limited to day sailing or, at most, weekending in the river on whose shores his home was located. Harry, however, was a Magellan at heart; he longed to cruise on the broad, blue bosom of the oceans, to put in, at the end of a long day, at such exotic ports as Oyster Bay, Eaton's Neck, or Price's Bend, all on Long Island Sound. His eyes glistened, his pulse quickened, his advertising man's imagination soared to undreamed heights as I told him of my experiences on the broad reaches of the Sound. So we agreed to sail together the following summer, Harry in his 23-footer, and Betty and I in *Merrimac*.

To rendezvous meant that Betty and I would go to Harry's

home, overnight there. The following morning we would sail
out past Sandy Hook, thence up through New York Harbor, the
East River, into Long Island Sound to Orienta in Mamaroneck.
We would take off from there the next day in both craft on
our cruise.

Betty and I entrained in New York, enjoyed the ride down
through New Jersey, arrived duly, were met at the station by
Harry in a large station wagon. The three of us sat in front, and
in the back of the car were three dogs.

"You must like dogs, Harry," I said brightly.

"Emily and I love *all* animals," Harry replied amiably. "In
addition to these, we have a few more at home—cats, too."

Betty nudged me. She likes a dog, too, when someone else
owns him. But cats? Her skin visibly crawls when she is near
one. It's not the cat's fault. It's hers, of course, but that's always
been the way it is.

Conversation about the impending cruise engaged our
attention as Harry drove us home. But talk faltered as he
stopped the car in front of a high iron gate that guarded the
entrance to an estate.

"This is where you live, Harry?" I asked, agape.

"Yes," Harry replied. "You see," he laughed, "we have to
keep the gate closed to keep the animals in." And with that, he
got out and went to open it. We sat and stared, speechless.
Stretching away in both directions was galvanized fencing that
was fully six feet high.

As Harry approached, there emerged from every nook and
cranny, from behind bushes, trees, and flower gardens every
kind and description of dog and cat that the Lord at his most
profligate ever created. There were little dogs, middle-size
dogs, and big dogs, each one in his own manner and pitch
greeting our host as though he were the father of them all. In
addition, the three at our backs set up a barking and baying

the likes of which we had not heard since once we had visited a dog pound looking for a pup for our children.

Harry, surrounded by dogs and a few cats, hurried back to the car, leaped in, and moved slowly through the gates. "As long as I'm here, they'll all come back into the yard," he shrieked. With that he drove inside, leaped out once more, ran back, and secured the gate. Not one animal escaped. And we drove up to the front door.

It was a lovely house, a mansion, in fact, situated not a hundred feet from the banks of the river, but we saw it only at a glance, so taken up were we with the canine crowd surrounding the car.

"H-how many have you got, Harry?" I asked, more in alarm than interest.

"Twenty-eight dogs, at last count," Harry called back. "And 11 cats. Let's go." With that he opened the door and leaped out. A veritable Pied Piper for four-footed kids.

He retrieved our overnight bags from the wagon and escorted us to the front door.

The first words Betty uttered were "Oh, oh," ominously.

"What did you say?" I needn't have asked, for just then my foot slipped.

"Too late," Betty replied. "You've got it all over your heel."

With that we were swept into the house; Harry, dogs, Betty, and me, to be greeted by Emily, who held two cats in her arms.

"Emily," Harry roared, "this is—down Rags, away with you, Toby—this is Betty and—Emily, Touser did it again—Jim!"

Emily smiled, held out a hand with a cat in it, mouthed something, and proceeded down the hall and up a flight of stairs.

"Your room," Harry called, pointing. "Emily will show you the way."

"Oh, Lord," I heard Betty moan. Her lips continued to move, but whether she was silently praying or actually speaking I couldn't tell. The dogs were still giving tongue, racing ahead, around, and behind us up the steps. Harry stood at the bottom at a hall table, calmly glancing at the day's mail.

At the head of the stairs Emily, smiling sweetly, pointed down the hall to an open bedroom door. "Your room!" she hollered. Then, considerately she began to gather the dogs about her and we were relatively free to proceed to our room. We entered, closed the door, turned around—cats!

There were two on our bed—*making babies*, three others lying on the floor, and one on a chair watching the proceedings.

Betty sagged against the wall. I hurled open the door, dashed around the room hissing, "Scat!" until the last cat was gone. When the door was closed once more, we stood together, looking about us. It was a lovely room with windows overlooking the lawn and river. It was a hot day, a mist lay over the river. Harry's boat was moored a hundred or so feet offshore. Idyllic? Unfortunately, no. No breath of air stirred, and the room reeked of cat.

"The whole place is an inch deep in animal fur," Betty whispered. "There's no place to even sit down."

Harry's voice called from somewhere. "Come down when you're ready for cocktails."

We washed, changed, and, as if to reassure ourselves, kissed, before we proceeded back downstairs. Most of the animals by then were mercifully outside.

Harry led us to a beautifully furnished sunporch, from which we had a view of lawn, a small cove in the river, and the dining room. I noticed a huge dog lying in the corner by the bar from which Harry proceeded to offer us drinks. The dog was eyeing me intently.

"That dog, Harry, he's a big one."

"Yes, a boxer. Just a great creature."

"You—you and Emily surely do like animals," Betty ventured.

"Yes. We have no children, so I suppose our love has turned to dogs and cats," Harry replied, bringing the drinks to us.

I made a move to rise. GRRR, said the boxer. I sank back into my chair.

Harry laughed. "I don't think Sarge would bite you. At least he's never bitten Emily or me, so just relax and enjoy yourself."

I wanted to, but it's hard to when a hundred-pound brute has singled you out as his personal public enemy *numero uno*.

We tried to make conversation. Emily emerged from the kitchen, smiling as she set the dining-room table. The silver gleamed on the white linen cloth. The china glistened.

"Ho, ho, go to hell!"

Startled, Betty stared into the dining room and I stared at Harry.

"Emily," Betty began, "Is there something—"

Emily laughed. "It's just Bad Paul."

"Bad Paul?"

"An old parrot we keep in the dining room," Harry explained, grinning. "Those are the only words he knows."

Conversation resumed about the cruise. We had another drink (we needed it badly). I noticed Betty staring into the dining room. Her eyes sought mine. I looked. A large cat was calmly walking over the table, neatly stepping from plate to plate.

"Dinner," Emily called cheerily.

The drinks had lulled my sensibilities for the moment, and I arose, too quickly, it turned out, for Sarge was on his feet and making a quick dive for one of my precious legs. "Down, Sarge!" Harry roared, and leaped. He was almost in time, but not quite, for Sarge's sabers caught my trousers and ripped them from knee to ankle. It was a tense moment. Harry held Sarge and talked with him earnestly while Betty and I inspected me. Fortunately, Sarge missed my leg by the skin of his teeth, and we proceeded into the dining room, my trouser flapping.

"First time he's ever done that," Harry said sympathetically. Betty was pale and I felt pale as we set to eating a sumptuous dinner off plates where recently a cat had trod.

"Ho, ho, go to hell," said Bad Paul.

Somehow it all came to an end. A morning we never thought would arrive did arrive. Good-byes to Emily were said and another cruise began.

In spite of her 23-foot length, Harry's boat was powered by a four-cylinder engine, which, since there was no breeze, propelled us at a breathtaking six knots. I suspect that New York Harbor is rarely busier than it is on any given Monday morning, when the world's commerce leaps to life after a quiet weekend. And most of this oceangoing commerce gains access to either the harbor or the sea by passing through the Narrows, a mile-wide body of water guarded on one side by Brooklyn, at. the western end of Long Island, and Staten Island on the other. Now the Verrazzano Bridge spans the Narrows, but it was not there then.

As we approached the Narrows, we watched in awe as both oceangoing liners and freighters moved majestically through the lower bay. With our glasses we could catch such home-port names as Tokyo, Copenhagen, Liverpool, Melbourne, San Francisco. Tugboats, with towing cables stretched taut as bar steel, throbbed with the strain as their screws threw a boiling wake back at the barges they strove to tow. It was a scene of aquatic chaos, with vessels crossing and crisscrossing others' paths, shrill whistles shrieking, leviathan horns rumbling replies. This was commerce and industry and luxury, too, on a Brobdingnagian scale. Yawing, rolling, pitching in our cockleshell, we nudged our way into the midst of it.

"Look at that tug heading our way," Betty said. "Those barges it's towing look like mountains." The barges were empty, and their size dwarfed the tug that strained to lead them.

"We'll get over to starboard," Harry said, "so we won't—"

The sentence was left unfinished, for at that moment our engine died. There was no sputter, cough, or hiss; it simply quit. We drifted 20 or 30 feet, then stopped dead in the water. There was only a whisper of breeze.

"Quick!" Harry shouted. "Get the stops off the main."

It wouldn't do any good, of course, but it was something. Betty and I both jumped and ripped off the canvas strips that lashed the sail to the boom. In a moment the mainsail was hoisted, but the only effect was to steady the rolling sloop. The captain of the tugboat must somehow have discovered our engine's failure as soon as we did, for with warning blasts on his whistle, he turned hard to starboard about 130 yards away from us, but even though the tug was turned almost broadside to us, the barges continued to bear down. At last, we watched the forward port barge turn, almost reluctantly it seemed, and slowly begin to bear off. Out of the corner of my eye I saw a cigarette fall to the deck out of Betty's trembling hand. The barges were turning, but unless we could get out of their way immediately, no power that tug could exert would prevent them from bearing down on us, crushing our craft, and grinding us under their hulls.

"What's your guess as to what caused the engine to quit?" Harry asked.

"If it had been fuel, the engine would have sputtered a few times before it quit, wouldn't it?" I answered desperately.

"Then it must have been electrical," Harry replied.

I started to speak again, but my voice was drowned by a roaring, chopping sound and we all looked overhead. A police helicopter bore down on us, then hovered 50 feet or so over our heads.

"Want a tow to the Coast Guard base?' a voice came down to us through a bullhorn.

If I had not been completely overcome, I would have shouted, "Damn right!" But things were happening too fast for me. I just stared.

Harry, though, shook his head the wrong way. "No!" he shouted. "We'll manage!"

"We—we will?"

The sail was luffing furiously in the wind from the chopper, and we dashed to drop it. That done, we came back to the problem of the engine.

"Betty," Harry said, in a voice as quiet as a full moon, "have you got a nail file, one of those cardboard things?"

"Yes!" she shrieked, and dove for her handbag. In a moment she had it and handed it to him.

We pulled up the engine cover. Harry squatted down, pulled the cap off the distributor, inserted the file between the points, and scraped vigorously at them. The helicopter pilot, no more certain of our engineering ability than we were, continued to hover overhead. In a few moments, Harry finished filing, replaced the cap, and clicked the clips into place. I glanced up. The world was eclipsed by barges. Thirty seconds more and it would be too late.

One push on the starter button and the engine leaped into life. Harry opened the throttle wide, slammed the gear lever into "forward," and we moved. Would we, could we escape?

Five seconds, ten seconds, and we were safe. The last of the barges moved ponderously by. Then, like pricked balloons, we collapsed onto the cockpit seats.

Sometime later, with genuine wonder in her voice, Betty asked, "Harry, how in the world did you know what to do?"

"It was the *only* thing I knew to do," Harry answered, and there was wonder in his voice, too.

Three or four points to port of our bow lay the most famous skyline in the world, and abeam stood the Statue of Liberty. The harbor traffic was joined by ferryboats running between Brooklyn and Staten Island and Manhattan. It was a fascinating sight, but we could scarcely see it so busy were we keeping our eyes out for debris, everything from garbage to half-submerged railroad ties. We approached Governor's Island, lying to starboard, and the Battery to port.

"We're within shouting distance of a nine-hole golf course," Harry told us. "Right over there on Governor's Island is Fort Jay, an Army base. The course is part of it. The only one in New York City."

Dead ahead was the East River. We were hitting the flood tide, which sets eastward through the river at three and one-half knots. Shortly we passed under the Brooklyn Bridge. Close by to port were the canyons of New York City, the traffic-laden East River Drive. We picked out the Empire State Building, the United Nations, Gracie Mansion, the home of the mayor of New York City, familiar sights but all the more awe-inspiring when viewed from the deck of a small boat. The engine was running like a charm, but as we approached the piers of the bridges—Manhattan, Queensboro, Triboro, Bronx-Whitestone —we watched the water crash against the great blocks of stone and thought of what could happen if the engine were to quit again. But one episode of the kind was enough. Harry held the throttle at three-quarters open, and with the aid of the tide we rushed past Blackwell's Island, through Hell Gate and beyond Riker's Island.

Six miles more and we were off City Island, where suddenly we felt a fresh breeze on our faces. The city, its roar and stifling heat were behind us. Ahead lay the Sound. The engine was stopped, sails were hoisted. Now, physically and emotionally drained, without speaking, we sat and the only sounds that came to our ears were those of the comforting water gently lapping the sides of our boat. We sat back and let a soft southwesterly move us leisurely east past New Rochelle, Larchmont and then into the Mamaroneck outer harbor. We powered down the channel and around to the dock of Orienta Yacht Club, where we tied up and left the sloop for the night. Perhaps Harry has forgotten those two days by now; Betty and I never will.

eight

the cruise

The next morning we set sail in the two boats. Another cruise had begun. That cruise convinced us that our desires had outgrown *Merrimac*'s capacity.

I wish to make an emphatic distinction between capacity and comfort, for far smaller boats than ours have made far longer and more hazardous cruises than we ever contemplated. We were not out to cruise for the sake of cruising only; this was a vacation for us. It replaced a cottage on a lake or the oceanfront, or a motor trip across the continent. We wanted adventure, but we wanted a bit of comfort too, and *Merrimac*'s offering in this department was minimal. The head did function in its own fashion, but still, situated as it was in the central part of our cabin, it was the first thing that caught the eye as one entered or even peered into the cabin. More important was the fact that we were sick and tired of crawling over, around, under, or through.

We cruised with Harry for only ten days that August because the weather was abominable, hot, windless, and foggy. Day after day we sat in our cockpits, Harry in his and Betty and I in ours, powering here or there, perspiring torrents in a sun that glared brassily down through the low-lying haze. It was like a shroud over the Sound, and we waited in vain for a breeze to tear it away.

One morning a slight movement of air did wrinkle the water. We thought that perhaps this was the change we had been waiting for. We were anchored behind the breakwater at Saybrook, usually not a comfortable anchorage, but at that time we could have anchored in the very center of the Sound and not felt a ripple. The air came from the southeast, so we weighed anchors and headed out for Fisher's Island's West Harbor. We intended to power out toward the middle and then sail east, but hardly an hour passed before the breeze expired and impenetrable fog enveloped us. It was as though we had wandered into the center of a jar of marshmallow whip. We talked to Harry and he talked to us, but whether we were 15 feet apart or 50, we could not tell. We shut off the engines, for it was foolhardy to continue. There is heavy barge and freighter traffic in the Sound, to say nothing of high-speed pleasure traffic, and as long as our engines ran we were not only blind but deaf.

After sitting and drifting east with the tide for ten or 15 minutes, Harry's voice began to fade. We felt it would be twice as bad to be lost separately as to be lost together. At that point he switched on his power and, by following our voices, found his way back to us. We decided to try to find Saybrook breakwater again, so rather than risk parting, he tossed us a line and took us in tow. Fortunately, we had taken careful compass bearings, but all the time we had been powering and drifting we had been carried east by the current. Now it fell to Harry to try to bring us back. There is a powerful horn on the end of the breakwater, but even though Harry shut off his engine every five or ten minutes it was the better part of an hour before we could hear it. At last we came within its range; Harry cut his power almost to an idle, and Betty and I, 20 feet astern and so able to hear clearly, guided us back by sound alone. Our relief at being back was mixed with frustration. We had hoped to get perhaps as far as Stonington. All we could do now was settle back and wait.

The fog held all through that day and night and until noon of the following day; fog and, of course, no breeze. During the morning of the second day we held a consultation—it was more like a council of despair. We decided to run up the Connecticut River, the mouth of which was just on the other side of the breakwater, and proceed to Hamburg Cove. In their cruising guide, Duncan and Blanchard stated that "here is absolute quiet with only sky, water, trees and two houses to be seen." Unfortunately, the gospel according to Saints D and B was not entirely accurate, although I hasten to say that this was the only time. For when we arrived there, after a delightful run with the current up the river, Hamburg Cove had more boats than the Motorboat Show, and more were coming in all the time. Apparently our inspiration to escape up the river was not unique.

Betty and I found a space which would permit us to let out adequate scope and yet swing with the current. Then we settled down to the din of ship-to-shore radios on every power boat, the shrieks of children aboard sail boats, and thunderous roars of countless engines, inboard and outboard. Along toward evening a heavy-timbered cutter came in, powered through the fleet for five minutes or so, then glided in to a stop about 60 feet dead ahead of us. Since the water at that precise spot was about 20 feet deep, the skipper of the cutter could let out very little scope or he would be down on us. And very little scope was what he let out.

Betty and I watched askance. When the boat was little

more than 35 feet ahead, I suggested to the gentleman that, if a breeze should come up during the night, we just might get cozier than either of us wished to be. No man, whether on land or sea, desires to have his judgment impugned, particularly in front of his wife and several children, and the cutter skipper was a man. He assured me he knew just what the hell he was doing. This being only my second season of sailing, I guessed that probably he did. However, before I crawled into my cocoon that night, I gazed long and with some trepidation at the cutter's boomkin.

During the night a breeze did come up, the cutter's anchor did drag. Betty and I were roused from peaceful sleep by the heavy thump of the boomkin ramming our bow. Our anchor was yanked out by the roots and we in turn careened into a blissfully sleeping group astern of us. It was like a traffic accident on a Los Angeles freeway, where anywhere from 50 to 150 cars crash into each other. When it was all said and done, a lot was said and the night was done. We haven't graced Hamburg Cove with our presence since.

There is a type of fly indigenous to the Connecticut River, at least the part of the river from Hamburg Cove down to its mouth, that is roughly the size of a small horsefly. It has the bite of a tiger, and in the stillness of our morning flight down the river, we were attacked. Like Prometheus, who was doomed by Zeus to be bound to Mt. Caucasus and have a vulture consume his liver, Betty and I, with nowhere to hide, sat in the cockpit, swatted and missed and were all but devoured.

The last night of our cruise was spent back at Black Rock. There was no wind, not a breath—typical, of course, of the entire cruise, if cruise you could call it. It was Harry's custom to come aboard *Merrimac* for dinner. For this last occasion Betty had prepared a repast fit for Lucullus. We had just begun to eat when I spotted a mosquito on her bare shoulder. As I disposed of that, Harry slapped at one of his own. Then I had a couple, Betty had three and Harry, four. With mosquito bites piling on top of Connecticut River fly bites, all insect repellent gone, we gulped dinner and retired to bed. It was another hot, breezeless night, but we spent it under blankets anyway for they were the only protection we had.

The following night, ashore, Harry took Betty and me to dinner. Over a marvelous steak we vowed that our next boat would have screens. It was at dinner that evening that we decided there would be a next boat. But the adventures of *Merrimac* were not quite over yet.

At the tag end of summer Sterling and Connie accompanied us on a weekend sail. We arrived off Sheffield Island late on Saturday afternoon, swam off the boat, and gazed once more with awe at the great white flag with the red rose on Tavern Island. Dusk fell and we sat in the cockpit exchanging gossip and small talk, thoroughly relaxed, contented with ourselves and the small world in which we existed at the moment. Drinks were handed up from the galley and then passed down the hatch. I was sitting facing Sterling, and the women were beside us. Sterling's gaze passed over my shoulder, halted, riveted, and quavered. His eyes grew round, his Adam's apple bobbed, and his jaw dropped.

"How many drinks have I had?" he asked tersely.

"What?"

"Just tell me. How many drinks have I had?" His tone was belligerent.

"Why, perhaps three."

"That's what I figured," he said. After a pause, he continued. "Listen. I saw this car coming down from a road over there. It ran straight off the road, across the beach—" His voice trailed off.

"So?" Connie stared at her husband.

"Well," he continued with an effort, "the damn thing didn't stop. It kept going—into the water. Turn around and look, and if you don't see what I think I see, then I'm either drunk or I'm going crazy."

We didn't want to look, but we did. There, in the middle of the harbor, quartering away from us, was an automobile. An automobile! It was moving at perhaps four miles an hour, half submerged, with headlights burning brightly.

"Well?" Sterling demanded.

"It—it's a car, all right," someone replied.

"And it's running through the water," Betty added. "Down the channel."

We stared speechless. The car rode serenely down channel, a young man and a blonde its sole occupants.

"You all saw it, right?" Sterling demanded again. We all nodded. "But I don't believe it," I answered. I tossed in my bunk that night. I knew Betty was awake, mulling over this strange sight. If Sterling left the cockpit at all that night, I wasn't aware of it.

Happily for our tortured minds, a man from a nearby boat rowed past in his dinghy the next morning. We hailed him and asked if he had seen what we saw.

"Sure," he laughed. "That's an amphibicar—a car that runs on land or water. The joker who owns it lives over near Norwalk. He waits until boating people have had a drink or two and then he drives by. He gets a lot of his laughs that way."

"I'll bet he does," Sterling added slowly. "And I'll tell you something else about him. Either that guy drives a lot of people to drink or he helps a lot of them swear off." He shook his head slowly. "Last night I thought I was gonna have to swear off."

nine

enter hornpipe

After two years of sailing, we had arrived at some definite conclusions about what constituted a good boat for us. We wanted another sloop because of the ease of sail handling. We wanted an engine with enough power to move us smartly against an adverse current or in a seaway and one that could push us along at five or six knots on a windless day. We were determined to have full headroom; storage space, a hanging locker, an *enclosed head*, a good weather helm. And our boat should be handsome—with "character," whatever that is. Incidentally, we could not afford to pay a premium price. All this may seem tantamount to demanding Rolls Royce qualities at Volkswagen prices. But the surprising thing is, we found it. Rather, it was found for us.

We had been making the rounds of brokers' offices and boatyards for about two months when Sam Schreiner, a good friend, told me that his father-in-law had seen just the boat for us. She was a modified H-28. She was sloop-rigged, a departure from the classic ketch rig of the boat, was powered by a four-cylinder Gray engine, enclosed head, etc. etc. etc. To take liberties with Julius Caesar, we came, we saw, we were conquered.

The Hereshoff 28 (28 feet long overall) was cradled in the Bedell yard in Stratford, Connecticut. Bill Bedell came down into the yard with us and said, "If you're looking for a fine sailing craft, there she is." There she was, too, with her lovely sheer, a fine entry, the classic outboard rudder, spoon bow. We found a ladder, climbed it, lifted the winter cover enough to go into the semidarkness below. The galley was immediately to starboard, with two bunks forward. And, praise be, under the galley was an icebox. On the port hand was a bunk; forward of that was an enclosed head, and then another bunk. In the fore-peak was a chain locker. Aft, under the cockpit, was the engine, which was freshly painted. As our eyes grew accustomed to the gloom, we could see the soft, almost living glow of mahogany; the bulkheads and cabin roof were painted pristine white. I glanced at Betty, and there was no question; we had a boat. But there were many things I didn't know. The boat was planked with cedar on oak frames. The fastenings, instead of being the almost universally used screws, were galvanized nails, driven through and clenched. When I mentioned this to Bill Bedell, he assured me that those nails would still be holding tight long after we were all dead and gone.

Well, maybe so.

Once more I went to Sterling, and the following Saturday, Sterling and another good friend, Fred Werber, and I drove back to Stratford. Fred Werber knew boats and boat construction and he, like Sterling, could detect a cracked frame, a spot of dry rot, a piece of faulty rigging, or a worn-out engine as quickly as the best marine surveyor. With Bill Bedell's permission, the three of us went out in the yard to where *Hornpipe* lay under her winter cover. We untied the tarp at the stern corners and peeled the cover forward. Consternation! The entire boat from rubrail up had been sprayed with an off-white paint. The combing, companionway doors, cabin trunk, deck, ports, even the varnished oak tiller had caught some of the spray.

"Someone sure was in a hurry," Sterling remarked.

Fred produced a knife and carefully scraped a bit of paint off a companionway door. "There's mahogany under this mess," he said.

Sterling was similarly engaged in a patch on the combing.

"Mahogany here, too," he announced. "If you should buy this boat, you and Betty are going to be buying gallons of paint remover next spring."

I had been standing on the deck surveying the off-white expanse. As I did my spirits sagged. How could this be? If this was the kind of care *Hornpipe* had been given on the surface, what could she be like beneath the surface? Betty and I, of course, hadn't seen all this, but could we have been so terribly wrong in our appraisal of what we had seen?

We slid the hatch cover back and went below. My hopes rose slightly. There was the soft patina of mahogany and the glistening white paint. The cabin was spacious, clean and sweet-smelling, just as I had remembered it. Fred and Sterling were favorably impressed, and then both turned to the engine. They squatted down and stared at it, muttered and went h'mmm at it. They took sparkplugs out and turned the engine over with a hand crank. Wiring was subjected to scrutiny, the distributor was gazed into and the propeller shaft turned and shaken. At last, like consulting physicians, the two of them conferred and pronounced the patient sound. Ah.

Next the cabin sole was raised, knives were driven into normally suspect places, rib ends and planking, in the bilges. Sound. Fred, who was young and slender, crawled forward and tested the stem and forward ribs. While Fred was at this, Sterling was busy outside going over the hull, planking, plank ends, deadwood, transom, rudder. Already I had assumed a certain possessiveness toward *Hornpipe* and each jab of a knife blade was akin to a thrust into my own flesh. I bled a bit but I bled in silence, for they knew what they were doing and they were doing it for me. Bill Bedell came down with the sails, working jib, Genoa jib, and mainsail. All Dacron, and perfect.

With hopes soaring once more, we all went over to the spar shed where the mast, fittings and rigging (both stainless), standing and running rigging, were inspected. All of us, that is, but Fred, who was standing 60 feet in front of *Hornpipe* looking at her bow on. When Sterling and I came out of the spar shed, he called us over.

"Do either of you see anything funny about her stem?" Conversation ceased. I caught my breath. Now, after all the time we had spent poking, probing, testing, examining—now could there be a weakness, a fault that would snatch this boat out of my grasp?

Sterling and I squinted. "It's absolutely straight for about the first four feet from the deck," Fred said, and paused.

"I see what you mean, Fred," Sterling replied. "From that point on down it seems to bend, doesn't it?"

Even I saw it. But the bend was slight!

"That's right," Fred answered. "That stem is warped."

Damn Fred! Damn Sterling! We hunted around and found Bedell, brought him with us, and planted him where we had stood.

"She's surer'n hell got a little twist in her all right," Bedell said, after due study.

"What would cause it?"

"I dunno. Never saw such a thing before."

"Will it get any worse, do you think?"

"Not a chance," Bedell answered emphatically. That was all I needed to hear.

Hornpipe in her cradle at Riverside Boat Co., Newcastle, Maine

Sterling, Fred, and I withdrew and conferred.

"If you and Betty don't mind the work of getting that paint off above decks," Sterling observed, "I'd say she's a fine boat."

Fred, in spite of the stem, was also affirmative. "I'd buy her."

"See what his bottom price is," Sterling advised.

I am not the dickering type, but there are certain conventions one must observe in all of life's functions, and haggling over price is absolutely essential in buying or selling a boat. I hitched up my pants and walked over to Bedell, who represented the owner.

"What's your lowest, very rock-bottom, absolutely minimum price?"

"The price I quoted to you is it," Bill said with finality. "The owner set it and I know he can get it."

Talk about sails losing wind. I thought of making an offer, but I could tell by Bedell's expression it would be useless. I couldn't think of the next line in a dicker. "Not a dollar less, huh?"

"Right, and she's worth every cent the owner is asking."

"Do you really think so?" I asked weakly.

"Yep. This boat's been on the market just a week. She'll go quick at that price, whether you buy her or not."

Whether Bedell knew it or not, he was a great salesman. At least, he knew how to handle me. Nobody else was going to get that boat.

"I'll buy her," I announced.

"Knew you would all the time." Bedell grinned. "If you hadn't, your wife would have," he added.

Fred and Sterling were as pleased as I was, and we shook hands all around. This was nirvana. I couldn't stop grinning, for somehow I knew we would never need—or find—a finer boat for our purposes than *Hornpipe*. Both Betty and I lived to rue the day we ignored that conviction.

We must have worn grooves in the Connecticut Thruway that winter. No work could be done, for the bitter wind whistled across that table-flat boatyard in breathtaking icy blasts, but we just wanted to *be* there. We went to the yard on any pretext or no pretext, and usually ended up in Bill and Betsy Bedell's kitchen, talking boats.

Four generations of Bedells had owned and operated boatyards on Long Island Sound, and Bill's own recollections went back half a century, and a hundred years or so in the lives of his forebears. We sat in the kitchen, drank coffee, and looked out the window at the deserted yard. But instead of seeing winter, we saw great four-masted whalers and the J-boats of Sir Thomas Lipton's and Commodore Harold Vanderbilt's days. Bill had seen them. In addition, he had sailed and fished the waters of the Atlantic from Sandy Hook to Grand Manan Island, and his tales were told with the simplicity and drama of a modern-day Alexander Woollcott.

Hornpipe is living in Maine now. She was sailing in Casco

Bay the last time I heard. Eventually the Bedells sold the yard and moved, to the tiny village of Ama, well inland on the Sheepscot River, in Maine. *Tempus fugit.*

Fortunately for us, besides the monumental task of removing paint above decks, there were no more than the routine jobs of preparing a boat for water to be done that spring. Sterling was almost right about the quantity of paint remover needed for the chore, for we were determined that where there was mahogany to be seen it would be seen. We spent countless hours on our knees scraping, scraping, scraping. Where paint remover could not do the job to our satisfaction, we used pieces of broken glass. Eventually we got the results we wanted. We worked through blasts of frigid wind. We worked together, side by side, talking, laughing, grumbling, exclaiming delightedly over some minor accomplishment. And there were long periods when each was too busy to say anything. At first we were alone in the yard, but as the days lengthened and a warmth came from the sun, others appeared; covers came off boats, sanders commenced their high whine. The hymn to spring from the Song of Solomon came to mind: "For lo, the winter is past, the rain is over and gone; the flowers appear on the earth; the time of the singing of birds is come, and the voice of the turtle is heard in our land."

We made new friends. They admired our boat and our work and we, theirs. No longer did we eat lunch alone in the cabin or the cockpit. Now we joined with others. Over sandwiches and iced tea or hot coffee we exchanged tips and suggestions as to how best to do this job or that. Saturday was always the day when most would be done, for we were fresh and physically rested. By Sunday our knees hurt or shoulders and arms ached. We worked, but there was much conversation, too. Generally we packed up and left for home by midafternoon.

At last *Hornpipe* sat like a gleaming jewel in her cradle. The day came when Bill Bedell brought his great traveling crane over, hooked padded straps under her belly, and lifted her gently but quickly away and set her down in the Housatonic River. During the following week, the mast would be stepped and rigging set up. We could sail her home the next Saturday.

Our son, Michael, was now a junior in college. He had seen *Hornpipe* only once, during the Christmas holidays. Now he wanted to come home to take the maiden voyage with us to Mamaroneck. But why try to make it in one day? We would make a cruise of it. We'd stay overnight in the little cove at Eaton's Point. Carol, fifteen years old at the time, agreed to come too, but reluctantly, for she had never cared about cruising. As it turned out, she did not come. There wasn't room.

Sterling had agreed to drive us all up in our car on Saturday morning. Friday evening we drove to the Mamaroneck station and met Michael. But he had a surprise in tow, a friend.

"Mom and Dad," Michael announced, after kisses and hugs, "I want you to meet George. George plays tackle on the football team."

We reached up and shook the great paw that was George's hand.

"You—you sure are big, George," I said, thinking of the six-foot-two-inch bunks in *Hornpipe*.

"He's six five, Dad," Michael announced, "and he weighs 245 pounds."

"Yeah, I'm skinny," George rumbled down to us. "Coach says that I have to weigh 260 by this fall."

"He must want you to play both tackle positions at the same time," I replied, with a weak smile.

"Have you eaten any dinner, boys?" Betty asked.

"We haven't had a bite since noon," Michael answered

quickly, as though he meant noon of last week. "And, boy, we're starved."

At ten o'clock that evening I went out to the kitchen to where Betty was charging around in a frenzy. There were stacks of food on the table. "What's this for?" I asked, knowing what this was for.

"That boy wants to get up to 260 pounds this weekend, judging by what he ate at dinner," Betty replied. "I'll have to take about twice the food I'd planned on."

Saturday morning, May 7, dawned bright, but cold. Not just chilly, downright cold. But I, with my acute prescience, knew it would warm up and be a beautiful spring day. Nevertheless, Betty insisted that we take plenty of cold-weather clothing. I did not know it at the time, but she went up to the third-floor storage room and found an ancient muskrat fur coat, which she brought!

George and I occupied the front seat on the drive to Stratford. I truly felt he would have been more comfortable if he had it all to himself. I suspected George felt that way, too. Betty, Sterling, and Michael squeezed into the back and proceeded almost to bury themselves in extra clothing. The trunk was jammed with things we had forgotten to take during the week, extra blankets and extra food—for George.

When at last we arrived at the yard, Bill Bedell took one look at our guest and announced, seriously, I believe, "The only place for him to sleep's on the deck." Then as an afterthought, "But it ain't wide enough."

With a fine breeze — an icy blast—on our beam, we took off. *Hornpipe* sailed down the river as though this was the moment she had always waited for. She heeled over and the water foamed away in a manner that left us almost speechless with ecstasy. *Merrimac* had been fast, but she was only a boat; *Hornpipe* fled down the river like a bird that had been caged and now was free. Presently we were out in the Sound. We sailed broad off, for the wind was out of the northwest and we were heading southwest. It was then Betty went below and broke out the muskrat coat. Well, it wasn't precisely boating attire, but it was appropriate.

In all the years that we have talked about great sailing days we have always come to that one. The sky was blue as cave ice, and the sun, as though enjoying the day fully as much as we, plunged into and out of great pillows of clouds. The only trouble was *Hornpipe* made short shrift of the sail and we arrived at Eaton's too soon. But no one suggested we stay out longer; it was much too cold and it would feel good to anchor and go below to a stove-warmed cabin.

Once, I recall, George went below and Michael followed. I surmised that it was to use the head, but they emerged too soon for that. I gave the incident no more thought.

Dinner late that afternoon was one of history's all-time masterpieces, both in quality and quantity; Betty had made a careful study of the pressurized kerosene stove. That evening she used it as though she had never cooked on any other kind. It was with almost sadistic pleasure that I shoved food at George and he downed it until he, like the rest of us, could eat no more.

After an interval, the boys went up on deck, and Betty and I started to do the dishes. In a few moments Michael came below.

"We have to take the dinghy and go ashore," he announced.

"Go ashore?"

"You'll freeze," Betty said.

"George has to," Michael said, with some urgency. "He's too big to fit into the head."

We stood aghast.

"He's too tall to stand up," Michael explained with a mixture of impatience and embarrassment, "and his legs are too long for him to sit down."

Another memorable evening at Eaton's comes to mind, but for a different reason. It was a month or so after the affair of George and the head. Michael had finished his junior year and had been home for a few days packing a change of clothing before working with the Forestry Service as a smokejumper, based in Cave Junction, Oregon. We had never before even heard of that esoteric occupation, but a smokejumper is a man who is transported by airplane in the company of a small group of other jumpers to one remote forest site or another where a small fire has just recently begun. Where it might take ground crews days of heavy going to arrive at the site of such a fire (by which time it might be a raging conflagration), jumpers could get to the scene by plane in a matter of hours, or minutes. Once there they parachute to the fire and, with the aid of hand tools dropped to them by parachute, contain the fire until ground help can arrive. Few occupations contain more potential for serious or even fatal accidents, but Michael did it for many summers without mishap. This, however, was the first.

It was also the first real separation for our family. We had always been close. Now our son was going 3,000 miles away, to face we knew not what. At any rate, he, and even Carol suggested a weekend sail as a last family get-together for the summer. For a reason that now escapes me, I did not have to work on Monday, so the four of us sailed most of the day on Sunday. Then, late in the afternoon, came once more to Eaton's. Being Sunday evening, the weekend crush of boats had thinned out and we had the lovely little cove virtually to ourselves.

It was a perfect evening. After supper we went ashore and

walked along the beach, each with his own long thoughts. Betty and I worried about Michael's summer, but my own worries were mixed with a certain envy, for it would be high adventure. We walked along the beach, skipped stones, searched for shells, or simply gazed out over the quiet Sound. Finally we sat down, the four of us in a row, and watched the deep, mysterious, and, that night, melancholy beauty of the sunset. At last we boarded the dinghy and rowed back to *Hornpipe*. We stood for a long moment looking out at the winking lights of boats still out on the water, the lights of the distant shore and the stars themselves, silent, remote. The only sound was a distant outboard hustling its owner home in the night.

We went below. In a few moments we were in our bunks. No one was sleepy, but no one could think of much to say. All sound was gone, there was no breeze to ruffle the water. *Hornpipe* lay dead in the night. Then Betty reached over to the radio and turned it on. It was an inspired move, for the great music of the Mormon Tabernacle Choir filled the cabin. No one moved or spoke. We lay there letting the music and the words fill our minds and our hearts.

At last the program ended. There were sighs and the small noises of bodies settling down under blankets. We said our goodnights aloud and our prayers in silence. Tomorrow would bring separation, but tonight *Hornpipe* held us in a close embrace.

Eaton's Neck brought us a different kind of experience. On Father's Day weekend Betty and I anchored 50 or 60 feet from a 35-foot ketch. We didn't notice then, but we did sometime later that the ketch was occupied by two handsome, middle-age men. They, though, were not alone, for also aboard were two truly beautiful and shapely young women of

eighteen or so. This was in the days immediately prior to bikinis, but those young women already knew about bikinis. Not a
few men, myself included, abandoned routine boat chores to
gaze in open wonder at the delightful sight. I knew what was
going through my mind, but I didn't know what Betty was
thinking until she announced, "It's not right. It just isn't right."

"Huh?" I snapped my gaze back to the real world. "What
isn't right?"

"Those two middle-age men and those two young girls,
that's what."

"What's wrong with it? They're just here for a swim and
maybe supper."

"And all night, too," my wife said with firm conviction.
"Where do you suppose their wives are?"

Suddenly the girl-watching was spoiled. "I don't know
where the wives are," I snapped. "Probably on missions of
mercy, visiting sick relatives or something while those two
rakes live it up."

Daytime darkened into night. There was supper preceded
by drinks aboard the ketch, and nary a move was made to up
anchor and go home. As Betty had suspected, *they stayed all
night.* We lay in our bunks listening to the tinkle of glasses and
laughter and music on the warm, early summer night. Things
weren't all that warm in our boat; they were distinctly cool.

The following morning I put on shorts and a T-shirt and
peered out. It was a beautiful Sunday morning, quiet with only
a few boat sounds to disturb the peace. I took a mop topside
to swab off the dew on the deck and as I did so I glanced
over at the ketch. After last night there would probably be
nothing stirring.

I dashed down the ladder. Betty was still sound asleep.
"Betty," I yelled. "Come up on deck. Quick!"

Not one to linger in bed when the ship was either sinking

or afire, Betty rose from her slumbers and promptly bashed her head on a beam directly overhead.

"Oh, my God," she moaned, and fell back.

I gathered her in my arms and with deep concern and contrition attempted to comfort her. But as far as she knew *Hornpipe* might have been settling to the bottom and she struggled for release. "What is it? Where—why—"

"Everything's all right. Can you get up?"

"Get up!" she exclaimed, already up. "What's wrong? My head's killing me. Why did you call me like that?"

Gently and clumsily I led her up the ladder, apologizing the while.

"Look at the ketch," I urged. "The masthead."

There flying in the fresh breeze was a tattered white banner, cloth obviously torn from a bedsheet, and on it in scarlet lipstick were the words "HAPPY FATHER'S DAY."

"Those girls are their daughters?" Betty asked in some wonderment. Then, gingerly fingering the rising bump on her forehead, added, "Punishment for evil thoughts came pretty quick, didn't it?"

As New York steamed in July, *Hornpipe* opened up a new world for us, the world of friends aboard. On hot, humid days Betty called one or two or even three wives and invited them and their husbands out for an evening sail. With sandwiches, salads, and thermoses of drinks, we met at the club after work, powered out into the Sound, swam, ate, and sailed. Generally we were back by 11:00 o'clock, but there were times when we stayed out, sailing in marvelous breezes until one or two o'clock in the morning. We were tired the next day, but who cared? Those were times of relaxation and easy, fond companionship.

This was the year we planned to cruise out of the Sound.

We thought first of cruising coastwise through Fisher's Island Sound to Newport and then into Buzzards Bay to such places as New Bedford, Mattapoisett, Marion, and Onset. But that didn't quite satisfy us. We have visited some of those places by automobile at various times in our lives, so our thoughts turned to Martha's Vineyard. Neither of us had ever been there. Too, it would take us offshore and that thought had its appeal. Accordingly, we turned again to Duncan and Blanchard and their *Cruising Guide to the New England Coast.*

We read there about Cuttyhunk Island, the outermost of the Elizabeth chain of islands, which bear such names as Penikese, Nashawena, Pasque, Naushon. We read with fascination of the "holes," those narrow passages of rushing water between the Elizabeth Islands, and how one must negotiate them, particularly Woods Hole, with foreknowledge and caution. Currents through Woods Hole are so strong that often channel markers are dragged completely under the surface of the water. And then what does one do? Our reading did not reveal the answer to that question.

One hot evening at Orienta, we asked Orville Arnold, that noble gentleman who had saved our sanity at Branford. We knew he had sailed out to Nantucket the previous summer. We talked for some time about the various points of interest, the equipment we needed, the sudden fogs that roll in, unexpected and frightening.

"I'd advise you not to try to sail through Woods Hole." Orville laughed.

"Did you?"

"I sure did. We left Edgartown in the morning with a fair tide and a northeast breeze of, say, 12 to 15 knots, bound for Stonington. We'd powered east through Woods Hole and I knew the way well enough, so there was no problem about that on the return. I'd studied the passage and currents thoroughly, and I was hooked by the challenge of sailing rather than powering through a channel of that kind."

Orville glanced out at his big sloop lying at her mooring a hundred yards away.

"Just you and your wife?" Betty asked.

"Yes." He laughed again. "Just the two of us. The thing I didn't realize, and perhaps it isn't always the case but it was that day, is that the wind is funneled into the passage—compressed in a sense—so that the 15-knot breeze became a 25-knot wind, and we were into the hole before we knew it.

"Well, there isn't a great deal of room for maneuvering in Woods Hole, and *Zircon* was over on her beam ends and driving like a locomotive. I couldn't bring her up into the wind and it was too late to reduce sail. All I could do was hope I could see the buoys and that other boats would get out of our way."

He paused, and I tried to picture it.

"Could you, and did they?" Betty asked.

"The answer is 'yes' to both," Orville answered.

I looked at the towering mast on *Zircon*, and thought of it pointing almost horizontal, across the channel, threatening scythe-like anything in its way.

"The current was close to five knots. I guess we were sailing at around eight knots, so we were moving over the bottom at about 12 knots."

"I'd have jumped overboard," Betty said.

As we looked out now over the peaceful basin with a cool and gentle breeze blowing over us, the experience seemed almost unreal.

"We were heeled over so far the deck was almost vertical. *Zircon* would struggle to get back up on her bottom and she'd almost make it when over she'd go again. The wind seemed to pin her down for minutes at a time.

"But one thing stands out in my mind above everything else." He stopped to light a cigarette. "As we finally neared the western end of the passage, my wife and I both literally stiff with fright, a huge yawl came toward us. I could only pray they'd have enough room to stay clear. She was powering east and there must have been ten people aboard. Four or five of them were forward watching us." He paused. I could see the scene was fresh before his eyes.

"As we came abeam those people cheered, actually *cheered* us."

"You deserve it," I said.

"I don't know about that," Orville answered. "Perhaps they wouldn't have if they'd known how terrified we were."

"I think they would have cheered all the louder," Betty observed.

"Well, I'll never know," he spoke. "But the fact is they made every minute of the terror worthwhile."

ten

twice on the brink

The tide was dead low on the morning we took off on our cruise, and because of considerable shoaling around the Orienta Club dock, we were afraid to bring *Hornpipe* in to load the last-minute things. This necessitated several trips in the dinghy. On the final trip we had, among other items, a 50-pound piece of ice. As we laid alongside *Hornpipe* I started to heave it aboard. At the crucial moment, when Betty thought I still had the ice and I thought she had it, it slipped away from both of us and splashed into the water. Even though ice floats, it does not float on top of the water, with the result that all 50 pounds were submerged. Everything else was aboard. We were within moments of casting off; *this* had to happen. To make matters worse, a light but steady rain was falling.

Recapturing that cake of ice was one of the most frustrating experiences of life. But at last, after half-swamping the dinghy and thoroughly soaking myself, I managed to wrestle it aboard and into its proper abode. By this time, the sky was completely overcast. What air there was came from the east. It was in our minds to go back home and wait for another, fairer day. I tapped the glass of the barometer. The needle fell. We sat in the cabin and listened to the rain patter on the deck.

"Shall we take off?" I asked.

"Why not?" Betty replied. "We'll never be more ready than we are now."

In another moment we were cast off and powering down the channel. The cruise had begun.

In retrospect one is inclined to recall the happy times, the sunny days of a cruise with a fine breeze blowing and a boisterous, lace-fringed sea running. How fortunate for us poor mortals that this is so. It is only when one delves deeply into notes and recollections that the picture is turned over. The dark side is examined and, as one recalls the days, one wonders just why one's there at all. It is only then that a cruise comes into honest perspective.

It rained for two days and the mist never rose from the water. By early afternoon of the third day, we were off New London, still under power, and approaching Fisher's Island Sound. The east wind had picked up a bit, the haze was thickening. We knew we would be lucky to make it through the Sound before the weather closed down completely. By the time we came up on the breakwaters that guard the entrance to Stonington, visibility was down to 50 yards. Betty stood in the bow. With both of us straining to catch sight of markers or the sound of bells, we groped our way in. We had intended to go inside and tie up at the town. Instead, we turned to port inside the second breakwater and dropped anchor. With the engine stopped, we sat in the cockpit, listening to the cacophony of bells, foghorns, sirens, and boat whistles far and near. These are dangerous waters, with the eastern egress of the

Sound blocked by myriad rocks, ledges, and reefs. The rain ceased. Fog crept in. Radar was still so new that few boats were equipped with it and we, snug and safe at anchor, wondered how others would find their way through such places as Lord's Passage, Sugar Reef Passage or Watch Hill Passage. All about us perhaps were worried or frightened people. There was nothing we could do but sit and listen to the warnings of bells and horns.

Later, as we ate supper in the warm glow of kerosene lamplight, we became aware of the throbbing of a heavy marine engine, sometimes close at hand, then fading away but always there, somewhere, circling. After supper we went out once more to the cockpit where the stifling fog lay close about us. The heavy engine was throttled down low, but we could still hear it. I blew as hard as I could on the hand boat horn, but it did no good. I put my fingers to my mouth and blew. The engine stopped. Silence.

Then a voice floated over the water. "Hallooo there."

"Can I help?" I called back.

"Keep whistlin' and I'll come to you," the ghostly voice replied.

The engine started again. I whistled until I was dizzy. At last, at no more than 20 feet away, a 60-foot dragger loomed, scarcely moving. At the last moment the skipper reversed his engine and came to a stop alongside.

The fisherman stepped aboard us while his mate held us off.

"You're anchored?" he asked. He could not see our white nylon rope.

I told him we were and gave him our location. He studied the compass for a moment. "Well, thank God for you folks. Now I know where I am and what my heading should be. Never have I seen a worse one than this."

"Where's your harbor?" Betty asked.

"Why, for God's sake, it's Stonington, ma'am. Born an' raised right here an' I never been turned around in here before tonight."

He seemed embarrassed. Annoyed, too. I knew how he must have felt.

"We'll be goin' along now," and he stepped back aboard his boat. The engine started again. The huge, scarred black boat backed off. She turned about and headed away, this time with assurance. We hadn't done much, but we had done what we could. Shortly after, we went below and turned in.

We found out early in cruising life that we required longer hours of rest than we did ashore. This is due in part, of course, to the long days in sunshine and fresh air. Also it was because we did not sleep as soundly aboard a boat. No matter how deep the sleep, one's senses are attuned to any change of motion of the craft, be it ever so slight; the ears are alert to the thrum of the rigging and the slap and gurgle of water along the topsides. Each change of tone or frequency is noted by the subconscious mind and the sleeper comes awake listening, sensing. If he determines that the breeze has freshened or slackened a bit or if it is only that the boat has swung with the changing tide, he is likely to recede into sleep again. But if there is an urgency to the sound, he is instantly alert, if need be on deck to assess the changing conditions.

It was during the early morning hours at Stonington, two or three o'clock perhaps, that I awoke. *Hornpipe* had come to life. She was performing a nocturnal dance to the lilting music of tiny wavelets running by and the rigging tapping in the breeze. I went above and my eyes beheld a glorious night. The wind, light and cool, had driven away the fog. The moon drove her benign way through high-sailing clouds. The village of Stonington glowed with a moonstruck luminescence. The harbor was strewn with anchored craft—fishing boats, power-boats, sailing craft. Somehow they had found refuge and safety. But in the ensuing days and weeks and in different harbors we heard harrowing stories of adventures and misadventures that had taken place during that night of impenetrable fog.

With the earliest glow of light in the east we were bustling about, eager to be off. It was a new day, a new world, and we had no intention of wasting a moment of it. Chores were done, sandwiches made and wrapped in wax paper. Gulls were in the air. We felt as though they, too, welcomed the promise of fair weather. Quickly we ran the buoys that led us east, down onto Napatree Point Ledge, then a bit south of east magnetic, into and through the Watch Hill Passage. Now we were feeling the great rolling swells of the open Atlantic Ocean. We grinned to each other as *Hornpipe* rolled with a slow rhythm. Then, just as one act of a thrilling play follows another, a gentle south-west breeze came up. The engine was killed, main and Genoa hoisted. The sloop heeled as the sails filled and went to sleep. Neither of us spoke. This was the moment we had lived for. We were wise enough not to spoil it by words. The sun was a great red globe that rose in awesome majesty out of the sea, paused for a moment on the pencil-line horizon, and then moved some more. The little breeze raised goose pimples on the surface, and there was no sound save for the chortle of water sliding by.

At this moment all life was suspended. Neither of us broke the spell by speaking or moving. My eyes followed the curve of the deck to the bow and beyond, then back again and across the cockpit to where Betty sat. She was no longer smiling. Instead, her head was lifted as though she heard sounds and saw sights she had never seen before. Surely, she was part of the beauty of the moment, with a figure lean and strong, yet soft; legs, shoulders and arms burned golden and her hair bleached blonde by summer. But now the sun was in the sky, the white, blazing ball of early day was burning away the soft patina of dawn. The breeze strengthened a bit and *Hornpipe* heeled to her work; gulls no longer floated indolently in the sky. Day was come and there was fishing to do. Betty stirred.

"Honey, we have the jib sheet strapped in too hard. Ease it off a bit," I said. The spell was gone. The morning knew it, we knew it. There were things to do, places to go. One place was Cuttyhunk, about 45 miles away. It would be a long day if the breeze gave out, but it did not. By ten o'clock in the morning the breeze was up to ten to 12 knots. *Hornpipe*, not hard pressed, knifed through the water. She rode over the swells with the motion of a porpoise, over the top then into the trough, and the motion was an exhilarating experience.

Betty went below and began to strip bunks of bedding and the locker of clothing. Everything we owned was soaked by the days of rain and fog. Soon the deck was strewn with mattresses and blankets; smaller items were clothespinned to the standing rigging. At this point *Hornpipe* looked like an unmade bed, but the wind and the sun were doing their work. It would be good to be dry again.

Shortly after noon Betty took the tiller for a spell and I moved about on the deck to stretch my legs and body. I'd been standing gazing about for a few minutes when I caught sight of two odd shapes lying on the water dead ahead. A small sea was running. It was hard to make them out, but soon, with the aid of glasses, I saw that they were the dorsal fins of two huge sharks, apparently basking on the surface. It was impossible to judge their size, but I believed them to be eight to ten feet long. They gave us a good chance to see them, for they did not submerge until we were 50 feet or so away. It was a sobering sight. We were reminded that all about us lay things unseen and unsought.

It was at this moment that the breeze, which had held steady all morning, died with only a slight puff. We were becalmed. Cuttyhunk was still a good distance off. We handed the jib, brought the boom amidships and started up the engine. We had powered for only a few minutes when we noticed that the water surface suddenly was thick with seaweed and kelp. Just as we made that discovery the engine stopped. It didn't cough or miss, it stopped quickly, as though the ignition key had been turned off. There was only one place to look for trouble, and that was under the boat. Sure enough, long trunks of kelp were wound tightly around the propeller.

"Well, I'll get a knife and the ladder and go over the side to cut it away," I told Betty.

"You'd better take two knives," Betty replied. "One for the seaweed and one for the sharks."

Those damned sharks. It hadn't been five minutes since we ran down on them. Now the boat, dead in the water, rolled and pitched and the rigging creaked. Gone so abruptly was all the pleasure of the morning. *Hornpipe* and we were literally being held prisoner, and I knew of at least two sharks lurking in those dark waters below. How many more might there be?

"Could you reverse the engine and unroll the stuff from the propeller?" Betty asked.

"How the hell can I do that when I can't get the engine started?"

"Forgive me. I'm just a stupid woman," she answered.

No man, certainly not I, likes to go bathing when sharks are nearby, but the fact remained that there was nothing else to do. So with Betty standing watch above me, I went down and dove under *Hornpipe*. The propeller was only three feet under the surface, but it seemed like 30, and repeated dives were required in order to cut the kelp away. With each dive I hacked and watched, one eye for the job and the other for sharks. Once a piece of the kelp grazed my thigh as it floated away. An instant later I was on deck looking for teeth marks in my flesh. Betty was as frightened as I was. I *hated* to go back down. But there was no choice. At long last the job was done and once more we were on our way.

Late in the afternoon we ran down the buoys that mark the narrow channel leading into Cuttyhunk, and a short time later we were anchored in one of the snuggest and most serene harbors I have ever seen. It was a Sunday and there were boats of all sizes and from all points along the Northeast coast lying there. We brought drinks up to the cockpit and sat there resting, relaxing, enjoying the beauty of it all. Children splashed in the water. Sailing dinghies darted in and out and around the anchored craft. Across the harbor, which had a dredged area of 300 or so square yards, lay the tiny village, with small, neat buildings tucked in the folds of the hilly land. As we entered the harbor we saw a Coast Guard station on the port hand. Now we saw a Coast Guard lookout tower capping the highest hilltop. Part way up the slope we made out a small, square New England church, with its belfry pointing the way to Heaven. We learned from our cruising guide that a fort had been built on this little island of Cuttyhunk in 1602. That was 18 years before even the Pilgrims landed. So this place had seen civilization centuries ago, and all of us here were simply transients, bustling in and out to all points of the compass with some to return again, others to visit just once and then be gone.

Toward sundown Betty and I rowed ashore and walked through the tiny village, up the stonewall-lined street that leads toward the top of the hill. It was quiet. The strollers we passed, villagers and cruising people alike, spoke in low tones or not at all. Here and there folks sat on verandas waiting for the light to leave the sky before going inside. As we walked up the steep hill, the sound of voices in song came to us, faintly at first but stronger as we walked. Presently we came to the little church we had seen from the boat. Inside worshipers were gathered for evening service and they sang the great eternal hymns. We might have gone in and taken a back pew if we had been more properly attired; as it was we sat down on the curbstone and listened.

It was as though God had drawn a fine line where the heavens met the sea. And He said to the sun, "Set here on this line that I've drawn, sun." And the sun did. It moved lower, lower in majesty. A great red ball, reluctant to go. Even as it slid from view it cast up red and orange and yellow arms of flame to the sky. We watched. The colors paled into evening. The congregation sang on, then drifted to a stop. There were a few muffled words of benediction. We moved to go. But not yet. The organ wheezed into life again. There were a few chords and once again those in the church gave voice to their faith:

> Abide with me, fast falls the even tide;
> The darkness deepens, Lord with me abide.
> When other helpers fail, and comforts flee,
> Help of the helpless, O abide with me.

With the music still in our hearts we sought each other's hands and walked slowly down the hill. Overhead, stars like flung silverdust shone in the black vault of the heavens. The day ended as it had begun, in indescribable beauty.

Weather forecasts promised a spell of bright days ahead, so rather than spend them in a harbor, even Cuttyhunk, we decided to move on the next morning. It was our intention— taking due account of Orville's tale—to pass through Woods Hole from Buzzards Bay into Vineyard Sound. But it would be a long sail to Woods Hole and the tide would be turned against us by the time we arrived there. So we decided instead to run through the nearby Quick's Hole and make the 17- or 18-nautical-mile run to Vineyard Haven.

A friend, Gordon Davies, had come across the Sound from Woods Hole to Vineyard Haven by ferryboat. We met him at the ferry dock late in the afternoon, had dinner aboard, and spent a delightful evening (delightful for us, at least) telling him of our adventures to this point. The three of us spent the next day and part of the following walking through the town. Shortly after noon we got up sail and moved on.

The next harbor eastward was Oak Bluffs. Since it was only a short run away, we spent the afternoon sailing to a marvelous breeze in Vineyard Sound. It was a strange and welcome experience to be sailing for the sheer enjoyment of it and not with a destination to make. There were no charts to read, no compass points to check. We sailed hither and thither, laughed and chattered, engaged in impromptu races with two or three other sloops, thoroughly loving every minute of it. Toward the end of the afternoon thunderheads commenced to roll up out of the west. With some reluctance we headed toward shore.

The harbor at Oak Bluffs is actually a lake, Anthony by name, and it was made accessible to Vineyard Sound when a channel was cut through the beach. The entrance, protected by two jetties, is rather narrow but we sailed in and presently found an anchorage with adequate swinging room.

In spite of the fact that a thunderstorm was making up, Betty had supplies to obtain, so we rowed ashore. It was an odd, slightly tawdry resort town, its buildings adorned with nineteenth-century gimcracks. It reminded us rather of musical-comedy sets of a generation long gone by. But the activity was strictly modern. We entered a deserted barroom *cum* restaurant redolent of spilled whiskey. It seemed to be the only place serving food in the late afternoon. We ordered steak dinners. Wonder! They were superb. We saw that the thunderheads had rolled in. We barely got aboard the dinghy before the skies opened up. The quarter-mile row back to *Hornpipe* through squall winds, lightning, and thunder seemed endless, but in spite of the havoc wrought on our supplies, as paper bags disintegrated and groceries floated about in the rapidly filling bilge, we laughed and chattered like children playing in a mud puddle.

One of the ruined items of purchase was a copy of *The New York Times*. About the only thing salvageable from it was the crossword puzzle. After changing into dry clothing, we tackled it. *Hornpipe's* cabin was lighted by two brass kerosene lamps and a small electric reading lamp I had rigged up with a six-volt dry-cell battery. We hauled out a table and started, Betty and Gordon and I, to work on the puzzle.

In all this world I can imagine nothing quite so snug as a boat cabin with the warm, yellowish light of kerosene lamps bringing varnished mahogany to a glowing cherry patina. The rain drummed steadily on the decks and cabin roof. Even as we argued over the puzzle, we were alive to this rare moment when the world outside was washing away while we three mortals were warm and dry inside our small, beautiful cocoon. Now, in later years, when we think back to our sailing days, that fleeting moment is one of our sweetest memories.

Later in the evening the rain suddenly slackened to a slight patter. At almost the same moment we heard music, the sound of men's voices in perfect harmony coming to us from the blackness outside. We slid back the hatch cover and hurried out to the deck. At first we thought it was someone's radio. Then we spotted the port and starboard lights of a boat entering the harbor. As it came nearer the sound of the voices grew

louder, singing the great old hymn "Onward, Christian Sol-
diers." We watched and listened in awe as the fishing vessel—
for that is what it was—glided past us. Aboard her were 30 or
40 men. This was no ordinary fishing party. The voices were
trained; the harmony, perfect.

Betty solved the mystery. "Oh! In town I saw posters.
Something about a barbershop quartet competition tonight."

"What are we waiting for?" Gordon laughed.

This time we donned foul-weather gear before setting out
for shore and away we went following the running lights of the
singing boat.

The songfest was held in the "tabernacle," an open shed-
like building with only a tin roof. There were no sides to it.
When the wind and rain commenced anew, as they did
presently, we were chilled by the fine spray that blew in. But
we were unmindful of any of it as the group, called the
"Harpooners," if memory serves me, out of New Bedford, for
two hours sang first in unison, then in quartets, concluding
with the entire ensemble singing hymns of the sea.

The storm signaled a weather turn. The next day we
powered the two miles or so back to Vineyard Haven, for
Gordon Davies' stay was over. In fog and a chilling drizzle, we
saw Gordon aboard the ferry, then watched as she moved
ponderously out. A few blasts from her horn and she was
gone, enfolded by the fog. We became aware of horns grunting tidings of foul weather. The wind was into the east. We'd
be here for a while.

We were kept there, in fact, for six days, three days by
fog, three days more by a boisterous northwest wind that blew
down the harbor at velocities up to 40 knots. Two or three
venturesome souls attempted to get out, but no sooner were
they off their moorings than they were almost knocked
down by the gusts. One, a large yawl, handed her sails and

proceeded to power out. We could appreciate the sense of frustration that must have motivated her crew, for the violent pitching and rolling of *Hornpipe* were beginning to shred our own nerves. At last the wind slackened. Reference to the tide tables in Eldridge's informed us that we could make a favorable tide through Quick's Hole at noon the following day. As it turned out, we would have done well to wait another 24 hours.

On the morning of the fourth day of the northwest wind, we hoisted sails and made out through East Chop and West Chop.

The breeze was still brisk, down to 15 to 18 knots, but strong enough to heel us well over and send *Hornpipe* scudding down Vineyard Sound. Our intended destination once more was Cuttyhunk, for we had almost two weeks left of vacation and looked forward to a longer stay at the tiny island. It was a rare day for sailing. As we approached Quick's Hole, the idea of continuing down the Sound and proceeding to Block Island occurred to us, but that was a long leg toward home. The thought of another cruise coming to an end made our original plan look very good to us. Cuttyhunk it would be.

We arrived off Quick's Hole at the height of the ebb tide through the hole. It was our intention to sail through, but the breeze now was somewhat north of northwest, and since a long series of short tacks would be required, Betty went forward, dropped the jib, and put it in stops. As she did, I started up the engine and hauled the main boom amidships. Betty finished her work, turned to the cockpit, then stopped, turned back again, and stood like a bird about to take flight. My gaze followed hers. There, dead ahead, was white water, an odd sight in this otherwise quiet passage between Pasque and Nashawena Islands.

Later we learned what had caused this disquieting sight.

The heavy winds of the past three days and this fourth day, too, were piling water from Buzzards Bay through the hole and into Vineyard Sound. But now the tide, at the end of the third hour of its ebb, was forcing a driving, smashing collision of tide against wind-driven waves. We were heading right into the middle of it. As Betty quickly came aft, her eyes searching mine for an explanation of this unusual turn of events, I asked her to go below to close the portholes and secure the forward hatch cover.

By now I could get an intimation of what we were in for. The seas, though not high (they were five or perhaps six feet), were very steep and short. There was no definition to the wave tops. They were being curled over and blown off by the wind, surprisingly strong now, that funneled down on us. *Hornpipe's* bow rose to carry over the first wave. She did it nicely, then plunged down into the trough. At this point I was horrified to see that the following wave was rushing down on us at a distance of only 15 or 18 feet. Before our bow could rise to it the next wave broke over us and we were buried in crashing, foaming water. Betty was in the cockpit once more. She made a grab for a jibsheet cleat which was secured to the combing. I held for dear life to the tiller. I tried to angle off a bit to avoid meeting the waves head on, but it served little purpose.

I managed to throttle back the engine so as not to drive so hard into the seas, and at the same time the thought crossed my mind to come about and head back. No! Broadside, those seas would surely bring disaster. There was nothing to do but head into it.

Up our bow went over one wave. Down the other side we plunged. Then, before *Hornpipe* could rise again, the next one and sometimes two came roaring over us. I wondered about the pounding the hull was taking and the deck too, and whether or not we could stand up to it for very long. Another monster broke over us, and when I managed to clear my eyes of water, I looked over at Betty only to see her staring in disbelief overhead.

"The forward hatch cover's carried away," she managed to cry in a water-choked voice. I glanced up, but by this time it was gone, left somewhere far behind.

"Good God, we'll fill up!" I yelled. It was true. The hatch, just forward of the mast, was two feet square. We knew that with each wave over us we'd take gallons and gallons of water into the cabin.

Only a year or so before, the beautiful new yacht *Revonoc* had gone down somewhere between Florida and Cuba with all aboard lost. Nothing but a dinghy and perhaps a bit of bedding or such was ever seen. The cause of her foundering was the subject of much sad speculation. One theory advanced by an authority on the vessel was that the hatch covers were secured in such a way that huge seas might have carried them away. If such had indeed happened, there would be no earthly way to stop the seas of a storm from filling her up and dragging her to the bottom. Betty and I had both stood on shore and calmly listened to this possible explanation for a disaster at sea. At the time it was only speculation about something far removed from our present experience. Now the word *Revonoc* leaped to our minds. We knew that it might have been so. As *Hornpipe* plunged she rolled, and occasionally above the crash of water on deck we could hear our possessions in the cabin coming adrift and landing on the cabin sole. The chaos below matched that above.

How long all this lasted neither of us has ever been able to say. Was it ten minutes, 20, half an hour? We simply do not know. Sometimes occurrences of this kind can seem like an eternity even though they take but moments. I recall peering ahead once when *Hornpipe* raised her streaming bow to see how long it might be until we were out of it, but I could see only the next wave rushing toward us and the one after that. It was at this time that in a foolish act of desperation and terror I opened the throttle wide. I wanted to get out of it! The consequence of this was to drive her all the deeper into the next trough. It seemed as though she might never come back up. The two of us were almost battered overboard by the tons of water that cascaded over us. That was too close. I quickly throttled down again. Coughing, choking, gagging, we could only gasp for air between deluges. It was impossible to clear our eyes.

Then there was a lull. *Hornpipe* crashed down upon, but did not drive under, three successive waves. Up ahead we saw a monster rolling toward us. I'd racked my brains for something to put over the hatch, or something to stuff into it, but I knew nothing would hold, and the boat was becoming more sluggish all the time, moving slower, recovering from her plunges slower, acting like a creature that had battled almost to the end of her endurance. There was no way for us to know how much water was in the cabin, nor how much would be required to drag us under, but we knew *Hornpipe* couldn't take much more.

At this moment, Betty jumped from her seat, made a lunge for the handrail on the cabin top, grabbed it with one hand, and then grabbed the shrouds with the other. Was she demented? Where was she going? What was she trying to do? I tried to yell at her but nothing came out. Just as *Hornpipe* rose again to meet the monstrous wave tearing down on us she flung herself belly down over the hatch, wrapping an arm around the mast immediately behind and with the other hand clutched at the rim of the porthole in the forward center of the cabin trunk. A human hatch cover! *Hornpipe's* bow rose, but not very high this time, then plunged again, this time carrying

Betty down and out of sight. Then the wave broke over me. I could see nothing. I felt nothing but a dreadful, icy fear. The cockpit filled to overflowing and I was lifted up and carried out to the afterdeck. I clung to the tiller and clawed back aboard. Was she there? The bow was coming up again. Yes, she was there, head down, flattened out, with water streaming over her. In another moment she turned her ashen face toward me and yelled, "I'm fine!" Fine? Good God.

At least she was preventing appreciably more water from flooding into the cabin. But how long she could keep this up, gasping, choking, plunging again and again beneath the waves was something I could not even guess. My impulse was to dash forward and join her, although what good I would be to her I didn't know. If I left the tiller, the vessel would turn broadside to the waves and the chances were good she'd roll over and go down. There was no choice but to go on. Now time stood still. How long could this go on? My only thought now was that, if she went overboard, I'd go with her. We'd been married over 20 years.

At last the hole widened out. The waves were not so steep, and *Hornpipe's* plunging eased. Now I wondered how high the water was in the cabin. The engine was aft, of course, and set up on blocks, but if the wash of the water inside should put the engine out of commission, we'd back into the rip again. Please, God, it couldn't happen.

When, eventually, we came out into relatively calm water, the sun was still shining. I recall thinking of that with some surprise. Over in Buzzards Bay there were sailboats moving along in the good breeze. Betty raised up and, battered and dazed, dragged herself aft. The breeze caught the mainsail and I brought the bow over to port. I eased off the sheet, left the engine on, and we made our way to Cuttyhunk Harbor and thankfully dropped anchor there.

The cabin of *Hornpipe* looked as though a tornado had been spawned in her bow and had died in her stern. All four mattresses had been heaved from their bunks and tossed into the bilge, there to lie in the two and a half feet of water we had taken through the forward hatch. Locker doors had been sprung from their catches. Pots, pans, bottles, cans, and utensils were flung about, as had been the tools, nails, and screws from my own stores. A two-pound can of coffee had burst open. A canister of sugar was spilled into the bilge with the coffee, and a quart can of engine oil had split, adding its contents to the sorry mess. In all it was a dispiriting affair; we both sagged onto a bunk and stared. An almost-completed sweater that Betty had been knitting was caught by a sleeve at the foot of the mast. The rest of it lay drowned under the cabin sole. Perhaps it was the sight of the sweater sleeve or possibly it was oil that lay in a pool in the middle of a mattress. Perhaps it was those things and everything and the terrifying experience of Quick's Hole that caused it. Suddenly I laughed, then swore, then laughed again. It was infectious, for Betty began to laugh, then cry. Any listeners would have thought that surely two lunatics were loose, for we laughed and giggled as though what had happened in Quick's Hole was by all odds the most devastatingly funny thing that had ever happened to either of us. Then just a few words about how close we were to going down would bring us to a sober silence, only to break out again into gales of insane laughter, until Betty could laugh no more. She hurt too much from the pounding she had taken.

At last, and it was after a long time, we started to work. I operated the bilge pump until my arms and back ached too much to continue. Then I scooped the sloshing, oily mass with a galvanized bucket, handing each load up to Betty on the bridge deck, there to be saved for a later trip ashore. We knew we could dump it at a gasoline station.

Most of our food supply was spoiled and most of our wardrobe was ruined by muck and oil. While mattresses and blankets and odds and ends of clothing dried on deck we dug into the mess with our hands, saving what we thought might be salvageable, putting the rest aside to be discarded later. At the end of the first day's labor we turned on the radio and flopped into our bunks. Both of us were close to exhaustion and Betty's ribs and back pained her terribly. Toward the end of the afternoon the sun had gone behind a bank of heavy clouds and what breeze there had been died. The air was close and the cabin was hot.

We lay listening to music from WBZ, Boston, until it ended and a news program began. Suddenly the announcer spoke of a hurricane that was moving up the coast. It was still a long way from us, but its course was almost due north.

"That's all we need," Betty groaned. "A big fat hurricane."

"To hell with the hurricane," I said. "Tell you what. We need ice, so let's row over to the wharf, pick up 50 pounds, and get some fish for dinner."

It was something to do, a pleasant errand to get our minds off the mess in the cabin, the fright of Quick's Hole, and now the threat of an approaching hurricane. At the wharf, we got the ice and a pound and a quarter of thick, creamy swordfish steak, caught just that day. In addition, we bought a cucumber, some lettuce, and a small bag of charcoal (our own supply had gone into the bilge along with everything else), and rowed our purchases home. Our spirits revived. In a Bacchanalian mood Betty mixed gin and tonics while I scrounged around for the small charcoal-burning grill. I found it, filled it with briquets, poured kerosene over them, and touched a match to it out on the afterdeck.

Betty magically retrieved the salad bowl, found a small piece of garlic, and the last of the tomatoes we had brought from our garden at home. The cucumber, lettuce, and tomato salad she produced was an epicure's delight. Next she buttered the swordfish well, spread aluminum foil over the grill and laid the swordfish on it. At the last moment we slid the foil off the grill, allowing the fish to brown slightly over the glowing coals. Ah, that was a feast of unforgettable splendor. Let Zeus, god of the elements, do what he would. Once more we were happy, satisfied. That night in a euphoric haze we slid into deep and dreamless sleep. Tomorrow we would face the fury of the hurricane.

As we worked through the second day of cleaning up, we kept the radio on for weather reports. The sun was a brassy ball that glared down on us through a thick, encompassing haze. We both were bathed in sweat as we toiled in the cabin. When we did say anything, it was to talk of the hurricane. There had been only a few boats in the Cuttyhunk harbor when we arrived. Now those were leaving and no others were coming in. We surmised that everyone who could was heading for home and the relative safety of a heavy mushroom anchor. We discussed running, too, but where? Where in all of Buzzards Bay or Vineyard Sound was there a nice big mooring waiting for us to tie onto?

I got into the dinghy and rowed over to the Coast Guard station and asked a couple of guardsmen for advice.

"I reckon there's no use leavin', mister," one replied in a heavy Southern drawl. "If that ol' hummer comes this way, an' rat now it sorta looks like she will, best place for you to be is between a coupla them dolphins down the harbor."

I glanced over at the "dolphins," telephone-pole-sized logs driven into the bottom and braced by other huge logs.

"You can lay to your anchor tonight safe 'nough," the other man remarked in a Yankee twang, "but you'd bettah start layin' lines on them dolphins, fore an' aft, if she keeps a'comin'."

The first task was to find something, other than my heroic wife, to cover the forward hatch. The Yankee knew where there was a piece of half-inch plywood in a shed. In a few minutes we had it sawed out to fit. I rowed back to *Hornpipe* and tacked it over the opening. That would have to do until we got home, where the boatyard could fashion a proper cover.

We labored the rest of the day to put the cabin to rights. In the late afternoon we both went over the side with cakes of soap and scrubbed as much of the oil and filth off ourselves as we could. After a supper that interested neither of us very much we carried the radio up on deck and listened for news. By this time a wind had come up; soon we were driven below by heavy, drenching rain. Presently, I went above again and put out the storm anchor, a 30-pound Yachtsman's on 35 feet of ³/₈-inch chain. Since there was no one else in the harbor, I let out all the line on the anchor, 250 feet of half-inch nylon. That was it. There was nothing else to do. The hurricane, if it did strike, would not do so for another 24 hours, according to the various news sources. There was nothing to do now but turn in.

Soon I heard Betty's breathing turn deep and regular. She was asleep. Concerned though I was, I soon followed her. Several times during the night I came up on deck, but not for long. The wind was up to 25 or 30 knots and rain slatted down in chilling torrents. We were all alone. All alone! I recall looking up the hill at the Coast Guard station. Two or three lights glowed through the blackness. Perhaps I should waken Betty, get her into the dinghy, and row ashore. Forget about the boat. To hell with the anguish and torture of staying out here in this Stygian aloneness. But each time I turned back, went below, and crept into my bunk. The rigging whined and *Hornpipe* set up a devilish dance at the end of her tether as though she, too, wished to be off and away, away from this ominous threat of nightmare. But where? There was nowhere to go. We were here. We were stuck with it.

Dawn came. The wind slackened, the rain eased. Hurricane Cleo was on her way. We alternated between the deck above and our bunks below. Now there were definite assurances from radio stations all along the coast that Cleo would strike us that night. Of course! She wouldn't come in the daylight. We had breakfast, probably, but neither of us recalls it. About ten o'clock I started up the engine and powered across the harbor to the dolphins. We cast a line onto one, then proceeded to take the rodes off our anchors, one to go on the forward post, the other aft.

The wind stayed light. Now the weather prophets, with doomlike voices, informed us that Cleo was headed straight for Cuttyhunk. The very center of the storm was to strike us sometime during night. We tied and retied, looped and relooped. Did we have enough line on the forward post, enough aft? Had we allowed enough scope for the flood of water at high tide, for the seas that would flow when the wind was 100 miles an hour? Who knows? Certainly not I, an office worker who knew as much about hurricanes as Columbus knew about atomic submarines.

At last we were secured as best we could be. The wind picked up. It was late afternoon. Rain glistened in the gray light like Christmas-tree tinsel. I asked the question and Betty answered it.

"Should we stay aboard?"

"Why should we? The boat's insured. We've done the best we can."

At five o'clock in the afternoon we packed a few nightclothes, toothbrushes, razor into a bag, stepped into the dinghy, and rowed the short distance to shore. Part way up the road to the village we turned back to look at our boat. Perhaps we'd not see her again. She looked small, alone. We turned away and talked about where we could stay for the night. A short walk up the hill led us to a comfortable-looking house that had a lighted sign outside announcing "Room and Board." There'd be vacancies tonight, we knew.

We picked at some dinner, kept the radio at our sides, sat in the parlor for a while and made desultory conversation with the owner and his wife about the onrushing storm. The center would strike Cuttyhunk in the early hours of the morning. At nine or ten o'clock I glanced over at Betty. She was sound asleep in her chair. I roused her and we both climbed the stairs to bed. There was little sense in prolonging the agony of the wait. We'd know it when Cleo struck.

I rolled over onto my back. The room was light. Sun was streaming into the bedroom through the windows. A gentle zephyr ruffled the starched white curtains. Betty was lying on her stomach, dead to the world. My watch showed that it was late, later than we'd slept for a long time, 9:15 A.M.

I got up, being careful not to disturb her, and walked to the window. There, stretched out below were fields, backyards of houses, buildings down by the harbor, the harbor itself. We'd brought binoculars with us with the thought that through the chaos of the morning we might be able to spot our valiant vessel, to see if by any chance she'd survived the violence of the night. I picked them up, focused them, and looked. *Hornpipe* lay there in the harbor below, quiet, placid, becalmed. She looked like a lovely white moth entangled in the web a spider might have woven.

I turned to glance back at the bed. Betty had turned over on her back. Her eyes were open, but just barely. It always takes her a few moments to come awake. I walked over.

"Good morning, honey," I said softly.

Her eyes opened a bit more. She looked so young, tanned, fuzzy still with sleep.

"I don't know what happened, but the hurricane passed us by." If I had been listening, I might have detected a note of disappointment in my voice.

Her eyes rounded. She sat up. "The hurricane! *Hornpipe*— what happened?"

"I don't know. The only thing I *do* know is that nothing happened. It's a beautiful morning."

"You mean—" There was almost an accusatory tone in her voice. "You mean that the hurricane *didn't* strike?"

"It would seem that way." I turned on the radio we'd brought with us. In a few moments we heard it all. The great storm had turned east, out to sea, scarcely 20 miles south of the island. Nothing had happened at Cuttyhunk. We hadn't *wished* for anything to happen. But somehow it was as though we had rehearsed for a great play, a drama of messianic proportions, and the curtain had never risen.

My mind went back to a stormy winter night in Meadville, Pennsylvania. Meadville was a college town. The college was Allegheny. I was a student there, and so was Betty, by whom I had already been conquered. I was, for reasons too bizarre to go into in a book about sailing, sitting in my corner in a prize-fight ring, shivering. A standing-room-only crowd was waiting to see me fight—or be murdered by—Tony Canzoneri. Canzoneri, if memory fails me not, was the world's champion lightweight boxer. I, age eighteen years, height five-nine, had fought a kid once in the seventh grade. Well, I was good at football. And now, for consenting to let myself get belted by the great Canzoneri, I was some kind of celebrity around town. But where was Tony? Maybe he'd changed his mind. Maybe he'd never meant to come at all.

Then came the telephone call. Tony was in a ditch. He'd

skidded there in his car. The whole thing was off. Was I relieved? Yes. Was I disappointed? Yes. It was, like the Cuttyhunk hurricane, a nonevent. We all have them. And we go through life wondering. What *would* have happened? How *would* we have behaved?

I never stepped into a fighting ring again. But Betty and I were to meet, head on, another hurricane.

eleven

strange encounters

Most sensible sailing people of our acquaintance rarely left the relatively safe confines of Long Island Sound. Or if they did venture forth to bluer water, beyond Montauk Point, they went with other boats on the sound theory that in numbers there is safety. Often we were asked why we felt compelled to sail to Martha's Vineyard or Provincetown or Maine. Neither of us could answer, really, for we did not know. We could have sailed forever in the Sound, or outside with other boats, but it would not have been the same. Perhaps it was Thoreau's different drummer whom we heard.

It was not that we were ever truly skilled sailors. There were times when we got into difficulties that better sailors could have avoided, and other times we hesitated to venture forth when a more daring skipper would have. But we managed. We were a good team. As you may have inferred by this time, Betty performed the sail-handling chores aboard ship while I handled the tiller, to us a highly logical arrangement. Betty is a nimble, sure-footed, quick-fingered woman. She rarely wore shoes on a boat, for the native reason she felt she could get a better grip on any deck barefooted. Her hands and fingers were strong and far quicker than mine. She could handle lines, halyards, and sails with a deftness and speed I could not match. On the other hand, I could handle the tiller better than she. As a rule, the only time I went forward was to drop or weigh anchor or do some other chore that required masculine strength. It worked beautifully.

There were many times when Betty anticipated my thoughts. I would no sooner say, "I think we ought to get that Genoa in and the storm jib on," than she'd be hard at it. I would bring the boat up into the wind and we'd have the job done quickly and efficiently. Gathering storm clouds on the western horizon would set us to scanning charts for the nearest harbor. Sudden squalls and all-encompassing fogs unnerved us. We would often, like lost souls, try to retreat to the haven we had recently left.

Hornpipe was close to the perfect vessel for us. At 28 feet overall and sloop-rigged, she was not so large we could not handle her with ease. Yet she was large enough to take us comfortably, safely, and swiftly wherever we wished to go. Nonetheless, there were things about her we wished to change. We spent the winter months ripping the cabin apart, a process turned almost into pleasure by the artistry of Fred Werber, as both draftsman and cabinetmaker.

Almost before we knew it we were watching a wedge of honking geese fly over the boatyard.

"This is spring. Boy, it's what I live for!" someone would say. And now, with sails a-pull in a steady breeze of wind, and pennants snapping from mastheads, we were ready to sail again.

I recall one sunny day that year, a Sunday afternoon I believe it was, when Betty and I were coasting under a light

From left, Ellen Ditoro, Betty, and Peg Wyman aboard
Hornpipe, 1960

breeze. It was getting toward five o'clock and we were heading
west from Stamford toward Mamaroneck. I gazed out toward
the middle of the Sound and a strange rig caught my eye. A
sloop of something over 40 feet was gliding along. There
seemed to be a canvas dodger two or two and a half feet high
around her afterdeck. Then my eye caught a peculiar rig aft of
that, a short mast from which flew a tiny sail. There was one
more intriguing feature about the vessel. She carried a strange
flag at her stern. I switched on the engine and headed out
toward the sloop.

Betty, lying on the deck in the warm sun, sat up sleepily. "Anxious to get home?" she asked.

"No, but I am anxious to get close to that black sloop over there."

In a few moments we were close enough to read the name on the dodger, *Gypsy Moth III. Gypsy Moth? The Gypsy Moth!* Owned and sailed by Francis Chichester, the Magellan of our day? There was no one on deck as we approached, but the keen ears of the skipper, who was below, picked up the sound of our engine. In a moment a slight man of maybe 60 appeared from the cabin.

"Mr. Chichester?" I asked.

"I am indeed," he answered in a soft, clipped-British voice.

"It is a great pleasure to meet you. I—I've read your books."

"Thank you," he replied, "and I trust you will read the one I am now in the process of writing about my latest Atlantic passage, the passage I've just completed."

Because *Gypsy Moth III* was so much larger than *Hornpipe*, she sailed considerably faster, but by keeping the engine turning over slowly we kept abreast for half an hour or so. Chichester was a most gracious person. He answered our questions with patience and friendliness. But still, conversing with a man of his stature was somewhat similar to a kite flyer talking space problems with an astronaut.

"Where are you bound now?" I asked.

"Why, back to England," he replied.

Betty gulped. "You—you're on your way back now?"

"Yes. By way of Falmouth, Massachusetts. I'll take off from there."

I have heard Betty say she was going to the supermarket with more of a sense of adventure than this sailing man displayed at the prospect of recrossing the Atlantic Ocean.

Now Chichester took the tiller, disengaged a line or two

from his automatic steering device, and began to head slowly toward the Long Island shore.

"You're putting in to shore?" Betty asked.

"Yes, for the night," he replied. "Although she'd handle herself well enough through the Sound tonight, there's too much traffic to take the chance, and I'm a bit weary to steer her myself."

"Where are you headed?"

"Well, that's a bit of a nuisance, in fact," Chichester replied. "I've got only area charts. The only harbor I dare enter in this vicinity is Cold Spring Harbor. With this light breeze it will take me the better part of an hour to get down there, I'm sure."

"And even longer to get out in the morning," I added.

"That's the rub," he answered.

"What about Eaton's Neck?" Betty asked.

"My chart shows Eaton's, but no details and I'm chary of entering."

"Wait," Betty called, and dashed down the companionway ladder.

In a moment she was back on deck, a chart in her hand.

"Here's a chart of Eaton's, Mr. Chichester. It's yours."

It would be a gross exaggeration to say that we felt like Magellan, but we did feel like Magellan's navigator. Here was this intrepid man—the man who had flown an airplane from England to Australia back in the 1920s, the man who had sailed and raced single-handed across the Atlantic several times (who was later to circumnavigate the globe alone, then be knighted and become *Sir* Francis), graciously and gratefully accepting a chart from *us*.

"You can duck into Eaton's in 15 minutes from here and be back out in the Sound that quickly in the morning," I told him.

"And keep the chart," Betty added.

"I'll be happy to send it to you from England," Chichester said.

"No, no," I said grandly. "Keep it and remember us."

At last we came about and headed home. But the glow from meeting that lone, heroic man lasted long after the sun's rays that night.

Sometime later we received a lengthy letter from Francis Chichester in which he told us one or two of the highlights of his return voyage, but mainly he told us how much it meant to have spent that night at Eaton's Point. There was a long silence after we'd both read it. Finally Betty sighed.

"What a wonderful, thoughtful, heroic man," she said at last.

"Maybe you didn't know it, but he's married," I replied.

"He is?"

"Yep."

She stood up with the letter in her hand, then slowly put it on the table. "You could have waited and told me in the morning," she said.

That was the summer, too, of the Great Sea Rescue.

The weather was hot, humid, and breezeless when we left Stonington for Block Island. Then it began to rain, not a cool, refreshing shower, but a stuffy, steady, drumming downpour.

Dripping, we powered into the well-buoyed channel and headed for the area immediately off Champlin's dock, which we had been told had the best anchorage in the harbor. Apparently every skipper afloat had received the same news. So, as we had done on an earlier visit here, we continued east and anchored off the sandy strip which the chart told us was Indian Head Neck.

The second day a breeze came up out of the southwest and life became idyllic. The beach on the east coast of the

island is one long stretch of golden sand and we walked it
hand in hand until we knew every inch of it. In a day or two,
we discovered that clams could be had for the digging along
shore just a hundred yards or so to the lee of where *Hornpipe*
lay. One implement we lacked was a clam hoe, but where
there's an appetite, there's a way, and we dug with strong-
handled pans and spoons. Actually, it was better this way. A
hoe would have made it too easy, but because we had to
search and grub with our fingers, then dig with our awkward
utensils, each clam became as precious as a gem.

Clams became a way of life. We ate them raw, we ate them
steamed. We had clam cakes (too fattening), clam omelette
with chives (delectable), even clam pancakes (forget them).

Best of all, though, was the chowder. Betty diced a quarter
pound of salt pork, then put it in a frying pan over a low fire.
Next she sliced an onion, salted the slices so they would brown
evenly, and added these to the salt pork. The fat from the pork
became a liquid bath for the onion slices. For me no perfume
on earth can surpass that of frying onions. At this point I would
usually collapse on the cockpit seat in a state of nose-twitching
euphoria while Betty worked her wonders in the galley. To me
she was Amphitrite, wife of Poseidon and goddess of the sea,
or at least, the galley. Next she boiled a couple of potatoes,
then put about a quarter of a peck of clams in a big pan
and secured the lid. She never added water, and don't you
either, for the pure, undiluted juice of this lowly crustacean is
pure nectar.

When the shells opened, I was summoned out of my
reverie. We removed the necks, chopped up the bodies, and
added them and all the other ingredients to about five cups of
milk. The boiled potatoes were cut up into bite-size chunks
too, of course. The fire was turned down fairly low and this
marvelous concoction was set a-simmer. While you're about it,

and you're a fortunate person if you should be, add a few crumbled crackers to the chowder, continue to heat slowly.

Soon comes the true test of a man. When tasting and testing tells you the chowder is done, do not eat it. Put it aside. Let it cool. Let it rest. Read a good book. Take walks. Drink. Do anything, but let this ambrosia sit for at least a day, two days is even better. Your courage and fortitude and deprivation will be well rewarded if you wait, for clam chowder, like whiskey, improves with age.

One midafternoon while chowder was a-making, a small sloop came gliding down the harbor on a broad reach. We wouldn't have paid her any attention but for the fact that she had the appearance of great age, with sails mildew-stained to a dirty gray. She sailed down to a hundred or so feet to starboard of us, where the young man at the tiller brought her round into the breeze. In another moment the anchor was down. The man and a young woman, who we judged was in her midtwenties, deftly and quietly went about stowing the sails. They were clearly well aware of the poor quality of their sails, for they handled them with great care. After a bit they looked our way, waved, and we, in turn, saluted them.

Betty and I were both busy in the cabin an hour or two later when we heard a woman's voice hailing us. "*Hornpipe! Hornpipe!*"

We went up on deck. It was the woman on the old sloop.

"Have you got some bandaging aboard?" she asked.

"We do indeed," Betty answered. "Is something wrong?"

"My husband cut his foot," the woman replied. "It's bleeding some."

We gathered up the first-aid kit, jumped into the dinghy, and rowed over. The cut was jagged but not severe, although it was bleeding freely. Tom, the husband, had caught his heel on a nail head that had worked loose from the cabin sole. His wife, Bonnie, applied merthiolate to the cut, then bandaged it neatly while Betty and I stood by. The sloop, we were told, was 20 feet overall and something over 40 years of age. They had little money, few supplies, and no equipment to speak of. They were out of City Island and intended to start back the next day, with an overnight stop at Port Jefferson. The little ship had no inboard power, but I did notice a small outboard motor stowed under a bunk. After the usual amount of small talk, the young people thanked us and we returned to *Hornpipe*.

That night the weather forecast was ominous; heavy rain with near gale-force winds at times was predicted for early the next day.

"Do you suppose those young people have a radio?" Betty asked. "They're leaving in the morning, you know."

I glanced over at the darkened boat. "I hope so, but I doubt it."

"Maybe you should row over and tell them about the weather report."

"Tom might just hit me over the head with an oar for disturbing them."

I was to wish later I had taken that risk. Betty was concerned and so was I. But one just does not row over to a boat whose occupants have obviously turned in, rap on the sides, and announce that it's going to rain tomorrow. Nonetheless I was disturbed by a gnawing fear that they did not possess a radio, that I *should* inform them of the impending storm.

Neither of us slept well that night. I could hear Betty turning and sighing in her bunk. I churned in mine. As a result we both dropped into deep sleep toward dawn and did not awaken until we heard a heavy splatter of rain on the deck over our heads. We could feel the wind in *Hornpipe*'s rigging.

"Have Bonnie and Tom gone?" Betty asked, wide awake.

I jumped up and looked out a porthole. "Yes, damn it."

"They didn't have a radio, so they didn't get a report," she announced with finality. "What time is it?"

"Seven-fifteen."

"They probably left before daylight and couldn't have seen the storm clouds gathering."

Neither of us said anything as we dressed and bathed.

"The wind's getting stronger," Betty observed.

I wished she would keep quiet. My conscience was giving me enough trouble. We managed to get halfway through breakfast. "To hell with it," I announced. "Let's go out and look around. Maybe we can see them. If we can't, they're too far out for us to do anything about it."

The dishes were stowed unwashed. We got into foul-weather gear, reefed the main for use as a steadying sail, got up the anchor, and powered through the pond. The water here was almost still under the pounding rain, but through the channel we could see whitecaps rushing by.

"It must be blowing about 35 knots," I yelled.

"That's about 40 miles an hour," Betty translated for her own benefit. "I'm scared for them," she added.

I opened the throttle wide and we raced toward the channel, then we were outside. *Hornpipe* was slammed broadside by the heaving seas. But because we did not have the jib raised and the mainsail was reefed down, we were not uncomfortable. Though the clouds were heavy and low, there was a translucence about the air that provided a good visibility despite the driving rain.

"See anything?" Betty said.

"Nothing but water, but we might as well head southwest a ways."

We ran in silence for about ten minutes and the seas were beginning to build. They were now nearing three feet.

Suddenly Betty pointed to starboard. "There they are!"

Sure enough, directly abeam and not a half a mile away the little sloop pitched. The mainsail had been taken in but the jib was in tatters. I altered course and increased our speed. As we closed on them we saw they had put out a sea anchor of sorts and this held their bow into the waves. The little outboard motor was hanging to its rack on the transom, obviously lifeless.

Betty had gotten out a strong line for towing, but as we came alongside Tom was already handing his sea-anchor line and he tossed it over to Betty. Two streaming blankets served as sea anchors, and it took both of us to heave them aboard. Presently the line was secured and, with Bonnie and Tom calling and waving their thanks, we took off for the harbor.

"Poor things," Betty said. "Did you see that old raincoat Bonnie is wearing? And he's got just a sweatshirt."

"And no radio," I added.

"And no sails, I'm sure."

Bonnie and Tom, though, were wiser than we knew. After we were safely anchored once more, we heard the story. They had taken off shortly before dawn. They suspected that bad weather was on the way, but because Tom was due back at his job in two days they had risked it. There had been no breeze at first, so the little outboard shoved them along until they got outside the harbor, where they found a light southwesterly, hoisted sail, and stowed the outboard. Soon, though, Tom saw they were in for some weather and decided to head back to Block Island.

A sudden surge of wind canceled their plan. Providentially, they got their fragile mainsail down before it blew out. A wave doused the outboard. In another few minutes the old jib let go. Tom had just fashioned the sea anchor when we hove into view. Fortunately, they had another jib. That one was scarcely any better than the other, but it was usable. The next morning under a bright sun and gentle, very gentle breezes, they took off again.

"You know what we should have done?" I asked Betty sometime later.

"What?"

"We should have gone to the Coast Guard and let them pick them up."

"And miss our only chance for a rescue at sea?" Betty asked. "Anyway, the Coast Guard wouldn't have given them a radio," she added.

"No, they sure—what?"

"Oh, I gave them that little old transistor we never use."

"Wh—what about our foul-weather gear?" I stammered.

"Well, I must say I thought of that." She smiled.

It occurred to me to be grateful that our sails couldn't possibly fit the little sloop.

The day came when we became satiated with clams, hiking, and indolence, so we weighed anchor and sailed the 12 miles across Block Island Sound to Newport. This is the water where the America's Cup races are held, the water where the empire builders of another era luxuriated aboard yachts as large as their palatial homes. We rounded Castle Hill, on Newport Neck, proceeded up the channel, then came starboard into Brenton Cove, a bight in the southern part of Newport Harbor. A launchman from the Ida Lewis Yacht Club directed us to an unoccupied club mooring where we made fast.

An unforgettable ritual took place each day aboard a handsome sloop of some 42 or 43 feet moored to port of us. Promptly at noon each of the four days we were there two deckhands arrived by dinghy and proceeded to mop and polish every inch of that craft both above decks and below. Just as promptly, at two o'clock the club launch arrived with one or sometimes two young men in informal yachting attire, accompanied by a gentleman who we guessed must have been nearing eighty years of age. Each day he was impeccably attired in a white shirt with a dark blue necktie, deep blue yachting jacket and trousers, and dark yachting cap. He was infirm to the point where he was slowly and carefully handed aboard, then assisted to his seat at the wheel.

By this time the crew had got the sails bent on. After it was seen to that the old gentleman's needs were satisfied, the sails were hoisted and the vessel was cast off. On two of the days the wind barreled down out of the northwest, but it was always the same. He came off the mooring so quickly, so beautifully that Betty and I merely gazed in awed admiration. Off they went into Narragansett Bay for an afternoon's sail and it would not be until six o'clock or so that they returned. Always it was the same. This venerable man was still seated at the wheel. They flew down under full sail, rounded up under the mooring, and with marvelous precision he brought his ship's bow up to the float. The hand forward with the boathook merely reached down, snagged the loop, and took it aboard. There was never any frenzied snatching or fishing for the line. It was there, the ship's stem was brought up beside it.

Quickly the snapping sails were lowered. The old man was ceremoniously, almost reverently, helped to the side where the club launch was already waiting. The old man handled his vessel with consummate skill. We never learned who he was; we never asked.

twelve

down east

One does not cruise the Northeast coast too long before his thoughts turn to the coast of Maine. This rocky, beautiful, ever-dangerous shore has a magnetic attraction for the adventurous sailor. The moment for us to undertake it had come, our excitement was intense. We purchased charts to take us as far east as Penobscot Bay and spent countless hours studying them, plotting possible courses, and determining which harbors and coves we would like most to visit. A few of these we knew from the shore. Now we would know them from the sea.

As far as Cuttyhunk, it was familiar territory, if the sea can ever be called that. We spent a night at Cuttyhunk and by nine the next morning were bound for Onset, Massachusetts, a well-protected harbor that lies at the western end of Cape Cod Canal. Buzzards Bay was known to us only by reputation, so the flat calm of the morning's sail was not unexpected. But we had a sail of only about 30 nautical miles to make, so we dawdled along until about noon when a fresh southwesterly came up. Like a bronco responding to spurs, *Hornpipe* sprang to life. That boat was fast. Too fast, I would see now, for my calculations. I had intended to arrive at Cleveland Ledge Light just before slack water, but *Hornpipe*'s tearing along at full speed got us there a good two hours before the turn of the tide. Betty took in the jib, but if *Hornpipe*'s speed slackened, it was imperceptible. We arrived at Onset earlier than we had anticipated.

We had dinner aboard. Then, since it was still daylight, we rowed ashore in the dinghy and explored the town. A pleasant place, Onset. As we wandered about, we noticed uniformed men carrying musical instruments gathering at a small park. Then we spied a bandstand.

My home town had a bandstand—free concerts, too. But that was many years ago. How often such simple, pristine pleasures slip into the mists of time, to disappear, be gone and forgotten. But Onset had one. Its rear was to the harbor. The audience sat on a slight rise of ground, facing the musicians in their shell. As the band played—Victor Herbert, Vincent Youmans, Stephen Foster, John Philip Sousa—one's eyes slid to the harbor beyond. Here and there lights were winking on in boats riding to their anchors. A soft breath of salt-laden air came up off the water, and we were engulfed in nostalgia. At last, at dusk the concert ended. Betty and I rose from our seats on the grass and walked hand in hand back to our beached dinghy. In the softness of the evening I rowed into the darkness that hid *Hornpipe*.

In the quiet of the night we lay, one on each side, on the cockpit seats and gazed up at the sky. It was a cloudless night. High overhead twinkled Vega, the brightest star in the tiny constellation of Lyra, the Lyre of Orpheus. It was upon this lyre, legend tells, that Orpheus played his music and sang in a voice so sweet that even the birds were hushed in midsong and the babbling waters of brooks and falls ceased their sounds. There to the east is Pegasus, the horse; then the Great Square and attached to it is the constellation Andromeda. Between Pegasus and Lyra lies Cygnus, the Swan. By February, Cygnus is gone from our sky. By May it has returned.

All is ordered and orderly in that crowded sky, as timely and timeless as our own star, the sun. Without deviation, these awesome formations, which were named thousands of years ago by shepherds and other people of the night, wheel through the deep vaults of the heavens. Changeless they are, yet ever changing. The sky of an August night is not quite the sky of even a September night. Many of the constellations we see in summer are gone when the ground is white with snow. But just as night follows day, come another August, those same figures will be there. Our eyes will seek them out again, to watch, to wonder, without comprehension. World without end. Amen, amen.

We were up the next morning to a gray dawn. We hurried through our chores and errands, for we wanted to catch the favorable tide through the Cape Cod Canal. It behooves one in a vessel with only a 30-horsepower engine to travel with rather than against the tide through the canal, for the mean range of tide at the western, or Buzzards Bay, entrance is only about four feet, while at the Cape Cod Bay end it is almost nine feet. This difference causes strong currents in the canal itself, currents one does not knowingly challenge.

Before the canal was constructed (it was completed in 1914), vessels in these waters were forced to sail through the hazardous shoals around Cape Cod. The canal has reduced that voyage by as much as 100 miles. It is said that Captain Miles Standish, even in those long-ago days, wished for a cut through Cape Cod. Later, George Washington contemplated such a canal. Construction actually was begun in 1870, but was later abandoned. It was restarted in 1909, and the first traverse across the isthmus was accomplished by the august August Belmont. The land cut is slightly over eight miles. Volume II of the *United States Coast Pilot* states that "the waterway is 15 miles long from Cleveland Ledge Light to deep water in Cape Cod Bay." The canal has a water depth of 32 feet and a width of 450 feet. One more bit of information: one does *not* sail through the canal. As we were to learn later in a time of distress, one powers.

So we powered. It was a piece of cake, except for one exasperating experience. We were relaxed, enjoying the sights that slipped past us on either side of the canal. Suddenly a huge object caught our attention: an oceangoing vessel was approaching from the opposite direction. We braced ourselves against the bow wave that tumbled straight for us. It caught us, we slammed into it, rolled, and *Hornpipe* quickly regained her bottom.

That was easy. Fun, in fact. What we didn't take into consideration was that, when that bow wave struck the canal bank, it had nowhere to go but come back to us. It did. *Hornpipe* lurched, pitched, and I found myself half in the water, clinging for dear life to a cleat and a back stay. *Hornpipe* swung away and headed for the bank! "Get back in. We're running away!" Betty ordered.

"You think I *want* to be overboard?" I shouted back. "Steer!"

She did. I scrambled back into the cockpit, glared around to see what had hit us, couldn't find anything, shivered and shook some icy water off my shriveled hide, and glared at Betty, who sat at the tiller trying to control a fit of laughter.

In less than an hour, we were out in Cape Cod Bay, shrouded in a fog. Only the leaden heave of the water told us we were indeed in open water, not still in the Cape Cod

Canal. From the appearance of things it would be an all-day compass-and-engine run. We dozed, read, stretched, scratched, studied charts, ate, and sweated. The fumes from the exhaust curled up over the transom and engulfed us in a bluish smog. We both had headaches.

In the late afternoon as we approached Gloucester, still one of the world's great fishing ports, Betty's spirits seemed to lighten. I detected a faint smile playing with her lips.

"What're you smiling about?"

"Oh, was I smiling?"

But she had *something* on her mind.

At last we closed on Gloucester harbor and I heard:

> "'It was the schooner Hesperus,
> That sailed the wintry sea;
> And the skipper had taken his little daughter,
> To bear him company.'"

"'The Wreck of the Hesperus,'" I ventured.

She nodded.

"That's why you've been smiling?"

"Longfellow placed the wreck on the reef of Norman's Woe. The cove is just ahead on the left as we approach the harbor."

"Do you know the whole poem?" This facet of my wife's knowledge had evaded me.

"Once I did. A terrible thing happened."

"I sort of remember. It was a winter storm, or something, and they all died when they struck the reef?"

"The worst thing happened to me." She faced me. "I had to learn that poem and recite it before the whole school." She gazed over in the direction of Norman's Woe. "Well, I got halfway through it. Then, suddenly, well—the elastic that held up my sort of panty affair broke." She was blushing. "They fell down—right at my feet."

"I'll be damned."

"I picked them up and put them in my sweater pocket, and I finished the poem."

We moved along, both picturing the scene. "How old were you?"

"Twelve. 'On the reef of Norman's Woe,'" she intoned as we sailed past that cursed reef. The reef of Norman's and *Betty's* woe.

The next morning I arose early. We had planned to start at sunup through the Annisquam River, then sail the 65 or 70 miles of open ocean to Cape Elizabeth, Maine, and beyond to one of the lovely islands that dot Casco Bay. But the best-laid plans of mice and men, etc. I arrived on deck to the thickest, most peasoup, catatonic fog the elements at their demonic worst could devise. *Hornpipe's* white mast rose five feet from the deck and disappeared. The dinghy could have been in Hyannisport, for all I could tell. I sat down on the cockpit seat with a groan and rose immediately. Soaked.

There was nothing to do but crawl back to my bunk, wet pajama bottoms and all. We stayed in that cocoon all day.

We were already behind schedule. The next morning we were able to see 150 feet or so. All about us boat people were stirring.

"Let's go," I said. "We should have enough visibility to get a little way along." We made it to the eastern end of the Annisquam River. A few boats anchored near us, but the others passed on—out to sea, perhaps, but certainly out of sight. Another day lost.

The third morning we were still enveloped, but a weather forecast promised improving conditions. We felt we had to move. The air was breathless. I started the engine, hoisted the anchor, and got under way. Prisoners no more! We knew where the channel markers were supposed to be; we just couldn't find them. Where were they? There should be a buoy dead now, but...

Sssh. The sound of a ship's bow sliding into a sandbar. *Hornpipe* came to an abrupt stop. Quickly I reversed the engine, opened the throttle, and waited. Nothing happened. The engine alone couldn't pull her off. With Betty's help, I loaded the anchor into the dinghy, rowed well astern, dropped the anchor overboard, rowed back, and clambered aboard. Sometimes, I had read, one could "kedge" a boat off a shoal or sandbar. With the engine reversed once more and at full throttle, I hauled mightily on the anchor line. It's a neat theory. With the aid of the engine I should have been able to haul *Hornpipe* back off the bar. It didn't work.

We were aground in about three feet of water. *Hornpipe* drew something over four. It was half-tide now, and the tide was falling. Dear Lord, why did we ever start out on this cruise? I could be home, mowing the lawn, chatting with friends, watching the Yankees or Mets play ball, playing golf—anything. Betty thought of a few things she might be doing as well. Instead, we were stuck on a bar of river sand.

The time was approaching seven o'clock in the morning. Through the veil of fog I could barely discern the outlines of two channel buoys. In our blind groping we'd missed them by 75 feet. We heard the splashing of oars and turned. An elderly man clad in khaki shirt and trousers approached our stern.

"Gone aground, eh?"

It would seem so. "How long," I asked, "will it take for the tide to turn and float us off?"

He rested on his oars. "Well, sir, it'll be 'bout two hours 'til you're high an' dry. Another 20 minutes or so of slack water.

Another three hours 'til tide's high enough to git you afloat. That figgers out to be somewheres over five hours, I reckon." He gazed at us for another moment and rowed off.

We slumped onto the cockpit seats. This cruise was supposed to be fun, excitement, adventure. Well, one could call this adventure, but it wasn't what we had in mind. An early-morning flat tire at the beginning of a 600-mile trip by car could be called "adventure," too, I suppose.

Betty, the pragmatist, spoke through the gloom. "What will happen to the boat when she is 'high and dry,' as the man said?"

"She'll sit here. Nothing will happen—for five hours, anyway."

"But will she just sit on her keel when there's no water to hold her up? Won't we just roll over?"

I pictured our sloop slowly canting as the water receded around her keel; falling over on her side like a beached whale. My God! I thought of the havoc in the cabin as everything slid, crashed, tumbled into a chaotic mess. Worse, would the ribs and planking on *Hornpipe*'s side be strong enough to bear her great weight? Or would she collapse?

Stunned, we sat and stared at each other. Already *Hornpipe* had a decided list to starboard. The round bottom of a sailing vessel would roll, and *Hornpipe* had begun.

What to do? In all the reading, studying, practicing, question-asking of other sailing people, the subject had never come up. I clambered over the side and waded forward through the thigh-deep water. No question. She was going over. I saw, too, that the sand bar fell away abruptly on the starboard side. *Hornpipe* would not only roll over, but conceivably she could slide off the bar and sink into the channel!

My lower body was soaked with icy seawater. Above I was drenched in cold sweat. This must have happened thousands of times before. What did the others do? Did their boats collapse, crushed by their own weight? There must be some way to prevent that from happening. There was—wait! The anchors. The 18-pound Danforth and the big yachtsman's anchor. What if I lugged them out a hundred feet or so to the left, buried them in the sand, then secured both anchor rodes to the mast where it enters the cabin? Would they hold her up? I didn't know anything else to do, and time, like the tide, was running out.

I scrambled back onto the boat, hauled the anchors out, told Betty my plan, and stumbled through the water as she paid out the lines. Up on the beach I buried them as best I could in the sand, ran back to *Hornpipe*, hauled the anchor lines as taut as possible, and secured them around the mast. Now the water was scarcely two feet deep. *Hornpipe* had a heavy list to starboard. A few more minutes and she would have gone over. Now back to the anchors. They were dug in deeper than I had planted them. The lines were stretched tighter than I had fixed them. The anchors were taking the strain. We carried our most valuable possessions above the low-water line and deposited them on the beach; the rest would have to stay on the boat. At the bow once more I saw she had listed some more. Vaguely, I noted the warp in the boat's stern that Fred Werber had been disturbed about. It seemed worse. But *that* was of no consequence now.

Now, early-morning beach strollers were gathering. A few were genuinely concerned with our plight; the rest were idly curious. In fact, they were enjoying it. How could they? This was our *boat*. We were despairing of saving her. Betty joined me. The wait began. By now there was less than a foot of water at *Hornpipe*'s keel. No support at all. But the anchors were digging deeper and deeper into the sand. I began to feel confident they would hold.

Spectators came and went. It was like a carnival for them. But who could blame them. A boat didn't go ashore every day. They, as did we, waited to see what would happen. Would the anchors tear out of the sand? Would the lines part? For us, cold-sweat tension; for them, a pleasant divertissement.

The water was gone now. *Hornpipe*'s feet were dry. There were barnacles on her hull and here and there wisps of grass. Stricken but gallant, she was standing. That was the important thing. We held our breath and waited. How long? *How long?* Slowly, almost imperceptibly, the sea returned. An inch, then another. At last, at last. We had two feet of water. The keel was covered, small waves lapped at the hull. We gathered up our belongings, carried them through the water, tossed them back into the cockpit. There were smiles for us and wishes of good luck. People waved and disappeared up the beach, into the fog. They had stayed. Nice people. They cared.

I dug up the anchors and lugged them back aboard. *Hornpipe* could stand alone. In a half hour the sloop gave a little lurch; then another. Betty looked at me and I, at her.

"We're afloat?"

We were afloat. I started the engine, let it idle. Casco Bay was out, but we wouldn't stay here. I steered out into Ipswich Bay. In a moment Betty was spreading out chart #1206. The Isles of Shoals were roughly 20 miles east. We hadn't thought of them in our previous planning, but given the time of day, they'd make a good objective. A small breeze had sprung up from the south; sailing time. We cut the engine, unstopped the mainsail on the boom, hoisted it, got the jib on, and moved out. We set a compass course for whistle buoy W1. *Hornpipe*, like a parched creature freed from a trap, heeled to port and lapped noisily at the water. We both seemed to crumple into the seat cushions. The morning was a nightmare, but it was over.

The sun, which in the morning had waged a short battle

with the fog, had lost. We could see only a few hundred yards. Minutes earlier Cape Ann and the mainland had stood out fairly clearly. Now they were gone. All about us was the fog. *Hornpipe* lifted and fell with the slow, even surge of the sea. There was little to do now but watch the compass. Wavelets lapped *Hornpipe*'s bow and gurgled back along her flanks. Betty stretched out, sighed, and instantly fell into a soft, untroubled sleep.

"Sweet are the uses of adversity/Which, like the toad, ugly and venomous,/Wears yet a precious jewel in his head." This was the use of adversity. This was the precious jewel. The sails slept in the breeze just as my wife slept on the cockpit bench. The compass needle swept to 20°, then down to 12°. *Hornpipe*'s bow wandered with the heave of the sea. Never mind. We were on course. The anxiety of the morning was washed away by the euphoria of the present. I crept down into the cabin and found a waterproof jacket, laid it gently over my sleeping wife. A slight adjustment of the tiller put us back on course again. The boat's warped stem made a drag on the tiller. I'd think about that later.

An hour passed. Two. Then three. Betty stirred. Rubbed her eyes and sat up.

"I'm starved," she announced. "Where are we?"

"We should be coming down on the Isles of Shoals in an hour or so."

"I'll fix us a snack." Her voice trailed back as she headed down the ladder to the cabin.

We ate, sat back. Betty resumed her study of the chart. With the lunch she'd also brought the cruising guide to the cockpit. In the distance forward and to starboard we heard a half-moan, half-whistle sound. W1! On the nose. Our navigation works. We glanced at each other, pleased.

"All right," Betty announced. "We want to stay just about

on this same course. We should keep White Island to starboard. We can't cut it too close," she continued, studying the
chart. "There is a ledge and a big rock on our side of the
island."

I waited.

"There's a lighthouse on White Island, too. We won't be
able to see it, I suppose, but it's got a foghorn, so we'll hear
that."

Good enough.

Time stopped. The fog enveloped us in its gray cocoon.
Hornpipe rolled slowly to the rounded shoulders of the seas as
they swept beneath us endlessly, endlessly. There was no
sensation of forward motion. Instead, the sea came to us,
bringing with it seaweed, kelp, watermelon rinds, grapefruit
halves, a board, a drowned tree limb. And plastic. Cups, plates,
jugs, containers of all sorts and sizes. Mankind's detritus,
undissolvable droppings. All this the sea brought us on its
broad platter, swept by, and was lost. The sea, an endless
carpet littered by both man and nature.

Betty sat in her accustomed place, back to the cabin bulkhead, knees drawn up. She studied the chart. When the time
came to find our way to an anchorage among the Isles of
Shoals, she would be ready. She would know the buoys by
heart. She would know there was a ledge on the port hand or
shoal water to starboard. Quiet, sure, quick. She knew her job.
There was an instinct for the sea about her I never had. I was
the landlubber. Her ancestors came, generations ago, from
Wellfleet, on Cape Cod. Hardings they were, and they had
sailed the tall-masted vessels that brought fame and commerce
to America's shores. Eventually they had moved from Wellfleet
to Maine. But always they lived close by the sea.

My glance swept from my wife to the compass and back
again. Back to the compass. We should be coming down on the

whistler soon. But what if we missed it? What if my course plotting was wrong? Where would we fetch up? On a rock, a ledge? That, I guessed, was the principal difference between us. Betty trusted. You plotted the course with parallel rules, walked it off with dividers, allowed for compass deviation, consulted tide and current tables, made allowances, and sailed on. All would come out right. She knew it. I envied her.

Out of the fog whistle buoy W1 slid toward us and past, moaning and puffing in its lonely world. In a few minutes we picked up the heavy grunt of the White Island foghorn. There are no highway markers on the sea. No route U.S. 684. No arrows pointing right or left, no stop signs or traffic lights. But there are horns and whistles and buoys. And lighthouses, those great flaming beacons which have drawn the eyes of anxious men through seafaring centuries.

White Island, barely discernible, drew abeam, then diminished. Lunging Island was next. We continued for a few minutes, came about into the light breeze, dropped the sails, and started the engine. Our destination was Gosport Harbor. Star Island, with its summer hotel, would be to starboard. Cedar Island and Smuttynose Island, too, would be somewhere dead ahead, and Appledore Island would lie to port. Crazy names. Funny names. What did they signify? Who named them such? There is even a Malaga Cut. Malaga, Spain? We know that these tiny mounds of rock and earth have been inhabited for centuries. Fishermen and their families settled on Appledore in the early 1600s. Celia Thaxter, in her book *Among the Isles of Shoals*, tells us that over a hundred years before our American Revolution there were perhaps as many as 500 souls living on these tiny isles. They lived well off the sea, and such was the quality of their schools that students even came out from the mainland to learn their three R's.

The summer hotel on Star Island, named the Ocean Hotel,

is host through the summer to conventions of religious groups, mainly Congregationalists and Unitarians. If isolation is conducive to meditation, the profundity of their thoughts must truly stir the ear of the Deity.

I throttled the engine back to a mere murmur. The fog lay on the backs of the islands. The scene brought to mind an early American painting hanging in New York's Metropolitan Museum of Art. *Fur Traders on the Missouri* it's called, by George Caleb Bingham. Two fur seekers in a canoe. Soundless, motionless, arresting. We powered in between Star and Cedar, cut the engine. The place had the enchanting, waiting silence of a Christmas Eve. I broke out the anchor and lowered it gently into the sea. The breeze would back us down so the hook would find its home deep in the sand and the mud. Betty sighed and, like a tired evening wave collapsing on the beach, sagged into a cockpit cushion.

"Long day," I muttered.

She got up. Stretched. "Mind if I go below and lie down?"

I didn't mind. In a moment I could hear her soft, even breath of sleep. Half an hour passed. I wondered about supper. Perhaps we didn't need to eat. But we should. It was getting late. It would be dark soon. It was then I heard the soft rumble of an engine. A lobster boat ghosted out of the fog, slowed, and stopped beside a lobster float like an attentive mother. The fisherman hitched a line to it and, with the aid of a small block-and-tackle device, began to haul the trap.

I cat-footed down to the cabin, stole my wallet from a locker, got into the dinghy, and rowed over to the lobsterman. He didn't hear me approach and turned only when the bow of my dinghy nudged the side of his boat.

"Good evening," I said.

"Ayeh," he inhaled. To my knowledge State of Mainers are the only people who talk breathing in.

"Would you have a couple extra?"

"Never got extra lobsters." He talked and worked. "Never git 'nough, seems so. How many might you be wantin'?" He straightened up slowly. It was chilly and damp, but the sleeves of his blue workshirt were rolled above his elbows.

"Two," I spoke with hope, "if you can spare them."

"Guess I might at that." He turned to a large, weather-beaten box at his feet. It seemed to be filled with seaweed. He reached down, felt around, came up with two prehistoric monsters.

"Them two suit you?"

"They sure would. How big are they?"

"'Bout three, three an' a half pounds each, I figger. Ain't got none bigger."

My Amex traveler's checks were back aboard *Hornpipe*. I had only cash in my wallet.

"How—ah—how much are they?"

"Wal." He eyed me. "You look a mite peaked. Poorly, y'might say. Give me a dollar each an' I'll throw in the plugs I got in their claws."

I paid him quickly before he could change his mind, thanked him, and rowed back to *Hornpipe*, humming. I always assumed Betty loved me. I *knew* she loved lobsters. But seven pounds of lobster?

She never stirred as I rummaged around the galley for the biggest pot we had. Tiptoed out with it, brought out the kerosene stove, and set things up on the afterdeck. Lit the stove, dipped enough seawater to cover the bottom of the pot. Sat down and waited. It is more blessed to give than to receive. Surprise. Surprise. Surprise! I hoped she wouldn't waken. My heart thumped and I grinned hugely. The water boiled. In went the lobsters. My God, what a way to go. They thumped and banged their anguish against the sides of the pot and I had to hold the lid on. The thrashing stopped. I'd do them 20 minutes by my watch. There was a stirring below. Around the bulkhead I saw Betty move. She sat up.

"Something woke me. I was dreaming—*what are you doing?*" She came up the steps from the cabin like Mean Joe Green. "You haven't! You couldn't!" She snatched the lid off the pot. Stared, disbelieving. "Where did you get those beautiful, gorgeous creatures?"

"Well, there was this great big bird flying around. It looked like a stork. Yes. It *was* a stork. It brought these babies to us."

We gorged. We ate the claws, the tails, the legs. Sucked every ounce of flavor out of the legs. Then went to work on the bodies. The green stuff. The tomale. Finally we sighed and fell back.

Betty really did love lobster. And she loved me.

By early morning of the following day the breeze had backed a bit from south to east. The sea fog still held us in its cloying cocoon. But there was a different texture to it. It might lift a bit later on, and we could move. We *had* to move, for already we were a week behind our schedule to sail to Maine and home again in a month. I was mopping the deck and brightwork, using the fresh fog and dew as mop water. Betty was below, banging pots and pans and dishes around.

"Oh, oh."

The mop stopped in midswipe. Those two words. How short they are. How ominous. My dentist uses them. He gets that small metal pick in his hands, then goes exploring. He hums. He jabs here, hooks the pick into something there. Suddenly he stops.

"Oh, oh."

My heart jumps. He works the pick deeper. Oh, oh. I want to cry out. What is it, man? What horror have you discovered smoldering in that molar?

So now, with Betty. She's discovered a hole in the bottom, or perhaps the bow stove in, and we're sinking.

"What is it, dear?" I assume my calmest voice.

"We're out of ice."

"Out of ice?" Is that all?

She slid the hatch cover back, stuck her head out the companionway, and faced me. "You sound disappointed. But being out of ice means what supplies we have left in the icebox are going to spoil if we don't get some ice soon."

I sigh. No long sail today. No making up time. We study a chart and decide to put in at York Harbor. We'd get ice, gasoline, fresh water, and Betty would shop. In 20 minutes we had the anchor up, the sails on and were moving out, headed east.

East. Not to York Harbor yet. There was another place I wished to see. A place of minor tragedy in the saga of the American seacoast which, if Kenneth Roberts had not preserved it in book form, might be lost forever. Boon Island.

Boon Island is a short six miles offshore. Yet in the winter of 1710 it seemed to the shipwrecked souls on that dismal rock pile that those six miles might as well have been 600. In late September of 1710 the galley *Nottingham*, with a crew of 14 men, sailed out of Donegal Bay, Ireland, bound for Portsmouth, New Hampshire. She carried 60,000 pounds of butter and 300 Donegal cheeses. The weather in October was bad and in November it turned atrocious. The 13 crewmen and their gallant captain, John Dean, fought the savage seas of the North Atlantic valiantly, but in vain. On December 11, 1710, *Nottingham*, in a blinding, gale-driven snowstorm, fetched up on the rocks of Boon Island. Six short miles from Portsmouth, New Hampshire.

We sailed east in our *Hornpipe* on that quiet, foggy morning. In the distance the low profile of the island rose from the sea. We could see a lighthouse there, but not much else.

And according to author Roberts there *was* nothing else. Nothing but rocks, hoar frost, ice, and a pounding, driving sea. The shipwrecked sailors had dragged some timbers, a torn canvas sail, and a few cheeses ashore. And that was it. From the timbers and a few salvaged nails they fashioned a raftlike boat on which seven of the 14 took to sea, hoping to make the mainland. But the first big sea drove the craft back onto the rocks. The attempt was a failure.

They ate the cheese in a few days, then subsisted on seaweed and two or three mussels until, on December 23, one of them caught a seagull. One crewman died and they buried him at sea. There was no shelter except for a tentlike affair rigged from a tattered sail. Winter gales battered them with snow and freezing rain. Another member of the crew died. There was talk of giving him to the ocean that assaulted them, as they had the first. Instead, they lived off his flesh. Once more a raft was fashioned and launched. Two members of the starved company took off. They were never heard from again. All this while, on clear days the wretched creatures could see the mainland, and on occasion they could see, or thought they could see, people walking about.

That was Boon Island. Barren rock and ice storms that cut their flesh to ribbons. No fire, no warmth or protection but tattered clothing and the piece of canvas under which they huddled. On January 4, 1711, a shallop came from the mainland and rescued them. Twenty-four days. Ten men. A small saga when compared to many. But it happened on Boon Island, off Portsmouth, New Hampshire, and Kittery, Maine, a long time ago.

We sailed past, then turned west. York Harbor, Maine, where we could get ice and fuel and supplies. Boon Island receded into the last remnants and wisps of fog.

We dug out the *Eldridge Tide and Pilot Book*. With luck we

would make it into the harbor at slack water; at worst, the tide would just have turned against us. There is a rise and fall of nearly nine feet of water between mean high and mean low tides. Betty reads from the cruising guide that the tide in the York River "approaches awe-inspiring velocities at full strength." And "eddies swirl one about alarmingly." We glance at each other. Chart #211 shows that we go straight, then round one last nun buoy to starboard, and head up into the harbor. No problem there, except a gravel bank on the east. We would rather not run aground again.

Betty went below, checked supplies, and made a shopping list. We had a following breeze, fairly light but steady, and *Hornpipe*, as though she too had urgent business ashore, lifted her skirts and showed the sea a lacy froth. In short order we were at the channel entrance. Once more I fretted about the heavy helm. That twisted stem!

We came about, up into the wind, and dropped sails. Betty was furling the main, preparatory to strapping it down to the boom, when she stopped.

"What are those red things bobbing around in the channel?"

I turned. Gaped. "They couldn't be!"

"But they are!" Lobster buoys, on either side of the channel and *in* the channel!

"Lobster traps aren't allowed in channels," my fair lady protested. No damage would be done if we simply hit the floats that marked the traps lying on the bottom. But there would be a problem if the warp, the line that connects the float to the trap below, should get tangled up in our propeller.

I turned to the engine. Betty said, "I'll get up to the bow and guide us in." I pressed the starter button. The engine coughed, came to life. Coughed again. Died. I tried again. The starter motor whirred and whirred. Nothing. We were drifting closer to the channel entrance. I raised a cockpit seat, wrenched off the gas-tank top, grabbed the measuring stick. Dry! *We had run out of gas.*

"Betty! Get the jib up. I'll hoist the main!"

Oh, my God. Hurry, hurry, hurry. Sweat, sweat, sweat. It would be one thing to sail down that channel; quite another to do it and dodge those floats. We would have a following breeze. That meant we would gybe in. Fortunately, the breeze was not so strong as to threaten the mast. The mainsail boom would be swinging back and forth across the breadth of the boat with each quick turn. If I didn't remember to duck with each swing, I would be either knocked overboard or beaten bloody. Or both.

We got the sails up and swung away. What now? York was the only good harbor, with supplies, between Cape Porpoise— a long way off—and Portsmouth.

"Shall we go in?"

Betty looked at me. "We're out of ice, out of gas, low on supplies. It's all less than a mile away. I'm game, if you are."

That's my kid. Sure, why not. Once more we approached the channel. I trimmed the mainsail so the boom would swing only four or five feet off center each time it came over. But the sail would partially block my vision forward.

"Okay," I said, trying to keep the trill out of my voice. "Take the jib down so we'll have only the main to bother with. You've got to guide us in from the bow." I paused. I had to go to the bathroom. "Forget the nautical terms. Just say 'left' or 'right.' Or 'hard left' or 'hard right.' Okay?"

She had the jib down already. "Right," she called back.

"You mean 'turn right' already?"

"No. I mean, right, You're right. And shut up. Don't confuse me."

Thirty seconds passed. "First buoy coming up. Turn right." Done. "Now—turn left." I stood at the tiller. The mainsail and boom slammed over. I ducked. "Hard left!" The wooden float scraped *Hornpipe*'s flanks. "Still left, but ease off some." Did that, too. "Now—we're getting close to the left side of the channel." *Hornpipe* swung right. The mainsail started to swing left, hesitated, luffed. "There's one I didn't see! Hard right—hard, hard." The boom knew what to do this time. Bust the old skipper above the right ear. "Quick!" Betty shouted. "Lort! Lort!" Lort? That's "left" and "port" put together Betty style. She'd been saying "port" and "starboard" too long. I'd confused the matter by suggesting she say "right" and "left." Bang! We struck the heavy chunk of wood head on. It scraped the length of the bottom. Would it catch the prop? No. I watched it stream aft.

"Okay, get ready." What does she mean by that? I'm so "ready" I've sweated out all the water I've drunk in the past week. And I *really* have to go to the bathroom.

"Hard peft now." Peft? "I mean lort! Left. I'm so nervous I can't talk right."

All I heard was "right." I turned right. The boom swung. I ducked. It parted my hair. "Don't turn right! Who told you to—all right! Now—hard right. Bang! Another buoy. Rattle, rattle, scrape. Gone. "Now—turn left. Left, hard. Right. No, don't turn right!" she hollered. This time I saw the boom coming. Ducked—ducked so hard I plunged the end of the tiller a foot into my right eye. I hadn't been crying before. Now I was.

Betty whirled. "Are you going to steer this thing, or aren't you? If you don't do what—turn starbright! I mean stright. *Point this damn thing toward the land.* Now—porst!"

"What's porst?"

"Don't argue with me. Porst, lort, pest. Starbrid, left, right. You've got me so mixed up I—turn that way!" She pointed. "Quick." I pointed the boat where she pointed. Crash. Another buoy. "You aimed us right for that one!" I hollered.

"I did not. If you think—quick. Porft. Lorft. *Left.* Port! I could cry." And she did. That made three eyes running like burst hoses. "You've got me all mixed up," she sniffed. "Don't cry! Aim us!" And she did. Lort. Peft. Damn. Bam. Cry, cry. Sniffle, sniffle. "We're out of the channel! Steer starbight. Right. *Steer this bloody boat right!* Oh, I don't care." Sniffle, honk. "I don't care if we hit a rock and everybody drowns—*drowndes!* You wouldn't care. You'd just make fun of me. I—you're hitting one." Bam. Rattle, scrape, bang, bang. "There, I *told* you!" She sounded glad.

We made it. We steered our way in and around moored boats of all descriptions until we found a vacant mooring float with the word "Guest" painted on it. Tied onto it. Tidied up a bit, found the shopping list, a gasoline can, ice bag, wallet, and rowed over to the marina dock. We could have taken *Hornpipe* in, but not under sail. We'd had enough adventure for one day.

A man loafed over as we scrambled out of the dinghy. He was short, dressed in seaman's boots, scruffy overalls, the ubiquitous blue-denim shirt and a long-billed cap. The dockmaster.

"Hi," I grumped.

"Quite a breeze o' wind you was kickin' out there in the channel." His eyes twinkled. I thought he'd laugh if we would.

"Guess so," I tried to be civil. "Do they always set lobster traps in the channel here?"

"If they've a mind to," he answered. "You two folk sounded like a bull moose an' his she, bellerin' an' shoutin' down the channel. Thought I'd bust out laughin' a coupla times."

I looked at Betty. She looked sheepish. Later she told me I did, too.

"Ah—have you got ice?" It might be well to change the subject.

"Shuah. Ice an' gas, too. You out? That why you sailed her in?"

Not all New Englanders are Calvin Coolidge quiet. I nodded. "And we've got some grocery shopping to do. Can we leave this gas can and the ice bag here until we come back?" "Yes, suh. Right straight out, you was, comin' in. Right sma't job o' sailin' you done, mistah, dodgin' all them buoys." I smiled. This was better. I thanked him and we started across the dock.

After a moment he called. We turned. "Just one thing. What direction is starbright?" At that he slapped his knees and doubled up with laughter. We laughed, too. But a little slowly at first.

Betty found a telephone and called Carol, who was working as a waitress at Newagen Inn. We shopped, picked up the ice and fuel. Among other treasures, I bought a bottle of Scotch. I needed it.

That evening the yellow light of our kerosene lamps threw soft color onto the mahogany and white of *Hornpipe*'s cabin. York Harbor was millpond-quiet. Betty wrote postcards and I, drink in hand, started a letter to Sterling.

> Dear Sterling: [drink, drink]
> It's been a great cruise. [drink] All the crazy things you've evermagind have hapned$_{\text{to}}$ us. [drink] We ran$_{\text{out of}}$ gas [drink, hiccup] and thees$_{\text{crazy}}$ lobtsers up here in Maine — they must have seen us$_{\text{com}}$ becasu they had their crazy trapsin the middle of$_{\text{the}}$ [drink] crazy riveran. . .

The pen dropped from my fingers. Betty grabbed the unfinished drink as it, too, started to slide. She put me to bed. Later I assured her I had simply gone to sleep. She had her own opinion.

The east wind of the past days had taken on purpose. Outside York Harbor we found heavy, thrashing seas running

and a 25-knot southeaster that seemed almost to overpower
Hornpipe. We took a reef in the mainsail and headed down east.
The expression "down east" seems to be a contradiction in
terms. If one travels to New England, he goes *north,* north and
east. And north is up. Up to Canada, up to Alaska. But Maine
people speak of "going up to Boston," which is in reality south.
The reason for it all derives from sailing. With prevailing winds
from the west, as they are, one sails downwind along the New
England coast. Thus one sails "down east."

It was cold, raw, damp. *Hornpipe* was laid far over, on her
beam ends. Her lee decks were under water a good portion of
the time and spray torn from the tops of whitecaps soaked
every part of us not protected by foul-weather gear. *Hornpipe's*
twisted stem presented difficulties. Sailing vessels of good quality tend to head up into the wind. *Hornpipe,* on the other hand,
fought to fall away, and the stronger the breeze, the greater
was her tendency to do so. Finally, with some difficulty we
took the jib in; that eased the strain on the tiller. Within two
hours the rains came, heavy, lashing, almost overwhelming.

Betty went below to study charts and the cruising guide.
Despite the good speed *Hornpipe* was making, conditions were
too severe for us to continue for very long. Within minutes
Betty's head appeared at the companionway. "We could make
for Cape Porpoise," she shouted. "But if we thought there were
a lot of lobster traps at York, there are more at the entrance to
Porpoise."

"Then let's keep going," I shouted back. Bad as things were
out here, they'd be worse if we got tangled up in lobster-
trap lines.

Biddeford Pool seemed the most likely anchorage, about
two sailing hours farther on. The wind-blown rain drove at us
in thin gray streamers. There was nothing for Betty to do on
deck. Wisely, she folded herself into a bunk on the lee side.

Such was *Hornpipe's* angle of heel, Betty lay more on the bulkhead than in the bunk itself.

At long last, soaked through and stiff with cold, we rounded Fletcher's Neck and Wood Island. We came up into the wind, dropped the main, and started the engine. Without the steadying influence of the mainsail, *Hornpipe* rolled fiercely. But we would be safe soon in the quiet of Biddeford Pool. Or so we thought. As we closed on the entrance a man in oilskins at the wheel of a lobster boat approached us. "No room in the Pool!" he shouted. "Anchor behind Wood Island."

"In this sea?"

"Good holding ground," he shouted again. "You got no choice 'cept Cape Porpoise." He waved and the boat rumbled away.

So near, so far. We peered into the placid waters of the harbor, opened the throttle, and turned *Hornpipe's* bow into the heavy seas. While Betty stood at the tiller, I went forward. It would take every bit of the chain and 150 feet of nylon line to keep the Danforth buried in the mud. I dropped it overboard, paid out line as *Hornpipe* backed away. I felt the anchor grab. Paid out more, and kept some tension on it. At last all our line was out. I secured it and went back to the cockpit. I lined up a rock and a tree on the island and waited. If the anchor were to drag, the angle would change. The rock would be lined up with something else. I watched for five minutes. *Hornpipe* was secure.

The storm raged the rest of that day and through the night. *Hornpipe* pitched and rolled and plunged like a terrified horse at its tether. We peeled off our soaked clothing, put on something somewhat dryer, and got into our bunks. Gusts of wind were so strong at times the boat shuddered. I could see the rock and the tree through a porthole. The man was right. The holding ground was good. How strong was the half-inch nylon? Strong enough, no doubt. But I wondered. How much reliance man places on the things he makes. He stakes his life on a shackle. On a cotterpin. A rope. We talked of the peace and quiet of the Pool as we lay in our bunks, rolling and pitching with every roll and plunge of the boat.

We had something to eat. As night fell I lined up two lights on the mainland. Watched again. The anchor must be three feet deep in the bottom. Good. But one doesn't sleep on a night like this. At least, this one doesn't. Doze, perhaps. Or, surely. But each slight shift in the wind, a sudden, sharp, different motion brings the eyes wide. The body tenses. Then relaxes slowly. *Hornpipe* resumes her plunging. The waves slap and hiss at this side of the boat, only three-quarters of an inch away. That is the thickness of the planks. Three-quarters of an inch between safety and disaster.

"You awake?" I ask.

"If you shouldn't get an answer to that question, you'll know I'm dead," my soulmate replies. "I sure won't be sleeping."

Bad nights, though, like bad times, do end. It is just a matter of waiting them out after doing the possible. Sometime during the early hours of the morning the wind subsided. Instead of slashing at *Hornpipe*, the rain fell softly onto the deck and the cabin roof. We slept. The sea, calmed by the gentle fall of rain, rolled the boat quietly. *Hornpipe* was our cradle.

Toward midmorning the rain changed to a mist. The wind became an offshore zephyr and a watery sun sent down a promise of better days ahead. We rowed ashore, walked to stretch our legs, found a telephone booth and called Betty's cousin, Rich Howison and his wife, at Falmouth Foreside.

"Come on down here," they asked. "Stay with us overnight. You can get baths, get your gear dried out, and tomorrow we'll put on a clambake!"

"What day is this?" Betty asked. We thought. Saturday. Good luck. We'd lost track of time. Back aboard, we turned on the portable radio. The local meteorologist promised clearing weather this afternoon. Tomorrow would be beautiful.

Rough reckoning indicated it would be a 14- or 15-mile run from Wood Island, out around Cape Elizabeth, down Hussey Sound. There was plenty of space at a Handy Boatyard float to tie up. Richie had assured us of that. The night receded from our thoughts. It would be remembered as a rough night. But that was all. One remembers the time of pain, but the pain itself cannot be relived. The soaring human spirit.

We got the engine on, powered out around Wood Island, and hoisted sail. The breeze was west-northwest. The sun grew stronger. Instead of the waves rushing savagely at us as they had the day before, they danced now and invited us to join their play.

Low-lying cloud cover could be seen far out at sea. Overhead there was nothing but blue sky and blazing sun. We shed our still-damp clothes. Here we come, Rich and Jane. Here we come, lobsters and clams. Hi, there, blue-green ocean. Greetings spruce-clad mainland. We rounded Richmond Island, kept flasher 22, which marked Old Anthony Rock, well to starboard. There is Cape Elizabeth to port and Alden Rock to the right. Ah, such a beautiful day. Did last night live? Naw! It died with the first shift of wind. It died at dawn. Here we are, humming, chatting, smiling, bare feet slapping the clean deck. God's in His Heaven, all's right with the world.

Into Casco Bay we sailed so prettily. We left Gong buoy 1 to port and hurried down Hussey Sound. Peaks Island over there to port, Long Island to starboard. Sails, white as white-caps, dotted the waters. People waved and smiled as they neared us, flashing froth. Now the harbor seals appeared. Sleek, rounded heads and dark-brown, staring eyes. Were these the progeny of the seals that watched us when we had that first knock-down in the Snipe? Gulls wheeled and cried and settled on the waters about us. Waves slapped and gurgled and hissed against *Hornpipe*'s flanks. Dark ducks speckled the water. A skier towed by a boat bearing three or four young people dashed by. Betty and I watched the wonders around us. It was great, great, great to be alive. And ahead—a clambake! A bath. A bed instead of a bunk. Jubilee time!

Let's see. Red right return. Keep the nuns to starboard, the cans to port. Past Clapboard Island. As we came in, Betty uncased the binoculars.

"Jane and Rich are standing on one of the floats," she cried. "They're waving." And Betty waved back.

"All right," I announced. "We'll come around, round up to the float, and as we come up into the wind, drop the jib."

Okay. Betty got fenders out of a locker. We were going to do this right. Sail in. In Casco Bay, where all this started. We did. The mainsail luffed, *Hornpipe* came in bow for the float, and at the last moment I brought it out again. Rich had to move only five feet to catch a shroud. We had lines, bow and stern, out, fenders over the side. We laughed, shook hands, slapped backs, kissed.

The word went out. Jane called Carol, at Newagen Inn. Carol got someone to substitute for her and was free for the day. She, in turn, got in touch with Michael. He had graduated from college in the spring. Now he was up at Charlestown, Maine, visiting a school with a name out of Dickens. Higgins Classical Institute. He would teach history there come the fall session. Someone called Betty's sister, Nancy. She and her son, Peter, were on their way from Jefferson, Maine, where they lived. There was Betty's Aunt Ruth. Betty's cousin, Ludwell, his wife, Dolores, and their children. And Jane and Rich's son, Bill. It would be a great family affair.

Richard and Jane Howison, 1947. Rich was an owner of Handy Boatyard in Falmouth Foreside, Maine.

Long before we were up, Rich had gone out to Sturdivant Island, a short distance offshore, to prepare. He built a circle of stones, with a few rocks in the middle of the circle. He put kindling wood there, and gathered driftwood. Rich and Lud had lobster traps of their own, which Lud emptied. The kids gathered rockweed and seaweed; the women rounded up potatoes and corn.

The family drifted in from here and there. Greetings, yips of delight. Laughter. Confusion. Suggestions. Commands. Bundles and old seabags full of things. Aunt Ruth produced two wash boilers. Holdovers from times gone by that she kept for just such purposes as this. Big, lusty clouds powered their way through the skies. The first hint of autumn was in the air. We lugged our belongings down to Town Landing. The boats came alongside and we piled aboard. An oceangoing picnic!

At Sturdivant, Rich got his small boat close enough to shore so we could wade to the island. The keel on Lud's larger boat required that he anchor offshore. But he towed a rowboat. With that we had ferry service.

"We haven't got enough potatoes!"

"We've got enough potatoes to feed the Irish."

"Mom, where's my bathing suit?" "Where's the camera?"

"Now everybody scatter and gather driftwood," Rich yelled.

We scattered. The small children frisked in the frigid water. We gathered driftwood, as ordered, carried it back to the roaring fire in armloads.

The morning passed. Busy. Loafing. Catching up on the news. "How's Aunt Grace?" "How's your Mother?" "Michael, you've grown *three feet* since I saw you last." "Carol, you're *beautiful!"*

Where there had been a roaring fire, there now were white-hot embers. The rocks on the perimeter of the fire and those in the middle were heated to lava state. Rockweed and seaweed were neatly laid on the bottoms of the wash boilers. Seawater was poured over that, then the boilers were placed on the rocks. The water boiled and the potatoes in their skins were thrown in. More seaweed. Then the lobsters, claws waving good-bye. Seaweed. Corn, in husks. Cover with seaweed. Clams last. Then put the covers on the wash boilers and wait!

We can't wait! We're starving. Let's just take a look. Please. I'm *sick* I'm so hungry. Just take the lid off one and look. At last. The lids came off. Steam billowed forth. Platters were passed around. The clams were open. Take some. Stand or find a place to sit. But eat. Now the process was reversed. Take the seaweed off. Find the corn. Butter. Salt. Man, get those lobsters out! Still starved. There are galvanized buckets. Be neat. When we leave, this place is going to look just like it did before we arrived. No paper lying around. No cornhusks or clamshells or lobster shells. Every scrap goes into the buckets.

"Here, little kid, let me help you with that claw. That shell is hard for little hands."

"Be sure and take that long, black stringy thing out of the tails. You don't want to eat *that.*"

The clambake—Betty (standing) and friends

Helping hands. Love. Good will. Warm smiles and burned fingers. Little cuts from the shells. Sighs and groans. "If I eat one thing more, I'll bust! But—oh, sure. Just one more ear of corn, then."

The robust northwest wind died toward midafternoon. We strolled around, cleaned up. Sat and talked. No one wanted to go home. This day should last forever. The sun blazed down and sunburn lotion mixed with sand was rubbed gently onto red shoulders, faces, and arms. In the lengthening shadows of late afternoon we picked up and packed up. Looked around. Is everything the way we found it? Ayeh. Aboard, everybody. The water was colder than before as we waded, carrying our gear. The breeze the boats stirred had a cut to it. Back to Town Landing. As you were, good people. Back to the things of the world. It was such a short while ago we were greeting each other. Now, good-bye, dear. We'll miss you. Oh, how we hate to leave this perfect place, this charmed day. Good-bye, good-bye. Pillows cradled tired heads that night. Tired, contented. "I really hated to see Carol go, Jim. And Michael. Wonderful as

this cruise is, I do miss them so much." A tear. A touch. The
lamps of night burn low.

Ah, the luxury of a shower. And the joy of a hot breakfast
with Jane and Rich before he left for work. One quick look at
the charts with Rich. He was born in this state of Maine. Bar-
ring an instant ice age, he will live out his life here. For him
and Jane there is no place on earth so sweet.

We got ice, gas, a few small items, and took our leave. The
breeze was westerly, light but steady. We sailed down on buoy
N6, left it to port, then rounded up into a narrow passageway
between Little Chebeague Island and Long Island. Into
Chandler Cove and out. Down another passageway into
Luckse Sound. Twisting and turning, sails crossing from
one side to the other. It was interesting sailing. Active. We
looked at the land and watched for channel markers. We
rounded a place called Outer Green and then Junk of Pork.
Junk of Pork?

"*You* know what that means." My rose petal looked at me
accusingly.

"'Junk of Pork'? Sure. It means a piece of rotten, poisonous
pork. It's junk. To be thrown away."

"It's perfectly good Maine usage. It means a piece of pork.
A 'junk of wood' is a piece of stovewood. A piece or a chunk
or a hunk is a 'junk.'"

"Thanks." I looked at her. Here we've been married all
these years, sitting around in this boat for all these days, and
she'd never told me that. What else did she know? She was
staring off into the distance. Hey, there, Betty. You, inside.
What are you thinking about right now, as you stare at the
ocean? Do you really love me? Are you holding something
back? Something inside you? Who lives in there? You could
have married an Annapolis man who ended up as an admiral
in the U.S. Navy. Any regrets? Right now you could be riding

The Clary Knoll farm in Jefferson, Maine (1921)

around on your own private aircraft carrier. Do you say to yourself, "Boy, look at him, and look at this jerk I married?"

"How do you know about that 'junk' business?" I asked.

"From summers at the farm." She turned back to me. "I remember once when Everett came in to the kitchen and held out his hand to Mother and there were two neat holes in it. One right in the center of the palm and the other in the back of his hand." She looked past me. "He'd been pitching hay and he ran a tine of the hay fork through his hand."

My stomach turned. "Did your mother take him to a doctor?"

"She wanted to, but Everett insisted that all he needed was a junk of pork for it. Mother got the pork and made a bandage to hold it on. In a couple of days the holes were closed and his hand was fine. All better."

Everett was the hired hand on the farm that Betty's parents, who lived in White Plains, New York, owned in Jefferson, Maine. Betty and her sister, Nancy, and their mother used to spend all their summers there. Betty's father would visit on

weekends and on his vaca-
tion. They had hired Everett
to run the place. Betty's
mother had been born in
Maine and was the life of
the farm. Its heart. When
she died, the rest of them
never wanted to go back, so
Betty's father sold it. But the
Maine blood runs rich and
strong in Betty's veins.

Betty's mother,
Ella Harding Peffer

My home is a small
town 12 miles north of Pittsburgh, on the Ohio River.
There is no ocean in my veins. Just Ohio River water. Steel
mills and coal mines. The very rich and the very poor. We
weren't *very* poor. But with six kids in the family, we never had
any extra clothes to *give* to the poor. My father had been born
in Ireland. He was a kind of a dreamer. My mother was no
dreamer. She kept the family going. She insisted—
demanded—that all four boys go to college. How was no concern of hers. And we all did, on athletic scholarships. I met
Betty in college. Allegheny. Another brother went to Amherst.
The third to Pitt. Another to Penn State.

Betty didn't have to play football to go to college. Her
father had enough money to send her. But did her mother and
father ever mind that their daughter wanted to marry some
poor kid from Sewickley, Pennsylvania? Steel-mill territory? If
they did mind, they never let on. At least to me.

When we were kids, we used to swim in the Ohio River.
There was a kind of sandy beach there, Walnut Beach. The
water was surprisingly clean, that is, if you didn't mind an
occasional dead dog or cat floating past. But it *was* clean. At

least it seemed clean to us. And on sunny, breezy days it even turned a sort of blue color, and it had little whitecaps. It was really slick. And when you came out from swimming around, *you* felt slick. A thin coat of oil. It was brown. An Ohio River suntan.

Years later I went back to Sewickley. My mother had died. Everybody at the funeral looked so old. They were different people from the ones I had known. They looked different. They were different. They had to tell me who they were. I never would have known. Except for one person. I looked past my mother's coffin and there she was. This person. I walked over to her and said, "Edna! You haven't changed a bit since we were in school."

And she shook my hand. "You mean to say," she asked, "that I looked 50 years old in high school?"

After the funeral I walked down to the river. I wanted to see it again. But I shouldn't have. Where once that river had been alive, now it was dead. It smelled, like death, I suppose. Oil and chemicals and feces. There was nothing to remind me of my childhood. I was the only person standing there. I turned and walked back to the motel. Betty was waiting for me there.

Hornpipe was humping up and down, bow rising and falling rhythmically. She reminded me of an elderly lady dozing before a low fire, head rising and falling with each gentle breath. But the dinghy had other ideas. It rose to the crest of a following wave, raced with the wave until it bumped our stern. Then, in the trough, it stopped. Like a puppy out for a first walk with its master, the dinghy lay in the trough until *Hornpipe*'s leash snapped it to attention. Once more it rose, raced a wave, and crashed into our stern. Tiresome. Annoying. I waited for it, reached astern, and warded it off. But it could play longer than I.

There were other things to take our attention. The sky.
The sun. The gulls, wheeling, mewing. The dip of the bow, the
rise of the stern. One could doze off. One did.

"You know something?" Betty said.

I roused myself. Stared at her. Sure, I know something. I'm
asleep at the tiller.

"We've left the dinghy. It's half a mile back."

"Wh—What?"

Sure enough. The little boat had gotten tired of the game.
It had snapped its leash and was now happily going its own
way. We could see it only when it bobbed to the top of a wave.

Scramble. Scramble. Haul in the sheets. Down hard on the
tiller. Bring *Hornpipe* around, up into the wind. Shorten up on
the sheets. Bring the jib in tight and the mainsail amidships.
Now we were going upwind. Sail to port, cross over, and sail to
starboard. Tack. Tack. If I had a switch, I'd paddle that little
devil's rear end. How far to port do you go before it's too far?
Okay. Come about. We'll be about right this time. No. One
more tack. Come about. We'll be about right this time. No.
One more tack. Come about quick. There! We came abreast.
The dinghy appeared chastened. I was just chasing a butterfly,
daddy. Or a wave. I just saw this sunbeam and I thought—

"Hand me the boathook! Betty! Bring *Hornpipe* a little
more up into the wind. There. Got it—no. Hold still, you little
— — —. There! Now. Grab a length of rope. Try to thread it
through the loop in the dinghy's bow. Don't jump up and
down. At last. Got it. I'll fix you so you won't go wandering off
again. I'll secure this so even the QE2 wouldn't get away.

"Okay," I said. "Now let's take a look at the chart and see
where we're headed." Islands everywhere.

We head to starboard a bit. We're coming down on South-
port Island. At this tip end is Cape Newagen, where Carol
works. And on the starboard hand is Damariscove Island.

Damariscove Island. There it lies, peaceful, quiet, somnolent. It was not always so. English and Dutch and French vessels used to put in here loading and offloading goods and wares. We know that the Pilgrims came upon hard times as they tried to winter on New England's frigid, inhospitable shores. And one of those Pilgrims, Edward Winslow, searching the barren coast for bits and scraps, came upon Damariscove. Later he was to write: "I found kind entertainment and good respect with a willingness to supply our wants and would not take any bills for same but did what they could freely."

This little island here, passing quietly to starboard. Damariscove. When, in 1675, Indians attacked mainlanders, killing, raping, burning homes to the ground, 300 souls fled to Damariscove. Found refuge and safety there. Later, in 1814, their descendants and others watched the epic battle between the British frigate *Boxer* and the American *Enterprise*. They battled to a British surrender. The two young commanders of the vessels, British and American, died in the fight. They were buried side by side in a cemetery in Portland. American history. *Early* American history.

Now, after these fleeing centuries, there are only two permanent residents of Damariscove. Only two. But they are permanent. One is a fair, fair maiden who has been seen on many a moonless night. Wandering, wandering. She has been seen walking into the bottomless pond on Damariscove, the pond into which Captain Kidd dropped his treasure of brooding gold and teardrop diamonds.

The other is a headless man. Betty and I have no time to loiter. But if you, dear reader, were to sit down on a Damariscove beach to enjoy the sights of the endless sea, you would not sit alone. For this headless man is lonely. He needs company. He might join you. He is quiet, contemplative, like you. Do not take fright. He is the ghost of Captain Richard

Pattishall. Captain Pattishall was murdered by Indians aboard his ship. The year was 1689. He was beheaded and cast into the sea. His body found a home on this lonely island. He dwells there yet. The Captain and the fair, fair maiden.

We glide abreast, stare at Damariscove Island. And pass on.

Boothbay Harbor does not let one dwell long in the past. We're back in the twentieth century. Put the dinghy on a short leash and drop the sails. One doesn't sail down Fifth Avenue close-hauled at high noon. The Boothbay Harbor Yacht Club is accommodating. We are directed to a guest mooring. We appreciate that.

We change clothes, board the dinghy, and row ashore. We walk about and find a laundromat. Boothbay? Well—it's Brooklyn, Scarsdale, Beacon Street, Michigan Avenue, State Street, Main Street, Belgrade Lakes, and Great Falls, Montana. Boothbay Harbor is America. But it isn't Maine. Or, to be more precise, it isn't the Maine Betty and I know. I strike out for the library. It's been *weeks* since we've read the news or even *cared* about reading the news. I find a week-old *Time*, a two-week-old *Newsweek*. *The Portland Press Herald* reports that a moose stood in the middle of a highway up Bangor way, wouldn't move, and held up traffic for an hour. The professional football exhibition season will begin soon. That means autumn is moving in. Vacation time is running down. We've got to make a decision. If it's to sail *Hornpipe* back home, we should prepare to move. We'll be sailing upwind. Tack. Tack. It will be slow going.

A heavy blanket of fog lies over the harbor the next morning. There's a small bite to the chill, and we wear heavy sweaters. Betty and I have learned that there is a time to talk. A certain time. A time to listen. A time to laugh, a time to cry. A time to live. A time to die. This is the time to talk. We sit in the cabin. Shall we end the cruise? Have *Hornpipe* hauled in a

Maine boatyard for the winter and have her twisted stem repaired? Or shall we turn back, sail for home? If it's the latter, we'll barely make it before the end of vacation. We discuss the stem. If it can be repaired, or replaced, it will be expensive. Can we stand the cost?

We decide two things. We shall stay. We can spend the remaining days sailing here, sailing there. Next, there's a good boatyard on the Newcastle side of the Damariscotta inlet. We'll sail up there. Have Creston Bryant, the owner of the yard, examine the stem and give us an opinion.

We discuss the stem in hushed tones. *Hornpipe* is the patient. One does not voluntarily discuss a serious illness in the presence of the patient.

By afternoon the fog had lifted enough to allow us to sail. "Sail" is not the correct word. We barely clear Spruce Point before the light air dies and the fog, a great bank of it lying just offshore, moves in. We turn to the engine, putt-putt along, and find the mouth of the Damariscotta inlet. It is fervently hoped that the fog will lift as we move up the inlet.

"Eerie," Betty says. "We should have stayed at Boothbay."

Too late. We're committed. But we don't have to make the whole passage up the river. We scan the chart and spy Christmas Cove. We make for Christmas Cove. Heading in, we spy a white spar with a red top. That is a guest mooring. We hook on.

Within an hour the fog lifts. We can see. We need a walk, a walk in the quiet country. We row ashore to a dock at the Coveside Inn and climb the small hill behind.

Christmas Cove is a lovely little land-enclosed harbor and we turned to look back and down. There's our *Hornpipe*. Other boats, too. But we have eyes only for her.

"I guess I forgot to tell you," Betty began tentatively. "I saw a few leaks up forward when I was trying to find my sneakers."

"Leaks around the stem, maybe?"

"I guess so. I hated to say anything."

"It must be pulling away from the planking."

I turned, then paused. An old man was sitting on a stump ten feet away. How long he had been there I did not know. He was looking at us.

"Hello. I didn't see you there."

"Watched you come in. Spend a lot of time just watchin' the boats." He sighed. "Ayeh," he breathed.

"Do you live around here?"

"Just over the hogback." He inclined his head. "Right smart sloop, you got there. Purty."

We thanked him. Betty moved closer. He must have been eighty years old. He was dressed in faded khaki. His cap had the long bill that fishermen favor. His eyes were faded blue, blue and misty.

"You know something about sailing boats," I ventured.

"By God I do," he replied with some strength. "Ought to. Sailed Friendships long afore the first big war."

"Friendship sloops?"

"Ayeh. Fished 'em."

"Lobstering?"

"Lobster an' shrimp. When lobsterin' was bad, went shrimpin'."

We waited.

"Friendship was the finest all-'round vessel ever built. Fust ones was built down to Bremen. [In Maine pronounce it "Brēmen."] They was called Muscongus sloops then. But Wilbur Morse, he lived over to Friendship. He shaped 'em up a bit an' called 'em Friendship sloops. That Wilbur. He said, 'A Friendship sloop is a sloop built in Friendship by Wilbur Morse.' Like to hear a yarn?" he asked.

We said we would.

"Well, 'twas durin' the war. Second one, that is. I was

fishin'. I had 'bout 50 traps. Fishin' was good." He paused, as though reliving the time.

"Well, I was fishin' shoal water. Them divils musta been watchin' me. As I said, the fishin' was good an' I had a good load of lobster aboard. Two hundred pounds. Was headin' back in, when all of a sudden—"

He paused. He'd told this tale before and knew how to get the most out of it. "All sudden like, this here submarine busts the surface."

Betty looked at me, I, at her.

"She was a German. She laid a hundred feet abeam. A lid come off the top an' by Godfrey Mighty, some one o' them hailed me through one of them megaphone things. Ordered me to come 'longside."

"And did you?" We were seeing the scene through the old man's eyes.

"Well now, I guess I did! One o' them divils was cradlin' a rifle in his arms. An' you know, they offloaded every damn lobster I had. By thunder they did!" He glared at me as though daring me to disbelieve. Then his face softened.

"But they paid my price. Full price. An' added a bit too. Them Huns. They had good eatin' that night."

Later, this story and others like it were confirmed by one of Betty's relatives, a cousin who himself was a lobsterman out of Friendship.

"You folks watch any of them Westerns on the TV nowadays?" The old man shifted gears pretty fast. "You know how them cowhorses always stand an' wait around while the rider gits off an' goes someplace?"

Well, he *was* old, and the minds of old people wander around a bit. Yes, we knew how the faithful horse always stood around.

"Well, a Friendship allus did that, too. With her two little headsails an' her big main you'd warp her up into the breeze alongside a lobster trap. Bring the main amidships, luff her up. An' that vessel'd stand there quiet's you please while you tended the trap. She'd wait all day if you wuz of a mind. Didn't need no engine power. Folks who lived on the island offshore, they all had Friendships. Work 'em hard all week, then take the womenfolk an' kids to town on Sat'day. Dry boat. Wear your Sunday go-to-meetin' clothes an' nary git a drop of water on 'em. High in the bow, low in the waist. Sheer. Purty. Last one I owned was 28 feet. Name of *Amy*. Long time ago. Long time."

"Amy was your wife's name?" Betty asked softly.

The old man pushed himself off the stump. He rubbed a spot in his back, straightened up slowly, tugged the bill of his cap lower over his eyes, as though the sun bothered them.

"Ayeh," his voice was just a whisper. "Fished her over 20 years. The Friendship, that is. The other Amy—my wife—married to her 53 years. She died, nine weeks ago yesterday."

The old man turned, straightened his back slowly, and on legs stiff with time, headed off to the house "just over the hogback."

N.C. Wyeth, father of Andrew, immortalized the part Friendship sloops played in the lives of Maine seacoast people when he painted *An Island Funeral*. Its locale is Teel Island, off Port Clyde. There is a Cape Cod house on shore. People stand in front of it. People stand on the shore, too. A few small boats are drawn up. A short way out are two Friendship sloops, bearing mourners. Somber. A quiet painting. Friendship sloops were there, in mourning or joy. In work or play. They were a vital part of coastal life.

Shortly after noon, we headed up the Damariscotta inlet. After the sea, an inlet is peaceful. The breeze, light and fluky, came off the ocean. An east wind. Rain would come. We gazed at the shore on both sides. At the houses. The pastures. The dark, wooded slopes. There are places where the river narrows down. Rocks and ledges. Treacherous. But we thread our way among them. Mostly, though, the channel is broad. We take our ease.

"Look!" Betty pointed over the side.

There, swimming along beside us, was a seal pup. Not ten feet away. It was swimming on its back, staring at us as we stared at it. I throttled the engine back and we watched. There was no fear in the creature's eyes. Only simple, innocent curiosity. Again that resemblance to a cocker spaniel. We'd owned one once.

"Blondy," Betty said softly. "An aquatic Blondy."

For two, three, or four minutes we exchanged innocence. Empathy. Finally, curiosity satisfied, the young seal flipped, dove. It surfaced again, 50 feet or so away. It didn't even look back. Are we that knowable? I wondered. Apparently it had learned everything it cared to about us in that brief exchange. Humbling. Deflating.

Ahead of us now was the bridge over the inlet that separated Damariscotta from Newcastle. To port was Creston Bryant's boatyard. We could not see any activity there, but we did spot a buoy. A guest mooring, we guessed. We tied onto it. It was as though a deity had wanted us to have a nice ride up the inlet. Now that we were here, the show was over. The skies had lowered and rain pattered down. We went below and closed the world out. Snug now in *Hornpipe*'s womb. We read, dozed, listened to the rain drum so close over our heads.

In the late afternoon Betty decided we'd have to go ashore. She "needed a few things." And we needed ice again. We walked the main street of the pretty town. Gazed into shop windows. It was nice to be among people again. Not too many people. Just enough. Most carried umbrellas. We felt superior, somehow, in our foul-weather gear. We're seafaring people. You can tell, can't you, by our dress, our deep suntans?

Oh, foolish ones. Oh, foolish, careless mortals. We had committed an unpardonable sin. We had forgotten to check the turn of the tide. After wasting a precious hour or so we got to the shopping. Taking our time. In the near dark we found our way back to the boatyard. And found the dinghy, high and dry. Someone downriver had pulled a plug and the water was draining away. The river and all that was in it was going out to sea! Our dinghy rested 50 feet from the nearest tiny lapping wave. It was one of those aberrations mentioned in earlier pages, a spring tide.

Well, hell. We dumped our precious packages into the little boat. I got out in front and hauled on the painter. Betty did what she could at the stern. This was no firm, sandy bottom we trod. It was muck. Mucilaginous muck. One foot down and an inch forward. The other foot down and lean on the boat to get them both out. By the time we got to the fast-disappearing river we were plastered from head to foot. Exhausted. We fell aboard and rowed out into the darkness. Left our once-proud gear in the cockpit to be washed by the rain. And sank into our bunks. The ice had melted, joined the river in its rush to the sea. And the groceries? In their paper bags? Early the next morning before we arose we could hear the seagulls squabbling in the dinghy, fighting over them.

This was the day Mr. Bryant was to look at *Hornpipe*'s stem. We picked him up in the afternoon, rowed him out. He leaned over the side and studied. Wordlessly.

"Well, I dunno," he said at last. "She's bent pretty bad."

We talked about repairing it. The cost of doing it. The cost of having him haul *Hornpipe*, storing her for the winter. The problems of getting back here by car in the late spring and sailing her home again. It all seemed too much. Mr. Bryant agreed to haul *Hornpipe*, and put her up for sale. We had only a few days left before we had to go home. We telephoned Carol. Her job would be finished at the time we wanted to go. We would ride back in her car. But first—let's finish the cruise.

It was bittersweet time. Our last days in Maine. Our last days of sailing *Hornpipe*. I recalled a time when Carol was just a child. Betty was being called away for some reason or other. She would be gone a week. It was evening. We were sitting in the living room. I was reading, I suppose. Betty was sitting on the couch, repairing something with needle and thread. She was leaving in the morning. Her bag was almost packed, on the cedar chest in the bedroom. Carol came into the living room from somewhere. She stood and looked at her mother.

"I—I miss you already." Her small voice quavered. "I know I shouldn't miss you, because you're still here. But I do. Oh, I really do."

All through life we live those times. Watching things slip through our fingers. Knowing they are going. Times of holding tight. Not wanting to let go, but letting go just the same. Facing the inevitable.

By morning the breeze had come to Damariscotta. It came with a clean white cloth in its hands. Wiped away the tears the low-lying clouds had wept on us and shooed them away. Like a gentle lady after her work is done, the late-summer breeze settled down in the west-northwest of her summer garden and breathed gentle, kindly breaths on us.

Once more we hoisted *Hornpipe*'s sails. We moved down the river. This land is changing. In the distance we could hear the tap-tap-tap of carpenters' hammers. They are building houses and summer cottages on the shores of this old inlet. Trees crash down to make room. Trees die ignoble deaths so summer folk can have a better view of the river and their neighbors. We looked, listened.

We peeled down to absorb the warming rays of a weakening sun. The burn was going out of it. Warm, yes. Down the river with the current. *Hornpipe*'s sails filled and she heeled to starboard. Gently.

Once more past Christmas Cove. We thought of the old man and his Amy.

Out in Johns Bay now. Pemaquid Point. One of the most spectacular places on the entire New England coast. The rockbound coast of Maine. Whoever coined that phrase must have been standing on those rocks, that glacial moraine, when it came to him. There is a lighthouse on the point. Where once it was manned, the light is now operated by remote control. A gift shop, an old hotel. Cottages. The town of Bristol has taken over the beach and charges a small admission for its use. Only seals can swim in that frigid water. Even on the hottest day of summer. Seals and small children.

Eastward lies Monhegan Island. We cannot see Monhegan, but neither could Captain John Smith when his vessel lay ten miles or so away. Monhegan is there. And it was there in the days of the Viking ships. Monhegan, Island of the Sea. Manana Island lies just west of Monhegan. There are runic carvings in the cliffs of Manana, proof to many that the Vikings visited there around 1000 A.D. Islands of Viking ships, islands of pirates, Pilgrims, Puritans, and pioneers.

We rounded Pemaquid Neck, and donned sweaters. Betty went below and spread chart #313 on her bunk.

"We could put into New Harbor," she called out. "But since we have the time, let's go on to Round Pond."

Why not? New Harbor would be easy to make, and it was chilly. I shivered. But if my passion flower and pilot down there in the cozy warmth of the cabin said we were to make for Round Pond, we had our orders, *Hornpipe* and I.

For a while we had sea room, space in which to tack and

tack again. But northeast of New Harbor, islands and ledges closed in on us. This was becoming hard work. Come about. Come about. Tack and tack. Betty emerged from the cabin and we dropped the sails. Furl the jib and with canvas strips lash it to the jib stay. Furl the main neat and secure. We tie it down to the boom with more canvas strips. Now we're neat and trim. Shipshape. Worthy of close inspection by sailors, lobstermen, and landlubbers.

Ahead and to starboard we see a ship. The hull is black, the superstructure is white. Black and white. Evil and good. The devil and the Lord. The devil part is down below, doing the dirty work. The white is above, pure like peace on earth. As she approaches we see her name, *Sunbeam*, painted in foursquare white letters on the black sides. And a white cross. *Sunbeam* is the vessel of the Maine Sea Coast Missionary Society. She is a lifeline, bringing hope and help from the mainland to people who live out their lives on offshore islands. Summer visitors see these islands in one light, sunbathed, sparkling, beckoning. The islanders see them in another. The light and dark of winter. Storm-lashed, bleak, cut off from succor when winter storms rage. Their sick may grow sicker and die. Their lonely may sink into troughs of despair. They cannot get to the mainland. But yes, they can. For here comes *Sunbeam*, driving through ice blocks and mountainous waves. *Sunbeam* is all steel. She is 65 feet long, 18 feet in the beam. She draws seven feet of water. Her main cabin can hold as many as 50 people. *Sunbeam* brings medical supplies, mail, furniture, hardware, Christmas presents, trained nurses to care for the ill, a minister to christen the newborn or to say final words over the new dead. *Sunbeam* is called "God's Tugboat."

She disappears astern as we head into Round Pond. There—shades of York Harbor—are lobster-trap buoys. But this time we are powering and there is no mainsail to obscure the vision. I look at Betty and say, "Peft." She gives me a tight little smile.

We move into the harbor, find room to swing to the anchor. Safe, snug harbor. And the Anchor Inn issued an unspoken invitation to dinner. We wash and change and row ashore.

There are Maine folk inside. No summer people now. We order fish chowder, two bowls. Betty continues to order. Halibut. I hesitate.

"This is Saturday, isn't it?" I ask the waitress.

She nods.

"Well, if we were back home in New York, my wife would have gotten some pea beans yesterday. She'd have gotten a junk of pork, too." Betty eyes me. Well, that's how they say it, by Godfrey Mighty. "She would have soaked the beans in water all night and baked them all day."

"And she would have served them to you tonight?"

"Ayeh," I inhaled.

"Well, the cook's a man, so he ain't your wife. But if you want baked beans the way your wife fixes 'em, we've got 'em.

"And hot dogs?" I ventured.

"With hot dogs," our kind hostess replied. She hesitated. "But just a word of wa'nin', sir. Don't say 'ayeh' like that while you're eatin' the beans. You might just choke yourself to death."

My first impression was of mosquitoes. Swarms of them. But mosquitoes couldn't make this much noise. Hornets? The Indianapolis 500. Or J.F.K. International at rush hour. *Hornpipe* was pitching and rolling. I glanced over at Betty's bunk. A long suntanned leg and haunch emerged from the covers. Wow! The foot braced itself on the cabin sole.

"Whatever you're doing, stop," she muttered.

A pale beam of sun peered through a porthole and found my eyes. I looked at my watch. Five-thirty! That noise. I groaned out of my bunk and up the companionway steps. A lobsterboat 20 feet away had its stern aimed directly at us. A sound like the *Damnation of Faust* blasted into our cockpit, down the hatch, and flooded the cabin. The lobsterman, heaving traps around, waved cheerily. Other boats were already taking off. At five-thirty? Why don't you give the lobsters a fighting chance? Wait until they wake up. I retreated into the cabin. Yawned. Scratched.

Betty eyed me. "So the Russians have finally come," she said.

"Yep. Squadrons of ICBMs. Multiple warheads. If they can bring Round Pond to her knees, the rest of the world will fall like a ripe plum."

Betty swung out of her bunk. The day had begun.

We washed, had breakfast, and studied the chart. We can't move without studying the chart. Are clergymen like this? Do they have to study the Bible before venturing out? Do lawyers have to study law books? Do airline pilots have to study maps of the U.S. each morning? Well, where are we going? Friendship? All right. So directly east of us is Louds Island and north of Louds is Hog Island. Betty wants to see Hog Island. Why? Well, because at the northern end of it is the Audubon Camp. To be precise, it is the Todd Wildlife Sanctuary.

We started the engine and hauled up the anchor. At that hour of the morning even the breeze hadn't stirred itself. Between Louds Island and Hog Island is a passage which the cruising guide says is the way to go. But Betty *wanted to pass by the sanctuary.* So that's the way we went. Hog Island, I am informed as we move along, is a mile and a half long. The only things that live there, besides the people who come in the summer, are spruce, pine, and hemlock trees. And animals and birds.

It seems that shortly after the turn of the century a Mrs.

Todd and her family were cruising the Maine coast when they
came upon Hog Island. There was an inn on the island and a
few cottages. But somebody was cutting down as many trees as
he could lay axe to. And he seemed determined to cut *all* the
trees on the island.

So where would the birds live? Mrs. Todd was determined
that they were going to continue to live in trees. And on Hog
Island at that.

Mrs. Todd fought a valiant battle to save the island. Upon
her death, in 1932, Mrs. Todd's daughter, Mrs. Millicent Todd
Bingham, took up the battle. She approached the National
Audubon Society. Would they be interested in establishing a
camp there? A camp where people could come in the summer
to live with and study nature? You bet. They were interested,
and the camp opened in 1936. Now the island is as it was
before white men began messing around. Unspoiled, uncut,
untouched. Evergreen trees march down to the very shores.
Animals walk around. Birds fly around. The only shooting is
done with cameras.

If one is sitting in his easy chair with nothing to do, he
might just reach over and pick up the United States Department of Commerce Coast and Geodetic Survey Chart #313. If
he does, he will discover that the passage between Hog Island
and Hockomock Point looks to be about two feet wide. Or
that's the way it appeared to us. With nothing but rocks and a
couple of can buoys. Particularly at half-tide. That's what it
was, half-tide. We could see one place on the chart where
there was 17 feet of water. Then 13 feet. Next, two feet. Two
feet? *Hornpipe* drew about four.

We approached this testing place with trepidation and nervous swallowing. I would have taken my darling in one last
embrace, but she was already up in the bow. The passage was
narrow. There *were* rocks. I always seem to sit light at times

like these. With maybe two inches of daylight between me and the seat.

"Steer to port," Betty called back. "Quick. Now, straight out. Port again. Straight again. Okay. We're fine."

I wiped my hands on my pants. Sweaty. And why do I always have to go to the bathroom at times like these?

"Starboard! Quick." She took a deep breath. "We didn't miss that one by much. Okay. Now straight! No! Straight." My hands must have slipped on the tiller. Almost through now. And then. . . to port. There lay a monstrous vessel. She must have been 200 feet long. She was actually 273 feet long, we learned later. Dismasted and abandoned. A rotting hulk. No doubt, in the mists of some distant time some other foolhardy captain had tried to make this passage and come to grief. How many of that crew died on this lonely shore?

"Did you notice the little birch tree—I think it's a birch tree—growing out of the bowsprit of that ship?" Betty asked.

Naw. She was seeing things. The strain was telling. But there *was* a little tree. And there *is* a tree—birch. And it grows in the rotten wood between the bowsprit and the bow itself. And the ship? She was a coasting vessel many years ago. When her sailing days were done, a Boston entrepreneur bought her and had her tied up to a Boston pier. She was to be a floating nightclub. But apparently, that failed. And then a Maine entrepreneur bought her. He had her towed up the coast and beached there. Her name was *Cora Cressy*. He drilled holes in her bottom. She was to become a lobster pound. But that didn't work out. And so there she sits. Abandoned. Rotting. A sorry sight.

There's Oar Island, to port. One nun buoy. Pass it. We're through, safe. Betty returned to the cockpit and smiled. My expert seamanship had gotten us through another tight one.

Friendship, Maine, is a fishing town. One winter day, many

years ago, Betty and I bought lobsters for 35 cents a pound in Friendship. We had arrived by land that time. This time we sailed in, anchored off a long pier and rowed over to Friendship Island to go clamming. We got about a peck of clams and hung them over the side of *Hornpipe* to let them pump themselves clean. Later, Betty made a sauce and we ate clams on the half-shell. Memorable moment.

That evening we visited ashore with our old friends, the Williamsons. Hanging on the wall was a print. It was Andrew Wyeth's *Christina's World*. A painting of a girl sprawled on the rough grass of a field that sloped up to an old, weathered house. That house, one could tell, was home to the girl. We had seen prints of the painting before, but never the original.

"I can't show you the original painting," Andy said. "But you can see the house, if you wish." We did, and Andy showed us on a chart how to get close enough by *Hornpipe* for a short walk.

The next morning we sailed out to the bay, then into the St. George River, and northeast. It's a truly beautiful river. Past Pleasant Point Gut and Turkey Cove and Maple Juice Cove. Beautiful, evocative names.

Just beyond Maple Juice Cove is Bird Point. We dropped anchor and rowed ashore. A short walk and we stood where Christina had sprawled, and we looked up over the field at the old house, as she did. Stark, lonely on its hilltop, like so many old Maine houses. But this one is different. Andrew Wyeth, by painting *Christina's World*, made it so. It is probably the best known of all his magnificent works.

Now controversy has brought the place more fame; worse, notoriety. After Christina and Alvaro Olson grew old and died in the house, a motion-picture director and art collector, Joseph E. Levine, bought it. He spent a fortune in restoring the place. In 1971 he opened it as the Olson House Museum. It was to house many of Wyeth's great paintings. Tourists came, hordes of them; as many as 500 cars would arrive in one day. Cushing is a small Maine town. The townfolk wanted it kept that way. And so the museum and the town steered compass courses in opposite directions. Collision. The museum was closed. No one won. Everybody lost something.

It was time to hoist *Hornpipe's* sails once more. We caught the current and tacked away. The cruise was ended. Tomorrow we would take our boat back up the Damariscotta river. And leave her there.

Last supper aboard. The kerosene lamps glowed yellow. We read a bit. Made desultory talk. Stared about us at the work we had done, thought of the plans we had made for this cruise long months ago. The cold crept up from the bilges and we searched with our legs for warm spots under the blankets. At last I got up, turned the wicks of the lamps down low, then blew them out. The riding light still glowed in the cold night. I kissed my wife and crawled back into my bunk. Tomorrow, Mr. Bryant, you may have *Hornpipe.* Tonight she is still ours.

Centuries before this night, *The Tempest* bespoke our thoughts: "Our revels now are ended. These our actors, as I foretold you, were all spirits, and are melted into air, into thin air; and like the baseless fabric of this vision the cloud-capped towers, the gorgeous palaces, the solemn temples, the great globe itself, yea, all which it inherit, shall dissolve."

Betty sighed. She didn't speak. It had all been said.

thirteen

old squaw

Suppose you are sitting in your living room reading this book. I don't wish to do anything to take your mind off the book, but just put it in your lap for a moment. How long is your living room? Eighteen feet? Twenty-five? If it is 25, it's a pretty long living room. Now just imagine 11 feet longer than that. Well, that is the length of the next boat we bought. Thirty-six feet. She had a bowsprit that was about three feet long, and a couple of feet of boomkin sticking out back. The boomkin is an arrangement of wood to which are attached pulleys. Lines from the mizzenmast go through those pulleys. Sheets, they are. More than 40 feet of wood! And I was captain of it all. Frightening.

She was 11 feet wide. The part that was underwater went down almost six feet. She was a ketch. A ketch is a boat with two masts, the shorter one in back of the taller one. Not way back. That's a yawl. The shorter mast, mizzenmast, is forward of the tiller. If you think 36 feet is long—and it is—think of the mainmast. It was 48 feet! That isn't as high as the Empire State Building. Nothing like that. But once Betty had to go up to the top of the mainmast. After she got down and stopped throwing up, she said if she could have looked, she is sure she could have seen Spain from up there. So that was our next boat. *Old Squaw* was the name on her before we bought her. We should have changed it. People sailing by would point to Betty. "Is that her?" And laugh. One woman yelled across a hundred feet of water, "If I was your wife, I'd brain you." I couldn't tell her I hadn't named the boat after Betty.

The winter after we sold *Hornpipe* we searched boatyards from City Island, New York, to Stonington, Connecticut. We really didn't know what we were looking for. A newer, sound version of *Hornpipe*, I guess. But we never found it. We examined a number of sloops. Sterling joined Betty and me on many weekend searches. Sterling and his icepick. There's one, we would say. That's a beauty. A 30-foot sloop. Where is Sterling? We would come on him eventually, shaking his head. He would have his icepick buried to the handle. Oh, well. We considered fiber glass. But there were few second-hand fiberglass boats on the market, and the ones that were had obvious, glaring faults or cost too much.

Finally, one day our broker—boat broker, that is—called. He was Fred Gade, of Cos Cob. Fred had just the boat! She was sound as a nut, large, sea-kindly, and at our price. So up we went. To Stamford, Connecticut. And there she was, *Old Squaw*. She huddled under a canvas cover that must have come from Ringling Brothers. She was for sale for a price we could afford—we, and our kindly, encouraging banker who wanted to make another large loan. She was a ketch, a rig that could be trimmed to sail in any kind of weather. With all sails flying, she carried almost 800 square feet of sail. But take down the main, Fred explained, and you sail in a whole gale on the jib and mizzen sail alone. Betty and I looked at each other. Sail in a full gale? Not if we could help it!

Sterling checked the engine. It was fine, as far as he could tell in a boatyard. But he did have one reservation. It was only a 30-horsepower job. And *Old Squaw* was a mighty big boat for an engine that size to shove around. But, of course, Sterling, we replied—I guess I replied—we'd need the engine only for getting in and out of tight harbors. Hackmatack knees, Fred said. Hackmatack knees? Knees are large blocks of wood that brace places where frames meet. Hackmatack is a kind of wood that lasts forever. If Noah had had hackmatack, the ark would still be sitting there on Mount Ararat! And she was planked with long-leaf yellow pine. Sterling knew the qualities of that wood. Good, strong, and flexible. It's scarce now.

Fred saved the biggest surprise for last. We scrambled up on deck. "She's got a great brass bell," he told us. He had it at home because somebody might just lift it off the boat. But the surprise was here. Look! There! There, on three racks, one just forward of the cabin, and the other two, one between the shrouds on each side, were—what are they? Fred smiled. He was pleased we didn't know. Why, the mahogany things in those racks are belaying pins! Belaying pins? we all said. Yep. That's what they are. Fred was enjoying himself.

"I thought belaying pins went out with Long John Silver."

Fred turned his smile on me. "You won't see them on many vessels nowadays," he said. "But *Old Squaw* has them." He went on to explain that, instead of coiling long lengths of line and then trying to find something to hang them on, you simply hung them on the pins. Unlike the lethal weapons pirates bashed out people's brains with, our belaying pins were no more than 14 or so inches long. Not lethal, but genuine.

The decks were bare pine. Waxed and polished to a sheen. And big. If it weren't for the cabin sticking up there, belaying pins, shackles, and turnbuckles, you could land a small airplane on those decks. Really big.

We looked anxiously at Sterling. Tell us she's too big for two little old people like us to handle, Sterling. Sterling was smiling and shaking his head in wonderment. "I'll bet Columbus would have traded Queen Isabella for a ship like this on some of his voyages," our friend said.

Betty and I could tell that Fred really loved Sterling.

"Well," said Betty, at long last, "I'll tell you one thing. With only the two of us aboard, in case of accident I'll be the first one off. Women and children first, you know, and there won't be any children."

We thought about that for a while. Sort of laughed and joked about it, but there was a look in her eye. She *knew* something.

Fred added that the sails were new, Dacron. If we wanted to go over to the spar shed, we could examine all the rigging. And two other parties were looking pretty seriously at *Old Squaw*. Aw, Fred. I don't think I've ever bought anything that two other parties weren't looking at. But the trouble is, maybe they were. Fred Gade was a friend. He wouldn't tell us that if it weren't true.

On the way home we thought and talked. Betty suggested that we could hold dances on *Old Squaw* with a live orchestra. We could charge admission and help pay for the boat. The trouble was, Betty wasn't quite kidding. Woman's intuition.

Sterling did nothing to encourage or discourage us. It occurred to us to wonder if he might not be as tired of visiting boatyards as we were. Connie had hinted that she would like to see him one Saturday this winter. Also, there was the snow and rain and mud. One of us got a brand-new cold every weekend. It was time. Time to make a decision. *Old Squaw* wasn't *that* big. There are lots of larger boats. The *Lusitania*, the *Titanic, Queen Mary*, and both *Elizabeth I* and *II*. The America's Cup boats were *much* larger. Of course, they had

Bus Mosbacher, Ted Turner, and about a hundred young, strong, sunburned deckhands, too.

But we had Betty. Betty and I had Betty. She looked at me a number of times during those days. Sidelong looks. Questioning looks. I would be sitting in the living room reading. Betty would have a book, too, but she would not really be reading it. She would be looking at me. I would glance up suddenly and catch her at it.

"What are you staring at?" I would say.

"Staring? I was just thinking," and she would duck back into her book. In a moment she would look up again. "That sure is one big boat we bought." Then she would add hastily, "But I know I'm just going to love it." Her look would say, If you believe that, you'll believe anything. *She knew something.* Women do. My mother knew that my father would die if he went out of doors once more without his rubbers. And he did. But not until he was ninety-three.

The yard in Stamford required that they do all the work on a boat from the rail down. That meant they did everything except what was on deck. So Betty and I busied ourselves with the deck, the inside of the cabin, and the spars. We grumbled a lot about how much boatyards charge. We had to take another mortgage on the house to pay the bill. But we had to admit we could never have done all the work ourselves. Not and sail that summer. In some ways it might have been better.

At last *Old Squaw* was ready to be launched. It was a big day. Good friends came from miles around to celebrate. And to wonder, we both felt, if we had taken leave of our senses. But they brought champagne.

During the following week the yard stepped the masts and installed the rigging. Betty and I were appalled. There were enough cables to run telephone lines from Atlanta to Jacksonville. Heavy steel cables! And rope. Some of the lines led up to the tops of the masts. Clear out of sight. Others led here and there, around and about. What was it all used for? How could we ever figure it all out?

At last the yard towed *Old Squaw* out to her temporary mooring. There were two mushroom anchors, one fore and one aft. Our boat was hooked up between them, with a tieline between the two anchors. The foreman told us politely but pointedly that he'd sure appreciate it if we could get her off the moorings as soon as possible.

Betty and I practiced in the evenings, and eventually knew how to hoist the main, mizzen, and jib, and how to start and stop the engine.

The following Friday night we wore out two bedsheets, twisting and turning.

"Oh, did I kick you when I turned over?"

"Yep. That's the third time, in the same spot."

"Sorry. Now, that line on the starboard side of the main-mast—hey! You've got all the blanket!"

"That's not the blanket! That's my pajama bottom you're yanking!"

"Sorry. Now tell me again about the mainsail."

We heard owls hoot. We heard the last birdsong of the night and the first in the morning. The cat came stamping into the bedroom. That gave us a start. Some damn heavy-footed cat we have. Hey. Give me at least *part* of the cover, will you?

"Now, the mizzensail sheet leads through those blocks back there on that thing—the boomkin. Right?"

"Ouch. Your feet feel like you're wearing football shoes."

"We've got to load the dinghy on the top of the car first thing in the morning."

"We won't forget to do that. Remember last night? You tried to get it up there by yourself and it fell down onto the hood. It's still there."

During the drive up to Stamford the car seemed such a safe place. Good car. That Saturday morning it never heeled or rolled or pitched. We thought when we got to Stamford we might just keep on going. Put the dinghy in some nice little lake in Maine. That would be enough boat for us.

A neighbor had gone along with us. He would drive the car back to White Plains and then come over to Orienta to meet us when (if) we ever got the boat back there. This neighbor was a good, well-meaning friend. He sensed our nervousness. "After all the sailing you two have done," he would say, "this new boat will be a lead-pipe cinch."

Arthur had never been aboard a sailboat. I could tell he didn't intend to sail with us, either. He helped me carry the dinghy down to the float at the boatyard and helped carry the rest of the duffel. When I pointed *Old Squaw* out to him, his Adam's apple bobbed.

"Yeah, I sort of see what you mean," he said. "Maybe you should have two or three more people to help you."

"Like you, Arthur?"

"I—I've got to drive your car home." Just plain chicken.

We stalled around, stowing our gear just right. But soon, far too soon, we were ready. We had *to sail that boat.* The moment of truth.

I started to haul the sails from their resting place on the forward bunks up to the deck.

"We're not going to sail right away, are we?" Betty asked. She looked startled. "Shouldn't we sort of power around just at first?"

It was decided. Unilaterally. One vote. We hauled the sails out of the sail bags. Miles of Dacron. We even got them bent onto the spars. Fortunately, there was a light breeze. Stamford Harbor is large. There was plenty of room for everybody.

"Okay. Cast off the bow," I commanded. "We'll let the bow

swing around and then I'll cast off the stern." Betty cast off the rope that held the bow secure. *Old Squaw's* bow swung around properly, as I had forecast. Then I cast off the stern line. The sails filled and we started down the harbor. Afraid yet to grin. The grins would come in a moment or two. Suddenly *Old Squaw* seemed to slow down. No, she didn't seem to. She did. The sails were filled nicely, but we were stopped.

"Oh, oh," Betty groaned. "Look at the dinghy."

I did. The painter, the line that attached the dinghy to us, was stretched tight. And the dinghy? Caught fast where the tieline is secured to the stern float. We were hung up like a cow on a tether reaching for a daisy two inches beyond her twitching nose.

A sloop passed us. Anything that moved at all could. Four people were aboard. They pointed, laughed, and waved. It was really funny. Ho, ho.

Betty was close to tears. I was just one sniffle behind. I let go of the tiller; *Old Squaw* wasn't going anyplace. I reached back and tried to untie the knot at the end of the painter. Nothing doing. *Old Squaw* was turning herself around. Okay. I pulled a knife out of my pocket and cut the line. *Old Squaw* lurched ahead. But I didn't see how we could sail a 36-foot boat 25 feet back to unsnaggle the dinghy. We dropped all the sails, started the engine. Other people sailed by, smiled and waved, and pointed out our dinghy. Yes, lady, yes, we know where the dinghy is. We circled around, made about four passes and finally corralled it. Betty gave me one of her meaningful glances. I tried to ignore it. If a boat 48 feet tall and 36 feet long can slink, we slunk out of the harbor. Under power. Well out in the sound, we hoisted the sails and got ourselves home.

We went out evenings during the following week and practiced. Our spirits rose. We gained so much confidence, in fact, that I invited my friend, Sam Schreiner, and his wife to go out with us on Saturday, which happened to be my birthday. Sam and Dory would be delighted. And they asked if Dory's father could go along. Of course. Dory's father wasn't old, but he was getting on.

Early Saturday morning Betty, Carol, and I took off for Darien Harbor in Connecticut, where Sam, also a sailor, is a member of the Noroton Yacht Club. It was a sparkling late-spring day. *Old Squaw* laid her lee rail over toward the waves and I noticed Carol casting anxious glances heavenward. All that wood and canvas up there! And it was sort of falling over. We reassured her, somewhat. In no time at all we were entering Darien Harbor.

It all goes a bit hazy here. We dropped the sails and powered in. To starboard were numerous boats bobbing at their moorings. And to port there were a couple of finger piers, with floats at their ends. We moved in slowly, waved to the Schreiners, who were standing on one of the floats waiting for us. We came in quite decently alongside. That is about all I can clearly recall of the harbor and the Yacht Club. We came back in, of course, when we brought the Schreiners back. But I remember only the things I don't want to about that.

Out in the Sound we sailed and had a fine picnic lunch. Sandwiches, salad, hot coffee, beer. It was a fine, bright blue and silver day. I remember that, and Betty provides confirmation. Toward midafternoon we decided we should return.

We came about and headed in. Everybody talked about what a simply perfect sail it was. And isn't *Old Squaw* just a perfect boat? She had about seven feet of headroom in the cabin. Just by running up and down the ladder from cabin to deck you could get all the exercise you need. Or by jogging the length of the deck a few times. At the entrance to the harbor, Sam said—now he denies he said it. He says I said it. But I am the one writing this book, so Sam said it.

Old Squaw at Orienta Yacht Club in Mamaroneck, New York

"Why drop the sails?" Sam said. "Let's sail in."

Betty's jaw dropped. Carol turned pale. Sam's father-in-law, up in the bow, smiled. He knew I had better sense than that.

"Okay, Sammy boy. We'll sail 'er in." Well, it was his harbor. He knew what he was doing.

Silence issued from all hands. Staring silence. What is going on here? those stares said. A couple of madmen?

Sam and I grinned. *Old Squaw* moved majestically down the channel. People waved from aboard their boats. Sam and Dory and her father knew them all. Sam and I waved back. Dory fluttered a hand. Betty and Carol and Sam's father-in-law just worried.

Suddenly, from Sam: "I think we've got a little problem."

"We have, Sammy boy?" Whatever the problem, I figured Sam could handle it. It *was* his home port. His idea.

"Yeah. There are a lot of boats tied up to the floats. We can't come in there." As I recall the setup, the float, or floats, were at the end of the pier, making a T.

"We'll have to come alongside the leg of the T," Sam said.

"Shall we come about and drop the sails?" I asked very quickly, sensing danger.

204 INNOCENTS AT SEA

"We don't have room to come full about. Start bringing her around to port. Head for the pier. Then, when we get in fairly close, head her out again, and move her right up alongside the pier."

My armpits flooded. "You—you want to try your hand at it, Sam?"

"It's your boat," Sam said tersely. "Now. Swing her hard to port!"

People on the pier and floats were watching. *Why do we always have an audience?*

I swung her. I pushed so hard, the tiller bent. Almost buckled. Like my knees. *Old Squaw's* bow moved ponderously, sliding by the pier. We weren't going to sail headlong into it.

"Sam!" Sam's father-in-law moved back from the bow. "The bowsprit isn't going to clear those pilings." I think there were two huge polelike logs standing close together at the end of one of the floats. The float was cabled to those pilings.

"Swing this son of a bitch!" *That* from Betty? I remember it clearly. She denies it to this day. We've never asked the others if they remember her saying it.

People scattered. Ran for safety. I thought of it myself. But we weren't close enough to the pier to jump. Because we had now been heading up into the wind, *Old Squaw* had lost her speed. She just sort of eased in. The bowsprit fitted as nicely as you please in between those two pilings and the stern swung just as nicely in against the pier. And there we were. Stopped. Wedged is more like it. *Old Squaw* sat quietly. She thought she *belonged* there.

Sam's face was scarlet. Dory dabbed at her eyes. Carol scrambled down the ladder into the cabin. *She* wasn't going to be seen in this mess. Sam's father-in-law sank onto the deck. I didn't dare look at Betty. She was against this operation from the *start.*

Well, the ball takes funny bounces sometimes. We must have gotten the sails down. I remember lots of people shoving *Old Squaw* around. We need three more men up here at the bow! Back her up a little more. More. Get there by the stern. Back. Hold it. Now all ten of us shove the bow out that way. Hey there. You in the cockpit. Sam! Tell your friend—the one in the coma—there to start the engine. She's got an engine, hasn't she? NO! NOT FULL SPEED! You'll smash... *There's a madman at the tiller*!

The Schreiner family was gone. We were alone, out in the Sound. The anonymity of space. None of these people on boats 'way out here had seen what happened. But, somehow, we sensed they all would hear. The word would spread.

That evening Betty and I had a little birthday—I don't know what to call it—not party. We wanted Carol to stay aboard and share the supper Betty had prepared. Supper and birthday cake—and coffee. *Hot* coffee. But Carol had a date. Or she made sure she found one.

We had a table that fitted into a track against the bulkhead. The outboard end of the table was supported by one folding leg. We had a nice supper. Betty cleared things away and brought out the cake. And with the cake she brought out a pot of steaming coffee. My outboard leg must have twitched. Nerves. Whatever. My outboard leg caught the table's outboard leg and it collapsed. Steaming coffee into my lap. I got hot coffee in places I can't tell about. But the cake formed a sort of poultice over it. The cake was in my lap, too. Upside down.

As the days of late spring passed into days of summer, the grass in the front yard grew longer and *Old Squaw* got to know us well. We never really got to know *Old Squaw*.

fourteen

old squaw triumphant

August brought cruise time. This year, however, we faced it almost with a feeling of reluctant inevitability. Neither of us knew why—at the time. We had no real destination in mind except one. We had arranged with Sterling and Connie and two other good friends, Ellen and Bill, to meet us at Onset. From there we would go through the Cape Cod Canal and probably to Provincetown, the outermost town on Cape Cod. After that we would just wander wherever our spirit and *Old Squaw* would take us.

We got a late start on the day of leavetaking. This was unheard of. Always before we had made it as early as possible. But that day we dallied. Because we cast off so late, we made it only to Black Rock. Unlike our previous visit to Black Rock, I was the personification of sobriety. In the morning—engine failure. It started, coughed, tried to clear its throat, but choked and died. Oh Sterling, Sterling, where are you? He had drilled one point at least into my head. If the engine stops abruptly, the cause is probably electrical. If it coughs and sputters, figure on the carburetor. One night he took a carburetor apart, described the function of its innards, and had me put it back together. I did, one way or another. Then promptly forgot almost everything he told me. And this time it was the carburetor. Never mind, I fixed it. Not without getting out every tool aboard and dropping most of them into the bilge. Even so, the repair was made. Sediment was the cause of the problem. I cleaned it out and the engine started. "My hero," Betty said. I feast on her praise.

Today the wind is coming out of the northwest. Fresh. A radio report said it was blowing 20 miles an hour with gusts up to 35. No sweat for *Old Squaw*. We bowled along, making good time. Great billowing pillows of cloud raced past, apparently anxious to get down east. As the afternoon wore on, the air got steadily chillier. We thought of putting in at Clinton, but decided against it. That was our first mistake. Instead, we settled on Duck Island Roads. I had the uneasy feeling that the bottom was said to be not too good in the Roads, that in heavy northwest wind an anchor might drag. But I wasn't sure I had heard that. "Anyway," I said to Betty, "the breeze usually seems to die around five or six o'clock."

Mistake number two.

We rounded a breakwater and headed in. The rocks and boulders that formed it were enormous. My scalp tingled a bit when I thought what they would do to a hapless boat that fetched up on them.

Thus began the wildest, blackest night we had ever known up to then. And we made our third mistake, which was to use the Danforth instead of the storm anchor we carried. But this was predicated on the second miscalculation. The breeze did not die. The Danforth was a perfectly able anchor for *Hornpipe*. For *Old Squaw*, double *Hornpipe*'s weight, it was not large enough.

We ate an uneasy supper, saying little, listening to the wind whistle, vibrate through the rigging. In her masts and spars and vast lengths of rigging, not to mention the bulk of the boat itself, *Old Squaw* presented an enormous resistance to wind. "Windage" it is called.

"I think we'd better haul up the Danforth and put the storm anchor down."

"I was thinking the same," Betty replied quietly. Now the radio reported wind gusts up to 45 miles per hour. They were strong enough to set *Old Squaw* back on her haunches, trembling. It was perhaps half an hour before sunset. I started the engine. It coughed, sputtered, ran for a few moments, and died. More sediment. No doubt it was coming from the bottom of the gas tanks. Little fingernail flakes of rust that lie in the tanks, quiescent until violent motion sets them afloat. I tried again. There was nothing to do but attack the carburetor again. With Betty's urgent attention, tools, and a flashlight I took it apart. The wind seemed stronger. But the strength of wind, I know, often is in direct proportion to one's apprehension. At last the engine caught. Lights were coming on in four other boats anchored there. We were all about a hundred yards from the breakwater. We could see shadowy outlines of figures on the other decks. Moving about. Checking lines.

"I'll move forward on the anchor, Betty. You hand it in, slowly, as we go." I opened the throttle halfway, and waited.

"We're not moving up," Betty called back. "I can't get any line in."

I opened the throttle to full. Waited.

In a few moments Betty called again. "The line's slackened a bit, but I still can't haul any in." We waited. There was a brief lull. She was able to get about four feet of anchor line. That was all. We'd moved up just four feet.

After five or ten minutes I shut the engine down. I remembered Sterling's reservation about *Old Squaw*'s engine. Now it could not move her against the wind. Perhaps there was a tide running, too. The only boat without lights at all was a sloop, a 25-footer, that lay some 50 yards to our port. No lights. No activity. But she had a dinghy at her stern. There must be somebody aboard. Perhaps not. I looked back. We were here. The rock wall was there. Only a slender cord of nylon and an anchor that either would or would not stay asleep in its bed of mud kept us apart.

I sat in the cockpit for a long time and got a fix on shore lights. If *Old Squaw* were to drag, I would know it instantly by looking at the lights. Betty went below for a few minutes to get out of the wind. Not for long. "I don't like it down there when it's like this." We sat together and listened to the waves slap against the hull. Neither of us knew what we were waiting for, but we waited.

So we sat. There was a bright, three-quarter moon. After a while the clouds seemed motionless. It was the moon that sailed among them. An hour passed. Two. Then three. We would stand up and stretch. Rearrange cushions beneath and behind us. Were we to stay this way all night? Watching? Waiting? It would seem so. Others on other boats seemed condemned to do the same. Still no one appeared on the darkened sloop. A sudden blast. *Old Squaw* shuddered alarmingly. Her bow twisted and turned like a fish trying to shake a hook. "My God," Betty said. I think it was said reverently.

At last she stood up. "I'll go below and heat up some soup. We need it."

I agreed. She closed the companionway doors behind her. The vigil required night sight, which light would destroy. In a while she called up that the soup was ready. She would spill it if she brought it up. Anyway, I needed to get warm. I went below. Night sight wasn't that important.

We sat at the table and consumed soup and crackers. From

time to time I stood up and lined up the shore lights. We were all right. When a boat is anchored in rough water, she pitches from stem to stern. I was about to return to the cockpit when suddenly there was a moment of calm in *Old Squaw*. The pitching stopped. Then she began to roll.

"My God, she's dragged the anchor out!" We both made a mad dash for the deck. *Old Squaw* had turned her flanks to the wind. We were being driven toward the breakwater!

"Betty!" I shrieked. "Haul the anchor line in. It'll foul the propeller!"

She dashed. I started the engine. It caught. We were rushing down on the breakwater. If we struck, we'd be killed. I pushed the tiller down hard to bring the bow up into the wind, shoved the throttle open to the last notch. Could she move up now where she wasn't able to before? She *had* to. We were 50 feet from destruction. I could see Betty up in the bow. Working madly. Hand over hand over hand. Please. Please. She's got to get it all in fast. And the engine must run. It can't quit.

Slowly the bow came around. Heading up into the wind. At least we'd gained that much. I heard the anchor crunch against the topsides. She'd gotten it in. Then it clanged onto the deck. At the same time Betty let out a little cry. What was that? I'd find out later. The wind softened for a moment and *Old Squaw* came full up into the wind. At last I could look for lights. If we could claw off that breakwater and move out, we'd be able to drop the storm anchor overboard. There was no use attempting it now. There must be *at least* a hundred feet of "scope." That much is necessary in a blow. Otherwise the anchor line is almost perpendicular and the anchor cannot get purchase on the bottom. We were now perhaps 60 feet away from the rocks. That brief lull had helped.

I lined up shore lights. An outside house light and a street light. Three would be better. Two were enough.

At last Betty came aft. "How are we doing?"

"Gained maybe ten feet."

Betty looked astern. I heard a little gasp in my ear. "We're so close to the breakwater."

I know. Better not to look back. Watch those two lights. See if we're moving. We were not.

"Have you got the engine wide open?"

"Yes."

Three or four or five minutes passed. The engine didn't miss a beat. *It couldn't.*

"Gaining?"

"Not yet. But we're holding our own."

At last. "What time is it?"

Betty went to the cabin door and opened it enough to see her watch. "Four-fifteen."

What time would it get light? Five o'clock, perhaps? I wondered how long the engine could race like that. Do engines seize up, "freeze" from running too long too hard? I hadn't asked Sterling that.

We waited. A brief lull again. The lights moved out of position. We had gained some, at least. The vigil continued. My back sagged against the seat. I thought of trying to get the sails on, Betty couldn't do that alone. I asked her if she would take the tiller while I got the jib and mizzen up. She said she would hate to. Later she said she thought that, if she took over, the engine *would* stop. Better not risk changing our luck.

We held on. At last there was a faint light in the sky. Another 50 feet and we could drop the big anchor.

Suddenly Betty's jaw dropped. At the same moment a particularly violent gust struck. "Look! The sloop!" she screamed.

I tore my eyes away from the new lights I'd lined up. The sloop was racing toward the breakwater. We watched. Speechless. The dinghy struck first. A moment later we heard the smash over the shriek of the wind in the rigging. The mast struck and was broken like a spine. The hull collapsed. The insides of the boat came spilling out. Disemboweled. We were sick. I turned back to the lights for a moment.

"Do you see anybody?"

"No. Nobody's aboard. Thank God."

My cheeks were wet. Betty said later that she cried. It was a horrifying sight, the destruction of a beautiful boat. And it could have happened to us.

Another 15 minutes. The sky grew lighter. Beautiful dawn. The wind slackened a bit. We were now 150 or so feet off the wall. The wind *was* lighter. This time Betty agreed to take the tiller. I went forward and dropped the Danforth over the side. No need now for the storm anchor. The danger was over. I slowed the engine down and put the lever in neutral. The engine would need to cool down before shutting off. Valiant work, engine. We love you.

We sat and watched the sun spread its fan of rose over the black jaws of night.

"When I dropped the anchor on deck I did something to my toe."

I looked. Her big toe was a blob of congealing blood.

"And you haven't mentioned it all this time?"

"It hurt when I did it, but I forgot about it. Until now. Too scared, I guess."

At last we turned and creaked down the companionway ladder. It had been a long, shattering night. Betty's entry in her log finishes: "I am emotionally unable to accurately write it down. I'm sure it doesn't matter—we'll never forget this night."

We awoke in midmorning, stiff and drained. We washed and dressed slowly, had some breakfast, not much, and went up on deck. We could see little of the wreckage of the sloop. A large motor-sailer that had been anchored perhaps 200 yards away was the only other boat there. She was moving out, but before leaving, she came over to us. There were three people on deck. A woman and two men.

"We're glad you're alive," one of the men called over.

So were we, I assured him.

"We watched your battle for over two hours."

I asked him if he didn't have anchor trouble.

"No," he replied. "I kept the diesels turning over most of the night. Just enough power to take the strain off the hook."

Two diesel engines. Oh, to have a couple of diesels—just in case. I thought of our 30-horsepower. No matter. We'd made it.

Betty's toe hurt more than she would say. We thought about turning back. But last night was enough to more than cover a whole cruise-full of misadventures. From now on it would be clear sailing. The weather would be fair. We— I—would make no more errors in judgment. Also there was Connie and Sterling and Ellen and Bill.

Betty put a light gauze bandage on her toe. It hurt. The air would help it heal faster. She kept warning me. "Stay away from me. Sheer off. If you step on that toe, I'll drown myself in the bilge." I didn't recall that I'd ever stepped on her toes, at least not since dancing days. But I stood clear.

We decided to sail. We'd had enough of Duck Island Roads. I attempted to hoist the mainsail. It wouldn't budge. The halyard was jammed. We flew an Orienta Yacht Club burgee from the masthead. Somehow, during the maelstrom the mainsail halyard and the pennant halyard had entwined themselves in an unassailable embrace. Unassailable, at least, from the deck. Well, we'd worry about that later. The breeze was still strong enough to drive *Old Squaw* well under jib and mizzensail alone.

We moved out of the roadstead into great, rolling swells that followed us from the northwest as we sailed east. I arranged the two sails so we would sail wing-and-wing. The mizzen to starboard and the jib to port. One pulled and the other pushed. It was a fine sailing day. The wind held. Great, puffy clouds were born in the west, matured overhead, and raced east. They seemed to rush. They had appointments to keep, far out in the Atlantic wastes.

Betty sat with me for a few minutes. She smiled. There was no need to ask how her toe felt. It hurt and it hurt. Her eyes showed it. Presently she went below. I hoped she would sleep.

I tried to think what to do about the mainsail halyard. *Old Squaw* was moving well, but without the mainsail she was a crippled ship. We had inherited a bosun's chair with the boat, but I'd never dreamed of having to use it. My mind didn't want to wrestle with more problems. I looked in at Betty. Her eyes were closed. Perhaps she *was* asleep.

Old Squaw pitched and rolled through the three-foot seas, past Orient Point, the easternmost tip of Long Island's north shore. Soon we were in Fisher's Island Sound. Off to port is Intrepid Rock. I tried to imagine the origin of that name. No use. Now I brought both sails over to starboard. *Old Squaw* rode easier. Watch for this buoy, then that one. There is the Stonington breakwater. We'd both had enough. I brought the ship to port, and immediately Betty's eyes opened.

"Stonington?" she asked.

"Yep." In another moment I cut the engine and heaved the Danforth overboard. Safe. Stand and stretch. And sigh. The water was quiet. It was so good to have a steady deck under us.

There is a fine line between wakefulness and sleep, a twilight zone, before one moves out of this world and into that other one, the strange world of sleep. Betty and I lived in that zone while we ate supper, made a few quiet remarks to each other, and sagged into our bunks. *Old Squaw* could have picked her anchor off the bottom that night and marched right back to Mamaroneck. We would never have known.

The next morning was Sunday. There was a boatyard in Stonington where we could get the halyard repaired, but it would mean a long day of waiting.

I studied the problem. There was a metal brace on the forward part of the mast, perhaps eight or ten feet from the top. The main and burgee halyards had become jammed in a small space between the mast and the brace. Perhaps a bolt had come loose. I couldn't tell. I tried to work them free. Nothing happened. Never mind. We decided we'd run up the coast.

It is unlikely that anyone has ever had trouble finding the passage at Watch Hill, Rhode Island, but we did. Our only excuse is that we had an area chart that covers perhaps 40 square miles. Detail charts are available. We didn't have one. We figured we knew where the passage between the land and a vast area of reefs should be. Right in the center of that, though, was something marked "Gangway Rock" on the chart. We'd made the passage before without difficulty. But perhaps we were still in shock. We could not find the channel. Perhaps it's over there to starboard. We headed that way. Several men were fishing from skiffs. Suddenly one of them saw us, waved us off, his mouth forming the words, "Go back! Go back!" At the same time we bumped. Hard. We were onto a reef. I jammed the tiller over. *Old Squaw* turned slowly. Another bump. Now we could see the reef, directly under us. *Old Squaw* wasn't caught yet. At last we came away. We were free. The man shook his head and waved again. Close. So close.

We were back in deep water. We *still* didn't know where the passage was. One thing, though: it wasn't here. We headed back toward Napatree Point, a spit of land that extends into Fisher's Island Sound from land. And at the same time we caught sight of a large yacht—she must have been 80 feet long—steaming east. She didn't hesitate. *Her* captain knew where she was going. She was making perhaps 12 knots to our four or five and quickly outdistanced us. But she showed the way. We found the passage and went through.

We sat and looked at each other. We had never had that trouble with *Hornpipe*. This boat did something to us. She caused strange aberrations. It wasn't *Old Squaw*'s fault. She couldn't do the navigating for us. *We* were the trouble. We knew it. But still . . .

Outside there was no noticeable increase in the wind. *Old Squaw* nodded, noodled, wallowed, and rolled in the long ocean swells. Without a mainsail, she lay almost dead in the water. Once more I started the engine. We decided to head for Point Judith, Rhode Island, roughly 20 nautical miles from Stonington. We puttered along and worried. Would there be a boatyard? How much would they charge to do the job at the top of the mast? Could *we* repair it? We stared up. The jib halyard ran through a block, or pulley, just below the brace. Close to 40 feet above the water. If Betty could haul me up on the jib halyard, I could work things loose. Maybe.

We arrived at Point Judith shortly after noon. Great stone blocks were laid to form breakwaters offshore to make this a harbor of refuge. If one could find a more protected place to anchor, one should take it. We should have tried.

I dug out the bosun's seat. It was simply a length of rope and a board. The board had a hole in each end. The rope passed through the holes and was hooked onto the halyard. One sat on the board. It was a precarious perch. We should have had a winch on *Old Squaw*, but we didn't. I explained the plan to Betty. So many things we should have had or should have done. But we didn't.

"What if I can't haul you up?"

I shrugged. No answer to that. A thought did sneak into my head, but I put it aside. I wondered if the same thought occurred to Betty. It had, of course, but neither of us mentioned it. Naturally, too, we were both aware that we had chosen another harbor of refuge. As though one—Duck Island Roads—hadn't been enough.

"Okay. Haul me up." I fitted myself into the seat. Betty heaved. I ascended a foot. Two feet. Only another 36 to go. That's as high as a four-story building. A *swaying* four-story building. I hadn't noticed how much *Old Squaw* was rolling until I was about six feet off the deck. The top of the mast swung to port, then to starboard; each time it seemed to hang ten feet out over the water. Betty was grunting with the strain of hauling me up. I tried to help by shinnying, but I couldn't use my legs without slipping out of the seat. Making matters worse, my hands were slippery. With sweat.

At ten feet progress stopped. "I can't pull you up another foot," Betty panted.

"Secure the halyard to a cleat and rest."

"No use. I won't regain my strength for a week. You're too heavy."

Back on deck. We sat and stared at anything but each other. Five minutes passed. "Feeling better, honey?"

No answer.

"H'mm," I said.

"If you think you're going to get me up that mast, you've got another think coming, buster." She always called me "buster" when she wanted to make a strong point.

"Okay. If we can find a boatyard, it shouldn't cost more than $50."

Betty looked up at me, then down. Fifty dollars was a lot of money. We hadn't counted on extras like that. I stared at Betty's feet. She stared at mine. My toes began to blush.

"You knew it would end up this way," my rose petal said.

"What way, sweetie?"

"Don't 'sweetie' me. How do I get into that thing—that seat?"

"Are you sure you want to go up, dear?"

"If you 'dear' or 'sweetie' me once more, I won't."

"I'll pull you up ten feet or so. If you don't want to go any higher, I'll bring you down."

"Then what?" she asked.

"Well. We'll find a boatyard."

"Haul," she said.

I did. At ten feet I stopped. She clung to the mast with both arms. "Let me down."

I did. She stood and faced me. "Have we got any whiskey left?"

"What!"

"Any—whiskey—left?"

"Maybe a little. But you can't have a drink and then go up again."

"It will give me false courage. That's what they call whiskey, isn't it? False courage?" She sat and had a drink. A small one.

"Betty," I said at last, "you can't go back up there."

"Why not?"

"Well—because. You can get yourself killed. One slip and you'd land on the deck, or in the water."

"You could have gotten killed if you'd gone up."

"That's different."

"Why is it different?"

"Because I'm a man."

"So you're a man. Because you're a man, does that mean you can order me not to go up, but you could?"

"You don't understand."

"What don't I understand? This doesn't involve physical strength."

"You're a woman! And women are—"

"Women are inferior? You mean to tell me—?"

"Aw, Betty."

"Hoist me up."

"Now wait. Listen—"

"Hoist me up this damn pole!"

There were little sparkles of fire in her eyes. She planted herself in the bosun's seat. I started hauling on the halyard. Five feet. Ten. At 15 feet I stopped. She held that mast in an embrace tighter than she'd ever held me. "Why'd you stop?" she called down.

"Are you sure you want to go on?"

"Hoist!"

"Yes ma'am."

Twenty feet. Thirty. My wife was something else. She looked neither up nor down, right nor left. My arms ached, but there were only a few feet left to go. She was up to the brace, swaying with the mast, far to one side, back to upright, then over to the other. I was getting seasick just watching. She clung to the mast with both arms and stared at the tangle. Well, she couldn't straighten it out with her nose. At last she freed one hand to work on it. She tugged. Gulls flew overhead as though to watch the show. There were two or three other boats anchored in the roadstead. People turned to watch. Thirty-nine feet above the water. One final tug. Both halyards were free, the burgee and the main.

"Bring me down," she called.

I did. She returned to earth, slid out of the seat, and walked slowly back to the cockpit. Loose-jointed. Fighting nausea. I joined her. There wasn't a word to say. All things and people were equal on our boat. Betty maybe more so.

The afternoon was wearing on. Betty's condition and my feelings persuaded us to make a short run for someplace where we could anchor safely, lie up, and lick our wounds. My wounds were only those of bruised vanity. I *should* have gone up that mast. Failing that, I should have found a boatyard. Well, it was done. We chose to run down to Newport.

Newport, Rhode Island. At one time it was a center of commerce greater than either New York or Boston. Later, Newport, with its "cottages," became the social center of the East, if not the entire United States. That era is past. Now Newport is one of this country's principal naval bases and one of the East Coast's great yachting centers.

The America's Cup races are run outside Newport; Brenton Cove harbors the competitors. Brenton Cove, too, is the rendezvous point for the Bermuda Race competitors. Every other year the Annapolis-to-Newport race is staged, and it is into this harbor that the boats straggle, often ravaged by storms and heavy seas. At the very center of all this nautical activity is the Ida Lewis Yacht Club. The club occupies a building that once was a lighthouse. The lighthouse, of course, was kept by the redoubtable Ida Lewis. She is reputed to have rescued 18 seamen in distress. Each one of those rescues is represented by a star in the club's burgee.

Betty and I found a guest mooring, cast onto it, and slumped. What next? we wondered. In just a few days we were to meet Connie and Sterling, Ellen and Bill. *Old Squaw* was secured to a heavy mushroom mooring. We would not go adrift tonight.

But *would* the cruise with our friends go well? Would our luck change? Connie and Sterling would have time only to make the sail from Onset to Provincetown. Ellen and Bill could stay a day or two longer. They would drive their own cars to Onset and leave them there for the trip home. We were all certain it would be a wonderful cruise. Only one of the four, Sterling, had had sailing experience, except for an occasional evening sail with us on *Hornpipe*, then *Old Squaw*. It would be exciting.

Now as we sat in our cabin we wondered about the "exciting" part of it. Please, God, forget that word. Make it fair. Pleasant. Fun. Easy. Just among the three of us sitting around here in the cabin. You, God, Betty and me. Let's make a little pact. Forget anyone ever said "exciting."

The following morning we rowed the dinghy ashore, where we tied up to a float at the Ida Lewis Yacht Club. From an outside telephone we called a cab to take us to The Breakers, one of Newport's "cottages." "Cottages" is the name given to the most palatial collection of mansions ever assembled in one relatively small area—simply a case of inverse snobbery.

Inverse snobbery does strange things to people. Betty and I attended a dinner party one winter night. It was bitingly cold. One of the women, the wife of a man of substantial means, arrived in what appeared to be a plain cloth coat. Later I remarked on it. Why would Helen come to a party in such a thin coat? She must have had something warmer. "Dear," Betty replied, as though talking to a not-very-bright child, "that is a full-length mink coat. Helen was wearing it inside out." I thought about that for a while. Stupid? No, Helen's not stupid. It must have taken quite a bit of time and energy to turn the coat inside out. It couldn't have been very comfortable that way. Why? Perhaps for the same reason Newport people called their palaces "cottages."

We took a conducted tour through The Breakers, the summer cottage of Cornelius Vanderbilt. There were four Vanderbilt boys, and they all built fancy houses for themselves. Cornelius II built The Breakers. William K. built a place called The Marble Palace, also at Newport. Frederick established a

600-acre estate at Hyde Park, New York. The fourth brother, George Washington II, erected "Biltmore," without doubt the country's most elaborate estate, near Asheville, North Carolina.

For those of you who might be interested in such things, as is Betty, William's hangout, The Marble Palace, cost $9 million just to furnish. But that wasn't enough. William's wife decided she needed a tea house. Maybe she didn't have just the right room in the cottage for such things. In all fairness, one must have the proper atmosphere for tea. So William's wife, Alva, brought some Chinese from China (where else?) to build the tea house. It was perfect. Exquisite. Except for one thing. Someone forgot to include the facilities for making tea. One might think that such an oversight could be easily corrected. Build a wing onto the tea house. Or get a simple two-burner kerosene stove and some tea bags. No, dear reader, that is not the way to do it. A miniature railroad was built from the main house, where the tea was brewed, to the tea house. On the tracks traveled a miniature railroad train, with open cars. And in those open cars sat liveried servants holding silver services. They arrived at the Chinese tea house and served the tea. How easy. Simple.

Betty and I toured The Breakers. Her big black-and-blue toe hung out. She limped around and people stared at it. That is some ugly, sore-looking tootsie, somebody remarked. Betty said yeah, brother, and just don't step on it. Those number twelves of yours can make a girl mighty jumpy.

The Breakers is not just your average big, gaudy house. The Breakers is 250 feet long. That's a home run in some ball-parks. It has 70 rooms and 30 bathrooms. That means that no matter where you are in The Breakers you have a bathroom handy. That's good, because you might be right in the middle of something, reading or eating, and want to take a bath. A servant appears. He's wearing a powdered wig, short pants with white stockings, a waistcoat, and a shirt with ruffles. "Forsooth," he says. That means there's a bathroom, with tub, right next to where you're sitting. In fact, you might even be in one of them. They're so fancy you might not even have noticed the facilities.

The ceiling of the great hall is 45 feet above where you're standing. It's painted blue, a pale blue. As you look up at it, you can picture clouds forming over there to the east. They move in fast. You hear thunder. A flash of lightning. Suddenly you've got a cloudburst, right in the great hall. All the tourists get soaked and demand their $1.50 back. (That's what it costs to go through the place.) Betty says that fresh water feels good on her toe. It wouldn't happen, of course. But as you look up at that sky, the ceiling, you think it could. It is that realistic.

The dining room is 58 feet long. Nowadays the servants would use skate boards to get around. Then they just jogged. But that was quite a trick. With a whole roast pig in their hands. And not to let the apple fall out of its mouth.

Betty thought I wasn't taking the tour seriously enough. I should be *interested.* There was a good-looking woman on the tour. Her skin was fair. Maybe she was a Rockefeller, seeing what the Vanderbilts were up to. I sort of winked at her a couple of times. She stared right through me. Didn't even *see* me. Betty caught me at it. End of tour. The wind was chilly that night aboard *Old Squaw.* But not as chilly as Betty.

Fog does not always come in on cat's paws. Sometimes it comes in like the smoke from the maws of cannon, rolling, roiling, engulfing. It did, sometime that night while we lay in Brenton Cove.

I awoke early. Betty lay breathing softly. Little puffs of steam—fog, it was—wafted from her nostrils with each exhale. *Old Squaw* was dead in the water. Not a tiny slap of water against her flanks. Fog. My feet felt the cabin sole. Wet.

I stumbled up the ladder. It was claustrophobic. Fish would be asking each other how to get from here to there. The silence was eerie. The world had died during the night. I stumbled down the ladder again. Betty had not stirred. When the fog lifted the day would begin.

At midmorning a breeze came to our faces from the west. Above, an artist was at work in the sky dashing streaks of pastel blue onto a gray palette. Then he brushed the gray away with his hand. Let the sun shine through. *Old Squaw* tried a tentative dance step. Then another. Her halyards tapped out the rhythm against the mast. The day was awash with light. Little waves, like a chorus line, moved in. Slap, slap, tap, tap. We were alive. The world was alive. The sun warmed our shoulders, dried the decks. We hoisted the damp sails. They joined the joyful music of the day. The sails luffed while they dried themselves. We cast off the mooring line. *Old Squaw* fell away, found her feet, heeled. We were off to Block Island. To Cuttyhunk. To Vineyard Haven and Edgartown. And from there to Onset to meet our guests.

Because it was a long sail, 34 or 35 land miles from Vineyard Haven to Onset, we were up early. We had to be, to catch a fair tide through Quick's Hole. This time we hoped for a fair breeze, too. Once through there with the wind against the tide was enough. It was too early for the morning breeze to have risen, so we powered down Vineyard Sound. The sun was not up; the sea was sleeping. Betty and I huddled into ourselves. It seemed as though the whole world was waiting for the light from the east.

At last we saw it come. First the small lightening of the dark. Next came a color like roses, slowly, slowly. Shafts of it grew into the sky above. No man-made alarm clock could be so gentle, so quiet, so majestic. Then it slid slowly up from where it had spent the night—China, Russia, Turkey, Scandinavia, Africa, Europe. It came from all those places to Betty and me. Once more the sun had kept its date with us.

Quick's Hole was a millpond, on that morning. We did not need to remind each other of our last passage through these waters. We picked up a breeze in Buzzards Bay and arrived at Onset in early afternoon.

In the evening our guests arrived. Connie and Sterling first, Ellen and Bill a half hour later. We greeted each other happily, with relief. They didn't know for certain, of course, if Betty and I would be there. Nor could we be sure that they would make it. An ill child, a sudden call out of town, bad weather. But they *had* made it. Betty took elaborate pains with dinner on *Old Squaw* that night. Grilled swordfish on charcoal, fresh string beans, a tossed salad, made with the tomatoes we carried on all our cruises. For dessert we had juicy, garden-fresh cantaloupe and coffee.

We talked late. They wanted to know every detail of our plans for tomorrow. We would have to take off early to catch the tide through the canal. Once that was accomplished, we would sail across Cape Cod Bay, thence in to Provincetown. Just as we had discussed it at home. *But we would have to rise early in the morning!* Betty and I were only too conscious of the limits of *Old Squaw*'s power. Why, of course. Everyone agreed. We would have a quick early breakfast and take off.

We sat in the cockpit. It was so good to have old friends around us. Betty and I realized how lonely for voices, particularly voices of friends, we were. It was so *good*, as though we had been away for months instead of just a couple of weeks. We had nightcaps. The night air was damp and chilly. We put on heavy sweaters and jackets. Onset was new and exciting to our guests. They asked questions about our cruise. We did not tell them about the night at Duck Island Roads. We did not tell them about Betty's voyage up the mast. Somebody noticed that it was beginning to rain. We moved below. *Old Squaw* looked her best. Betty had seen to that during the afternoon. The mahogany trim of the cabin took the yellow light of the kerosene lamps and turned it chocolate. The white paint bespoke a clean boat. Rain tapped its light fingers on the deck above our heads. This was an experience to be savored, not wasted by going to bed.

We talked, yawned, talked, and had another nightcap or two. No one wanted to go to bed. Feel the light motion of the boat. Listen to the gurgle of the water as it slips by the hull. And the rain on the deck. We miss so much of life in our fine, stout houses. This (yawn) is the way to live. At last, Betty showed the uninitiated how the pump in the head works. She turned down the bunks. At last everyone settled down. *Old Squaw* shifted around in her own bed, got comfortable, and slept. It had been a long, long day for us all.

I wakened first. Listened. The rain had stopped and it was daylight. We were late, late. If we hurried, we could catch the last of the favorable tide and the slack water before the tide turned against us. Failing that, it would be a six-hour wait until the tide was once again in our favor.

We hurried. Everybody hurried. Betty cooked the breakfast; Ellen and Connie helped. Sterling got the anchor up; I started the engine. We powered down the Onset channel and headed for the canal. With luck we would still have the tide most of the journey through the canal, and the end half an hour or so of slack water. With luck.

The green light was glowing at Wings Neck. We went in. *Old Squaw*'s engine purred. In a short time we were approaching the railroad bridge at the village of Buzzards Bay. Raised, it has a clearance of 135 feet. We swept under it. Raised. Slightly over a mile beyond is the highway bridge at

Bourne. There we noticed the start of a light breeze. With all of *Old Squaw*'s spars and rigging even a slight headwind would slow her down. And the tide was beginning to diminish. No matter. We would still make it comfortably if—if the wind didn't pick up. At the Sagamore Bridge, almost three miles beyond Bourne, the breeze *was* picking up and the tide, feeble. Our speed slowed noticeably. Another two, two and a quarter land miles and we would be free of the canal. But if the combination tide and wind overpowered the engine, we would have to turn back, back to Onset. We didn't want that.

I didn't express my concern. We would make it. Of course, we would. Slack water now. It seemed to me the breeze was a bit fresher. It seemed that way to *Old Squaw*, too. I pushed the throttle wide open. I needn't have bothered. It was there already. Betty glanced at me two or three times. She could read my face like a chart.

At last the end of the canal land cut was in sight. A strong gust struck *Old Squaw* and she slid a bit to port. I didn't want that. I wanted her in the middle of the channel. But she had been working her way imperceptibly to port. I brought the bow slightly up into the wind, but that slowed her down more. I brought her off the wind.

The United States Corps of Engineers pamphlet on the Cape Cod Canal states that the dredged, or bottom, width of the canal at this point is 540 feet. The channel, though, is somewhat narrower than that. At the eastern exit two long breakwaters extend out into the bay. The longer of the two is on the north side of the channel. It was toward that we were being gradually, inexorably blown by the southeast wind. I looked ahead at the nun buoy marking the port side of the channel. Instead of being well to our left, it was just dead ahead. We were being shoved out of the channel! The wall of rocks extending yet another 75 yards was too close.

What if—perish the thought. But what if the engine should die? It wouldn't, oh, it wouldn't. But it had before. The sails were securely tied to their booms by stops. It would take a long time to get them off. Anyway, we wouldn't have time even if we did get the sails hoisted, to claw off that rock wall. *Old Squaw* was barely making headway now. Sterling wondered if we would make it out into Cape Cod Bay. Bill looked at me. Connie and Ellen, fortunately, were up forward, enjoying the ride. There would be only one chance. *If* the engine should quit, then the bow of the boat would have to fall off sharply away from the wind, toward the breakwater. I would have to turn her in a tight radius. Without power that couldn't be done. But it *could* be done with the jib—maybe. We were still making headway. But if anything should happen—anything—we would be blown onto the breakwater.

I beckoned to Betty. She came back to the tiller.

"Quick. Loosen the stops on the jib. Get hold of the halyard. If I yell, haul that jib up fast." Sterling heard. In less than one minute the engine quit. Quit! Without warning!

"Haul!" I shouted. At the same time I grabbed the jib sheet. As Betty hoisted the jib I pulled the line in. Tight. Because the jib is at the bow of the boat, the wind caught it. *Old Squaw* hesitated. Then the bow swung to port, toward the breakwater. Later, there were six different opinions about how near we were to smashing up on those rocks. Twenty feet? Thirty? It seemed to take forever for the bow to swing. First it headed for the breakwater, then slowly turned, turned. At last we made it. I eased the jib sheet off and the jib ballooned out ahead, pulling us back the way we had come.

No one had spoken. We all sat transfixed by the proximity of disaster. Three of us could swim, the others could not.

We had hardly reached the inland end of the breakwater when a boat from the Coast Guard station came to meet us.

"Vessels are not permitted to sail through the canal," one of the men shouted.

We were dumbfounded. But of course they had not realized our predicament. We explained. We had two choices, they said; either sail back to the mooring basin on the north side of the canal and make our own repairs, or let them take us in tow to the Coast Guard basin. Sterling said he could fix the engine. I agreed that he could. We thanked them and made our way back to the mooring basin, another 500 yards or so west.

Now everyone was talking, giving his or her own version of what happened, where he was standing, what she was thinking.

Betty asked, "Whatever made you tell me to get the jib ready?"

In the long silence that followed the near scrape, and before the Coast Guard hailed us, I had wondered about that. What *did* cause me to tell her? I don't know to this day. I *do* know that if we had not had the jib ready enough, seconds would have been lost, so that we might not have made the turn. Sterling asked me if I had detected a miss in the engine. I had not. He had heard nothing, either. Extrasensory perception? Premonition? Perhaps it was simply a lack of trust in things mechanical. *That* thing beneath the floorboards of our cockpit, anyway.

Two minutes after we had tied up in the mooring basin, Sterling had the answer. Once more it was sediment in the carburetor. "Then why didn't it cough and sputter?" I wondered.

"Perhaps it did," Sterling answered, "and you were the only one who heard it." Well, perhaps Someone was looking out for us. Whatever, we got the jib up in time.

In five minutes the engine was purring purely, innocently. I glared at it. The dirty, rotten—but then I recalled how it had held us off the rocks at Duck Island Roads. We went up on deck and headed back for Onset.

Once more we were transiting the Cape Cod Canal. Once again there was conversation, laughter, small talk. But what is wrong? I wondered. Betty and I had talked about *Old Squaw* being jinxed. Neither of us believe such nonsense. But the engine in *Hornpipe* was of the same vintage as this one in *Old Squaw*. It never gave us trouble. We never dragged an anchor in *Hornpipe*. Of course, *Old Squaw* is three times as heavy. But *Hornpipe* never fouled a tie line. *Hornpipe* never fouled a halyard. *Hornpipe* never—oh well, I could pursue that train of thought endlessly. I looked up. Betty was looking at me. Was she wondering, too? Later, she said she had been having the same thoughts.

Ellen laughed. "It looks as though we've brought you bad luck," she said. "You've had perfect sailing until we arrived."

Again Betty's and my eyes caught. Should we tell them? No!

The tide and the engine whisked us back to Onset. We had an hour or two for ducking over the side. Then we all went ashore and walked through the town. Sterling and Bill said that dinner would be on them. They came back with lettuce and salad dressing, fresh vegetables and the thickest sirloin steak we had ever seen. We stood right there in the middle of the sidewalk and admired it. Oh, yes. They bought a bottle of Scotch, too.

So here we were, back in Onset again. Boards were placed athwart the cockpit, from one side to the other, and the grill was placed on them. We had done that last night, too. The grill was filled with charcoal and lighted. Like last night. The bottle was opened. Toasts were drunk to a great passage through the canal next day. No more engine trouble. We drank twice to that. But everyone seemed a bit more sentient this evening. Aware. They wanted to see the chart of Cape Cod Bay. They wanted to study the chart of the canal. We pointed out how far we had gotten, located the basin where the repair was made. We calculated that it was roughly 25 land miles, perhaps a fraction more, from the end of the canal to Provincetown. Also, that the bay was about the same distance across. We would be bisecting it, sailing across its middle.

Suddenly we were aware that this venture was no evening sail such as the ones we had taken outside Mamaroneck Harbor. Cape Cod Bay contains just one whole hell of a lot of water. And if a *very* strong wind came up while we were out in the middle someplace? Connie said she wished she could swim. Sterling reassured her. He said that, if things got *that* bad, swimming wouldn't help. We'd *all* go down, swimmers and nonswimmers. Everybody thanked him for introducing such a happy thought. One thing it did, though: it made everybody equal.

Betty and I, too, were suddenly aware that we had taken upon ourselves a responsibility. We had invited four people to share our fate, and our fate hadn't been all that good lately. H'mmm.

Betty and Ellen had the salad ready. The vegetables would be ready when the steak was. Bill slapped that beautiful piece of meat onto the glowing charcoal. Flames shot up into the darkening sky. Over there in the west, soon to set, was a planet. Venus. How do you know it's a planet? someone asked. Because the light is unwavering. It doesn't twinkle. Stars twinkle. Planets just sort of stare. Bill turned the steak and the flames leaped again. We lost the planet in the glare. It was just as well. People might begin to talk about eternity. How that planet had been shining down on this earth for hundreds of thousands of years. How short our lives are in comparison. As I said, it was just as well we could not see Venus.

Instead, we had another drink and watched the steak. At last it was flopped out of the fire and onto one of the boards.

Bill attacked it with a carving knife. While Bill operated on the steak, I took a large chunk of ice from the icebox, held it in the palm of my hand, and speared it with the stainless-steel icepick. Speared it too vigorously. The pick went cleanly through the ice and didn't stop. It went cleanly through the flesh of my left hand between the thumb and the base of the index finger. Scotch whiskey is a pain-killer. In addition, it eradicates inhibitions.

"Hey, everybody, look what I did." I held up the impaled hand for all to see. It really didn't hurt. That icepick was sharp. The point was sticking out the back of my hand.

Gulp. Gag. Choke. Gasp. Betty grasped the handle and withdrew the weapon. She poured some merthiolate or iodine on the point of entry. Sterling started to pour Scotch on the wound, but stopped. Use the merthiolate, Betty. Scotch is too precious to waste. Fine friend.

Well, said Betty's eyes, it's one thing to stab yourself. But it's an entirely different matter to make a display of it. Sometimes, my husband, you just aren't very bright. Her eyes said all that.

I allowed as how I agreed. To myself, of course. No words of that short exchange had been spoken.

We got a piece of gauze wrapped around old Jim's hand. Words of sympathy and solicitude were spoken. The bottle found itself being passed around. Old Jim's glass got an extra portion because of his mortal wound. Bill went back to surgery.

The steak was carved and served. Salad and vegetables filled the rest of the space on the plates. It was a happy evening. Occasionally someone asked if my hand hurt. It didn't. Betty told the story of Everett and the junk of pork. Ellen told about the time she had pierced her ears. Someone else told about a stabbing. Somebody else asked about tomorrow's weather. Connie said she sure wished she had learned to swim. I said we had life jackets for everyone. Betty said we wouldn't need them. The weather was going to be beautiful tomorrow. People have confidence in Betty. They have doubts about me. If they didn't before, all they had to do was look at my hand. Stabbed myself. What the hell kind of a skipper would do that, chipping ice?

There wasn't any question about everybody being awake the next morning. Everybody woke everybody else up—two or three times. Hey, Ellen. You awake? Yes. Bill? Yep. Connie? I didn't go to sleep for fear I wouldn't wake up. Betty? Been up for half an hour. Sterling? I've already been over the side for a bath. People scurried around, holding clothes in front of them. Into the head to dress. Out. Let someone else in. People bumped into each other. Betty manned the galley. Sterling and Bill inspected the weather. Ellen put her slacks on backwards. Had to start over. Bill took it upon himself to wake up the seagulls. It was that early.

Breakfast over, we just moseyed out the Onset Harbor. The tide hadn't even turned yet. But it did turn and we recommenced our journey through the canal.

We had oh'd and ah'd about everything there was to oh and ah about yesterday. Today we just watched the shore go by. We watched people in cars and campers watching us. We waved to them. They waved back. A huge freighter lumbered through, east to west. We braced for the bow wave, braced again for the bank wave. There was considerable idle chatter, followed by fairly long silences. Sterling didn't leave the cockpit. If that engine gave so much as a hiccup, he would be down there by its side, nursing it back to health. I noticed a screwdriver sticking out of his hip pocket. There would be no repetition of yesterday's near debacle if he could help it.

At last we came abreast of the breakwaters at the eastern end. Conversation started up again. Sort of nervous conversation. How close were we to those boulders? What would have happened if we had hit? Well, Sterling said, if we *had* hit and we *had* drowned, at least the tide would have carried our bodies back into the canal so the Coast Guard would have an easy time gathering us all in. Sterling, you are gruesome!

A breeze came up, a following breeze. Outside, we came up into the wind, cut the engine, hoisted the sails. Cape Cod Bay. This is more like it. We wouldn't have to depend on man's feeble inventions. We'd cross the bay by God power, the wind. God intended man to travel the natural way. Sails don't pollute. We're all environmentalists. By sailing across Cape Cod Bay we're helping to clean up America!

It was pretty obvious that everyone was glad to be out of the Cape Cod Canal. And they wouldn't have to go back through, either. Only Betty and I would. Lucky Betty. Lucky Jim.

The breeze came to us from northwest. *Old Squaw* frolicked. The farther out we got, the steeper became the waves. *Old Squaw* would hitch up her rear end and aim her bow down. A wave would slide under us. Conscious, perhaps, of an indecency, the stern would slide back into the water and the bow would rise. Two shipmates got seasick. Not violently. Just low-moaning, quick-swallowing cases.

Betty dashed below to the medical department, a small white tin box with a red cross on it. Her fingers visited the prescription counter, shopped around, and finally bought two Dramamine tablets. These, with water, were administered. Grateful, dog-sick eyes were raised to her. Sterling suggested that the patients should edge closer to the rail of the boat— *not both on the same side, for goodness' sake*—just in case.

A radio weather forecast from Plymouth, Massachusetts,. where the Pilgrims landed the second time—the first was at

Provincetown—informed us that the winds were up to 30 miles per hour. That's substantial. Cape Cod Bay, like Long Island Sound, is relatively shallow. In a breeze that strong the seas are steep and short. *Old Squaw* began to run downhill before she finished going up. We were taking a considerable amount of green water aboard. Guests and permanent residents alike were getting wet. All foul-weather gear available was called into use. All hands huddled in the cockpit. Connie gave me a quizzical look. "You and Betty really love this, don't you." It was a statement, almost an accusation.

I looked at Betty. Perhaps she would answer. She looked at me. Finally, I said, "We-l-l-l." We really did. Perhaps, though, we would love it even more if the breeze were only 25 miles per hour. Or even 20. But you take what is given and you are thankful it isn't worse.

Finally, Ellen, who had the binoculars, called out, "Land hoy." We explained that it was "land ho." It didn't matter. She had spied Race Point Light. Then we saw the Pilgrim Monument, standing 350 feet above water. Wood End Light was next. We were coming home. The seasick ones perked up a bit. They vowed that, if God would spare them this once, they would never even get into a bathtub full of water if the wind was blowing.

Perhaps the best way to describe the eastern end of Cape Cod is to compare it to the free arm and hand of a fencer. The arm from shoulder to elbow is horizontal. From the elbow to the wrist it is vertical. Then the hand and fingers curl in toward the head. At least, that's the way Errol Flynn did it. Where the hand and fingers curl is where Provincetown Harbor lies, beautifully protected against all winds except, possibly, those from the south and southeast. Our *Coast Pilot* informed us that the harbor has a diameter of about two miles. That is almost an inland ocean itself.

With a harbor so vast, we picked our anchorage at ran-
dom, a hundred yards or so from a wharf. There was a chop to
the water, but it was a relief to get out of the heavy, short seas
running outside. Everyone thought it would be a good idea to
go ashore, particularly our patients, so quickly as possible we
got things put to rights aboard. Since the dinghy could hold
only three passengers, it took a rower, Bill, three trips to get
the entire crew ashore.

The *Mayflower* landed here at Provincetown and remained for five weeks before proceeding on to Plymouth.
It was in Provincetown that the Mayflower Compact was
drawn and signed. The Compact preceded the Declaration of
Independence by over 150 years; yet the Compact is the base
upon which our democratic form of government is built.
Provincetown, along with such places as New Bedford and
Nantucket, harbored great whaling fleets. They're gone now,
of course, but many of the houses their captains built are
still standing.

It was not until the twentieth century that the monument
to the Pilgrims' stopover here was put up. President Theodore
Roosevelt was present at the laying of the Pilgrim Monuments
cornerstone in 1907. Another president, William Howard Taft,
was present in 1910 when it was dedicated. It was erected on
a 100-foot hill, and reaches 252 feet above the hill. It is the
tallest granite structure in the United States. Ah, Plymouth, you
have the Rock. But Provincetown, it has its monument.

We wandered about the town until our legs were tired.
Commercial Street is the main thoroughfare. Shops and restau-
rants, bowling alleys and bare feet. Far out, man. "No wonder
these kids have such long beards and hair," Sterling said at one
point. "It's all growing in inches of topsoil."

We had dinner ashore and returned to *Old Squaw* in the
small hours. Seasickness was forgotten. The rough passage

now was only a thing to be remembered. It wouldn't have been memorable if it hadn't been rough. In the morning Connie and Sterling took a bus back to Onset.

Ellen and Bill and Betty and I rented a car and drove down the cape to Wellfleet. Betty wanted to see the town of her ancestors. We found the town clerk's office to inquire if there were any Hardings around. "Hardings?" the clerk repeated. "Well, I guess so. You can find a whole passel of 'em right close by." And he gave us directions. We found them, in the cemetery. Thankful, Molly, Solomon. And there were others. Betty picked a tiny wildflower and laid it on Thankful's tombstone.

We arrived back in Provincetown late in the afternoon. A fresh breeze had come up, from the southwest. Clouds were gathering on the horizon. There was no hint of a storm in any forecast, but we had an uneasy feeling. With memories of Duck Island Roads fresh in our minds, I broke out the storm anchor and dropped it overboard 30 feet or so from where I judged the Danforth to be. Perhaps it was an unnecessary precaution. Now, though, there were four of us aboard. Two anchors would hold us even in a hurricane. We laughed at the thought. It would be exciting, though, wouldn't it? We had an outstanding dinner, talked late, and were finally felled into our bunks by sleep.

In the morning wind and rain were forecast. Only a few of the fishing boats had gone out. Those which did returned early. The rains came, almost horizontally. We watched the fishermen making things fast aboard their vessels. We did the same and twiddled the radio dial for weather forecasts.

Toward noon I donned foul-weather clothing and went up on deck. There was a short chop running. In addition, long swells were rolling in from the wide mouth of the harbor. So vast was the harbor it was almost like being anchored in the open sea. I looked about through the binoculars. The town wharf was devoid of life. Where have all the people gone? I wondered. There were many boats moored about us. Yet the harbor looked strangely deserted. The boats seemed small, empty, lonely. Perhaps it was because the harbor was so huge.

In 1849 Henry Thoreau of Concord and Walden had stood on the wide beach outside this harbor and watched the mackerel fleet round the cape. "Schooner after schooner," he wrote, "until they made a city on the water." Thoreau is quoted as having counted 400 vessels that passed into this place. My glasses peered here and there, then out to the harbor entrance. They moved, then stopped.

I took the binoculars from my eyes and wiped them as dry as possible, then looked again. An enormous ship lay outside. Smaller vessels were around her. An aircraft carrier and destroyers, I guessed. How many destroyers, if that was indeed what they were, I couldn't determine. I called Bill. He came up and looked. No doubt now. An aircraft carrier and attendants. We took turns passing the glasses back and forth. The ships lay dead in the water. There was no sign of life on any deck. Where were they all? Where were the fishermen? It was as though everyone else knew something we didn't know. The draggers tugged and tossed at their mooring lines. Bill and I were the only human beings in the whole world of Province-town. Everyone else had gone underground.

Just suppose—naw. That couldn't be. That's insane. But just suppose. Suppose this harbor is harboring 20 or 30 Russian nuclear submarines. They could have sneaked in during the night. God knows we wouldn't have known. Right now they're busy under our very keel arming their nuclear weapons. They are going to blow up the United States! And what were Bill and I and Ellen and Betty doing while those devils skulked into Provincetown Harbor? Sleeping. The battle was about to be joined! The Third World War was about to begin. Provincetown was the site. And we were sleeping.

Bill said to hell with this. It's raining and the wind is blowing. The waves are getting higher. It's cold and I think I hear my mother calling. I'm going below where there are beautiful women. I'm going to dig out a bottle of cold beer and organize an orgy. It's sheer madness to stand out here when down there in the cabin—ah-h.

He disappeared. I took one last look at the carrier, then turned to go below. If Bill wouldn't stand out here with me and watch the approach of Armageddon, I sure wasn't going to face it alone. I opened the companionway doors. There is a flagpole between the Pilgrim Monument and the harbor. Ever since yesterday a small-craft warning had been flying from its masthead. I glanced at it. Small-craft warnings simply mean that little boats should seek some kind of shelter. The warning is a red pennant. It flies from flagpoles when winds of up to 33 knots, or 38 miles per hour, are forecast. This time, though, there was no red pennant. Rather, there were two red pennants. Two red pennants mean gale warnings. A gale carries winds of up to 47 knots, 54 miles per hour. The rain was coming directly at me from the southwest. It didn't come from heaven, as most rain does. But it was hard to tell now what was rain and what was ocean. Tops were being torn off whitecaps. Little dollops of them were striking *Old Squaw*'s flanks. That and the rain combined were making it imperative that I, too, abandon the deck. The dinghy was at the end of its tether, straining to get to safer climes. In a few hours we, too, would be close to the end of our tethers.

I went below. No orgy there. Betty had gathered four life jackets and placed them on a bunk. The three of them, Betty, Ellen, Bill were sitting up very straight. Not at all relaxed. Even though it was still midafternoon someone had lighted the lamps. It was hot and steamy. Foggy, almost. Or perhaps it was the rain and salt spray in my eyes. The radio crackled. It sounded like someone frying bacon on a very hot fire. I shed my outer clothing and sat on the edge of a bunk. I sat up straight, too.

The seas in the harbor were short. *Old Squaw* raised her bow a short way, then plunged down with a jolt. I fitted a smile on, but nobody smiled back. Rain struck the deck over our heads intermittently like someone tearing a sheet. *Old Squaw* set up a humming sound. That was the extent of the music.

"Anyone like some hot tea?" Betty forced a smile.

"Ugh," said Bill. "I mean no, ugh, thanks."

"What's going on upstairs?" Ellen asked.

"Same as downstairs, only wetter."

A violent gust set the boat over on her port side. "You got any more anchors?" Bill asked.

"The only ones I've got are busy right now."

"Can't you fix that radio, Jim?" Ellen asked. "It's beginning to get on my nerves."

"The only way I can fix that thing is to throw it overboard." I snapped it off. The bacon was done.

No one said anything for a while. Just listened. There was a lot to listen to. The waves no longer slapped *Old Squaw*'s flanks. They pounded her. Whump. Crump. She lurched as though to get away. I hoped she couldn't. I put on my dripping rain gear and went up on deck again. I took some bearings on land things to determine if either anchor had dragged. Still safe. Nothing had moved but my stomach. It was heaving. The rain seemed to have eased a bit. I looked again at the flagpole. Whoever was manning those pennants was busier than a housewife with quintuplets. The two red pennants were gone. In their place was just one flag. I'd never seen one like it before. But I knew what it was. It was a square red flag with a black center. Whole Gale! Winds from 55 miles per hour to 72. I knew they couldn't be that high. Seventy-one, maybe.

I had read about whiteouts in arctic regions. That's when it is snowing and blowing so hard nothing is distinguishable. Everything turns white. This was a grayout. It was hard to tell where the sky ended and the ocean began. I thought about the dinghy. It was totally useless. With just one person aboard it would capsize. Someone was walking along the wharf, bent into the wind. If it stopped for a moment, he'd fall flat on his face. I waved and shouted. All I wanted now was to get us off this boat. The man never saw me. He was looking at his feet.

The rain slackened a bit, and even the wind eased. Perhaps the storm was ending. Once again I went below and doffed the rain gear. Bill was at one of the large, round portholes, Betty, at the other.

"Some fancy goings-on," Bill muttered.

"Navy people know how to live," Betty replied.

Bill pointed. "Did you see them when you were on deck?"

I couldn't see anything. Down here, at least, it wasn't raining. I looked where Bill pointed. Two boats—I learned later they were an admiral's barge and a captain's gig—were gliding in to the wharf. A dozen or more men were aboard the two craft. Ellen and Betty shared one porthole, Bill and I, the other. The boats were big, with powerful engines. They maneuvered for a few moments, then with the assistance of several willing hands on the wharf they came alongside, cast up lines, and were secured. The men scrambled onto the wharf and hurried ashore. The United States Navy. They did things in style. Our eyes lingered on the two boats bobbing beside the wharf. Beautiful, immaculate, ornate. Mothers back in Iowa and Nebraska and Alabama would have been proud of the way their sons maintained those boats—for the admiral, the captain, the commodore, and whoever else used them.

We turned away. It was five o'clock. Perhaps in an hour or so we, too, would get to go ashore. Maybe we could even catch up with the Navy and find out what's with the Russians. Failing that, they might lead us to some exotic place to eat dinner.

The Lord, though, He had other plans for us. Somebody tore up an old sheet, it sounded like. Only it wasn't. It was a curtain of rain striking the deck. *Old Squaw* started humming again. She bounced and bucked and struck the water with her bow and flanks as though by sheer force and weight she would flatten out the seas that struck her. But *Old Squaw* lost. She sawed at her anchors, first to port and then to starboard. She heeled sharply, as though a giant hand had grasped the tops of the masts to haul her over on her side. Pots and pans rattled against the doors of the locker that contained them under the galley sink. Suddenly the doors flew open; frying pans and kettles, a double boiler, the pressure cooker, all of Betty's cooking utensils spewed onto the cabin sole. Betty let out a small cry of dismay. But there were other, more important things to think about.

The entire boat vibrated, the wind shrieked through the rigging far above our heads. Betty took a life jacket in her hands, held it out. Ellen stood up, and they fitted it on and tied the bindings. Then she shrugged into her own. Bill and I did the same. Again *Old Squaw* ducked. She must have seen it coming, but not in time to avoid a roundhouse blow that sent her reeling. We were all thrown into and against the port bunks. The eye of the hurricane, or gale, had passed. That had accounted for the short lull. Now we were getting it from the other side. Winds of 75 miles an hour raged and shrieked at us. I caught Ellen's face out of the corner of my eye. Her eyes were closed. Either she was in shock or she was praying. Well, Ellen, baby, if you happen to be praying, make it a good one. I recalled the parable of Christ calming another storm at sea. If ever a quieting hand was needed to dampen down overpowering seas and winds, it was needed now. It was out of our power to help the boat. In fact, I didn't know how we could help ourselves. One thing was certain: we weren't accomplishing anything down here in the cabin.

The forward starboard mattress fairly leaped off the bunk and onto the sole, carrying with it blankets and pillow. The hanging locker door banged open. Laundry and shoes spewed out. I could see six eyes. Three faces. The eyes were dark saucers; the faces were gray, the color of a dead fish you might see lying on the shore after a storm.

I turned and plunged for the ladder. Once, years before, I had seen Everett, Betty's parents' farmer, with two or three rats in a metal trap. He'd caught them in the barn. He carried the trap to the horse trough and held it under water until the rats were dead. I didn't want to be caught in a trap like those rats. I headed up the ladder to the cockpit. The others stayed below. The wind tore my breath away. I turned my back to it and faced the stern. There, not over a hundred feet astern of us, was a boat. A Coast Guard boat! She was a 30-foot cutter, heaving and plowing through the eight-foot waves. An old double-ender. She was making heavy going of it. One man stood in the stern. He seemed intent on making it to the wharf.

When I was a kid I could put four fingers into my mouth and whistle a blast that caused ripples in graves in the Sewickley cemetery. I could blow out an eardrum at 60 yards. The wind was blowing from me to the Coast Guardsman. I put five fingers in my mouth—one for good measure—and blew. Betty and Ellen and Bill came up that ladder faster than the wind was blowing. They jammed into the cockpit, and I pointed.

The Coast Guardsman heard the whistle. He waved and brought the bow around in our direction. He couldn't head straight for us. The waves were too steep. He would have swamped in the first one. He quartered into them. Sort of rolled sideways into them. First to port, then starboard. The only way we could tell he had any control of the vessel was by the fact that the boat did turn from one direction to the other. If he was making progress against the seas, it wasn't apparent to us. But at least he wasn't going to leave us here!

Betty pointed astern. "The dinghy's gone!" she shrieked. It was. Our Dyer dhow, an expensive sailing dinghy. Fiber glass. A piece of the painter that had tied it to *Old Squaw* trailed over the stern.

The cutter came up slowly astern. One side, then the other. The man was working hard. The boat rolled from one side to the other, climbing over one cresting wave, then plunging down the back of it. I didn't see how he would ever get the boat close enough to take us aboard. I shed the life jacket. With that thing on I could jump ten feet. Without it, 20. Betty had taken her jacket off, too. I didn't know how good a jumper she was. I did know she was ready to give it a hell of a try.

I got Ellen out of the cockpit and over to the rail. She held on to the mizzenmast shrouds. Betty was beside her.

"When he gets close, jump!" Betty glanced at me. What did I *think* they were going to do, smile and wave as he went by?

The boat came abeam at last. As our stern went down his bow went up. There was a difference of about four feet. *Old Squaw*'s stern began to rise. I shoved Ellen. Betty jumped. They landed in a heap. "Jump, Bill!" He made a motion to. I jumped and landed on top of both women. Happy landing. I looked for Bill. The Coast Guardsman swore. "That other guy didn't jump!" he yelled.

Sure enough. There was Bill, still aboard *Old Squaw*. What was that about the captain staying aboard his ship until all others were off? Well, Bill could be the captain if he wanted to be.

The cutter fell away. The Guardsman was fighting desperately with the wheel. The engine roared for a moment, then he cut the throttle and the boat fell under *Old Squaw's* stern. He began maneuvering again. Quartering into this wave and the next, then coming about with a roar of the engine and heading across the back of the following one. It was harrowing. We huddled and waited.

"If that guy don't jump this time, I ain't tryin' it again."

Once more we came alongside, but this time too close. The cutter's bow rose, then crashed down on *Old Squaw's* rail. "JUMP!" we all screamed. Bill jumped, or fell into the cutter. We were safe.

In ten minutes of desperate maneuvering, we fetched up alongside the wharf. We scrambled onto it, waved to the man as his boat fell off. Once again the engine roared and he disappeared into the gloom. Thank God for the Coast Guard. (Later that same boat was to go down.)

It was a surrealistic scene. No painter could have captured it. In the weak wharf lights white water rose from green valleys. Water cascaded against and over the wharf, throwing sheets of spray 20 feet into the air. The tumult of sound was overwhelming, numbing. We stood for moments facing the storm, thankful, yet not fully realizing that we were safe. The wind drove us toward the land end of our haven, four drenched human beings.

We spied a dim, yellow light and, like moths, were attracted to it. The light came from the dome of an automobile. Pressing our faces against the glass, we saw a man sitting in the driver's seat, reading a newspaper. The man beckoned and we piled in.

"You look like somethin' dragged off the bottom," the man said. Then added, "Where you headed?"

We told him we didn't have any particular destination. We just wanted rooms for the night, the farther from the harbor the better.

"Ain't got reservations, I bet."

We said we did not.

"Money? Cash?"

Betty had grabbed her wallet an instant before she left the cabin.

"You ain't got a prayer of gettin' into an inn 'round these parts without a reservation," our discouraging friend said. He looked at Bill dripping beside him in the front seat and the two women and me in the back. "An' it's gonna take a month of Sundays to dry out the upholstery in this cab."

We felt guilty. But for the first time in many hours we felt secure. It was one chance in 10,000 that we had stumbled on a taxi.

"Isn't there any place *at all* where we could stay over-night?" Ellen pleaded. Even in her dire distress she managed a half-dazzling smile. It was an act of valor. We were all on the verge of tears.

The driver thought for a moment. "Got a friend might take you in," he said at last. "Mings. Takes in roomers sometimes."

He started the engine and wheeled away from the wharf. We were leaving the sea behind. Nobody looked back. The car climbed a small hill, moved down a street lined with modest houses. The driver pulled over to the curb at one.

"Mings lives here. I'll be back in a minute." Our savior, for the moment at least, pulled his hat down firmly on his head, clutched his coat, and dove out into the darkness. We watched him run down a walk along the side of the house. He never so much as paused at a door. Just pushed it open and burst in.

We were left alone with our wet skins, Betty's purse, and our thoughts.

"I don't know about this," Ellen said.

Betty agreed with Ellen. "We could be going from the frying pan into the fire."

Bill said fire might not be bad right now. No matter what we were getting ourselves into, we'd be warm and dry while it was happening.

The driver dashed part way down the walk, beckoned to us, turned, and ran back to the house.

For one short second we looked at each other, tumbled out of the car, and streamed down the walk to the open door. Whatever awaited us, we were running to get at it.

We burst into a kitchen. Plain, warm, homey. A sturdy, swarthy man smiled at us. Standing slightly behind him was a smiling, concerned woman. Portuguese, as was the driver.

"You brought no other clothes?" she asked the women.

They allowed as how they hadn't given clothes much thought.

The driver said three dollars would be fine. I paid him from Betty's wallet. We all thanked him. He left in a swirl of wind and rain. Our host's name was Mings. Gonzalves was the last name, we thought. But we were never quite sure.

Mrs. Mings led the women upstairs to a room and closed the door. Bill and I followed Mings to the next room. It contained simple furniture and a single bed.

"I get you some dry clothes," Mings said, and began rummaging in a closet. "Get them things off quick or you catch cold."

We did as he said. Apparently the women were doing Mrs. Mings' bidding. It turned out Mings and Mrs. Mings had two extra rooms, which they rented out occasionally. He did acknowledge that they were not usually called upon to supply clothing as well.

Later, the six of us gathered in the kitchen. Through

windows in the back wall we could make out the harbor. The storm still raged.

"I know your boat," Mings said. "*Old Squaw,* eh? Seen you this morning. I own a dragger. Went out early this morning. Come back early, too. Storm comin'. I know she be a bad one."

Mrs. Mings fussed over us. Had we eaten anything? We hadn't given it a thought. It was seven o'clock in the evening. We said we hadn't eaten. Mings left the room, but returned in a minute. He had a bottle of Madeira wine.

We now had time to look at each other. Bill wore a flannel shirt and trousers too short for him. The length of the trousers Mings had given me was fine; the waist must have been size 40. I just kept my hands in my pockets. No belt. I, too, wore a flannel work shirt. I don't know what Ellen and Betty were wearing. They looked rather odd in whatever it was. But they were warm and dry, and so were we.

Mrs. Mings fussed over the stove while the rest of us sat at the kitchen table.

"You want to see *Old Squaw,* huh?"

We all said Mings couldn't drag us out of this kitchen. Mings laughed. He got up, left the kitchen again, and returned with a powerful spotlight.

"While you drink the Madeira I show you *Old Squaw.*" He turned out the kitchen light. Mrs. Mings went on doing whatever she was doing at the stove, in the dark. She was cooking bacon and eggs, that's what she was doing. She didn't seem to need light to do that. Mings shone the light down on the water, flashed it around for a moment. *Old Squaw* appeared in the beam. We were astounded. Mings' house was not more than 200 feet from the harbor, with an unobstructed view of our boat, and his.

"*Old Squaw,* she ride safe to two anchors," he assured

us. His own dragger was secured to a mooring the entire Provincetown fleet couldn't pull out.

Mings turned the light on again. Mrs. Mings produced silverware, plates, eggs, bacon, toast. We already had glasses and the wine.

Mrs. Mings, you can do things with eggs that would amaze the smartest chicken. You are the two kindest people in the whole world. All this between and around mouthfuls of eggs, toast, and bacon. French vineyards in their finest years (gulp, swallow) never produced a wine as fine as this. I finished my plate and glanced at Betty's. Oh, no, you don't buster, she growled. Mings grinned and shone his light on *Old Squaw*. She rolled and pitched in the black seas. But that was out there. We were in here.

At last we sat back, replete. We grinned at each other, at Mings and Mrs. Mings. The wind seemed to bend the windows. Rain pounded tiny steel nails into the glass. But it couldn't touch us now. We were safe. The nightmare was over. One felt like saying, I had the weirdest dream today. I dreamed I was caught in a hurricane in Provincetown Harbor. If anything, the storm increased in fury, but it was only background accompaniment to the stories of the sea and Provincetown that Mings told us. He told of sea monsters of ancient days, of ghosts and pirates. He told of the blessing of the fleet, a daylong fiesta that occurs each year in June. The fishermen of Provincetown, the Portuguese fishermen particularly, are devout. The blessing by the bishop is of grave importance.

Mings asked us if we had heard of the submarine, the *S-4*. We had not, or if we had, had forgotten the story. The *S-4* sank off Wood End Light in December 1927. She could not rise again. A winter storm raged and rescue efforts were frustrated. There were 40 men aboard, trapped in 120 feet of water. The chief of Navy Operations arrived, as did the

Secretary of the Navy. Every type of rescue vessel known and available was assembled. But nothing could be done. A diver went down to the sub. He knocked on the steel hull with a hammer. There were answering knocks. Then, using code, they communicated. What are you doing up there to rescue us? We're doing all we can, but the weather.... A day passed. Has the storm eased? Are you doing all you can? We are down here in the black and cold. We need help. Another day. The third day came and the code messages became desperate. Urgent. We are running out of oxygen, and strength. Please. Please. Do everything. Do more than you are doing now. We want to live! No man should die like this.

The fourth day brought only little sound from the sunken sub. The urgent messages were gone. A pervasive silence was settling in. The men, all 40 of them, were doomed.

A month later the sub was raised, the bodies were recovered. Too late, too late. Mings was a boy then, but as he told the story we could see it all in his eyes. He lived it then. He was reliving it as he spoke the words.

The wind lashed at the window. One could almost drown out there tonight in this storm. I felt Betty shudder next to me. The *S-4* went down a long time ago, but a good storyteller can bring the past to life, to live once more in his words. The wine bottle was empty. The story was told.

Mings' wife fussed over us, told him he had no business telling us such stories at bedtime. And bedtime it was. We rose from the kitchen table, stretched, and followed Mrs. Mings upstairs to our rooms.

We slept late the next morning, late, that is, by the Gonzalves' standards. As we trailed downstairs, one by one, there was a sense of urgency in Mings' voice and manner. He had another story to tell, but he would wait until we all were there. We looked out the window. *Old Squaw* was still jumping. Mrs.

Mings served a sumptuous breakfast, and as we ate it, Mings told us another story. But this one didn't happen many years ago. It happened last night! Last night while we all sat here in this very kitchen.

Mings had arisen early. The storm had subsided somewhat, but it was still far too rough to venture out. So he had gone down to the wharf. He met other fishermen. Friends. Mings! You haven't heard? Where were you last night?

Well. That flotilla out there, outside the harbor. That's made up of one aircraft carrier, a 40,000 tonner, the *Intrepid.* And seven destroyers. And one submarine. They had been at sea for two weeks. They had been too busy during those weeks for many happy hours. So now it was happy-hour time. It had begun when we watched through *Old Squaw*'s portholes as the admiral and the other high-ranking officers had come ashore. They weren't concerned with the weather. Winds of 25 or 30 knots were forecast, but what was that to men who had braved the heaving seas of the Atlantic for two weeks?

The admiral and his men had a nice, leisurely dinner ashore. But while they were dining all kinds of things were happening down in the harbor. Well, said Mings, his eyes dancing, the Navy came back down to the wharf at seven o'clock or so and wanted to go home. But home was 'way out there in a hell of a storm and they were here. They looked at their own boats, the barge and the gig. No sir, buddy, we ain't leaving this harbor in those babies. We'll git us a *big* boat, that 95-foot Coast Guard cutter will do. Where's her skipper?

It so happened that the skipper of the cutter was a 23-year-old lieutenant. He was ashore, but somebody got him by telephone. The lieutenant came down to the wharf to see what was up. What was up was the Navy. They wanted to go home! Six- and eight-foot waves were dancing all over the place. So were all the little boats tied up at the wharf. So were all the

other boats out in the harbor, including *Old Squaw*. Even the
95-footer, *322*, was getting a bit uneasy about all this water
flying around.

The lieutenant could have told the admiral it was
too rough out there. But what lieutenant is going to tell an
admiral, "No way, mister." The lieutenant was a Coast Guard
Academy man, with a fine record in the service. He was a seaman. So he said, "Just hop aboard, men."

Well, Mings said, they got the cutter out of the harbor and
headed for one of the destroyers. The lieutenant was
determined to offload the gold braid. If it had been bad in the
harbor, it was infinitely worse out here. Waves like houses.
The *322* was going up while the destroyer was coming down.
But with the touch of a gem cutter he brought *322* in close
enough to get a couple of lines aboard the destroyer, the *Du
Pont*. Two of the officers even managed to get themselves
aboard by way of a flimsy rope ladder hanging down the *Du
Pont's* side. But that was it. Them Navy men knew a bad thing
when they seen it, said Mings. They backed off.

The lieutenant looked around. He reconnoitered. He
would just as soon have gone back home. He saw the carrier
setting there steady as an island. All hands agreed they should
make for the carrier. And that's when things really began to
happen. Gettin' that 95-footer in just right against the flanks of
that carrier was like maneuvering a tall ladder against the side
of a house in a gale-force wind. Somehow, the cutter's superstructure come up under the carrier's overhang. There was a
clangin' an' a bashin' and 25 feet of radar and radio mast was
hangin' over *322's* side like so much spaghetti. The lieutenant
thought perhaps he'd had enough of this. The Navy 'lowed as
how he figured right.

So they came back into the harbor. But what about this?
The *322's* sister ship, the *321*, was laying in *322's* berth.

What now, mateys? They ain't no room in the inn. The lieutenant had no choice. He came 'longside *321* an' put some lines aboard her. He'd just lie there until all this blows over. At this point the Navy decides they'll go uptown, have a drink, or take in a family-type movie until the storm blows itself out. *Then* they'll give the lieutenant another chance.

Them cutters, *322* and *321*, hitched side by side, they began the up-and-down business. One up, the other down. One shootin' forward, the other lurchin' back. The crews got out fenders, sort of cushions boats use, and put them between the two sisters to keep them apart. But they chewed them fenders up in no time at all.

Now the lieutenant *knew* he should have stood in town. He decided to move out, find some other place to tie up. So he started to move. Now *322* was beginnin' to really get into the spirit of things. Her port propeller (shades of *Old Squaw*, I thought) found some heavy iron chain danglin' down from somethin' an' wrapped herself up in that chain—tight. That chain wasn't just hangin' there doin' nothin'. It was holdin' a float. The float swung free, knocked into a gangway. The gangway in turn tore out a lot of electric cables. So now the lieutenant not only had a propeller wound up with chain, he had fireworks from the tore up cables. Next a big water pipe busted. So he had a big water fountain, an' fireworks to watch it by.

The lieutenant, though, he didn't have much time for watchin' the display. The cutter had went clean out of control and was backin' fast into a fish-packin' house.

Breakfast was forgotten. Mings had told us some stories last night. But this! He looked at us and came back to his own kitchen. Until now he had been reliving every traumatic moment of the night. He shook his head. "An' here we sat," he said, "through all that. With me tellin' ghost stories. Holy Mother of God."

Well, the poor lieutenant, he went on. One propeller was all wound up in chain. The other was thrashin' around doin' nothin'. An', of course, the wind was howlin' at 60 knots. That's somewheres near 70 miles an hour. An' them waves? Mings shook his head sadly. Them waves kept drivin' that cutter into the fish house. An' one thing the lieutenant didn't need was *fish*. He had a big enough stink on his hands as it was. Well, he got *322* out of there after knockin' down a wall and then he busted into a coupla floats. It wasn't his fault. Just one of those things. Mebbe a dozen of those things. A few of them was other boats. Quite a few was chewed pretty bad. But at last the lieutenant got *322* hogtied.

Betty poked at some food on her plate. I watched *Old Squaw*. Over there to the right, just beyond our vision, was the wharf where it all had happened. The waves were down now to perhaps three feet high. The wind was still gusting.

Mings looked around at us. "You said a Coast Guard 30-footer took you off your boat last night?"

We said that's right.

"Well, she went down this mornin'."

We stared at him, dumbfounded.

"Sometime 'round seven or eight o'clock. The lieutenant tried to move the cutter outta where he'd got her hogtied.

But she wasn't going to budge. So he got the 30-footer to hook onto the cutter's bow. They got movin', but somehow the cutter shot forward, dragged the 30-footer a ways, an' down she went."

Anybody hurt? We were thinking of our young rescuer.

"Nope. Coupla men got a swim they didn't need. In all that business nobody got hurt. Nobody got killed. Thank God."

We sat around for a while longer. It was time to leave, but we were reluctant to leave these kind people.

"Mings," Betty said. She sounded tentative, almost reluctant.

He smiled at her.

"This may sound like an odd thing to ask. But do you think a boat can be jinxed? You know—can a boat have some kind of bad luck attached to it?"

Ellen and Bill looked surprised.

"Ho ho," Mings laughed. "You betcha your life. I had one —no, two. Two boats I thought was jinxed. Brought me all kindsa bad luck." To him it was not a surprising question. Jinxes were a part of life at sea. I thought of the albatross and the Ancient Mariner.

"Had one boat," he continued, "she wouldn't fish worth a damn. Other fishermen were bringin' in good hauls. I couldn't fish nothin' with that boat." He paused, remembering.

And the other?

He laughed. "The other. She was like that *322*. Allas gettin' into trouble. Trouble this, trouble that. Engine trouble. Chains and blocks foulin'. Weather? I get well offshore. Boom. Storm come up. Tear up nets. Stuff like that. I get rid of her, quick." He laughed again. "Sure. Boats is jinxed sometimes." Then he added, "But just for one fisherman, mebbe."

Just for one man?

"Sure. 'Nother fisherman here, he liked the second one. Bought her off me. Never had no trouble of any kind. Good boat—for him."

"What about the first boat?" Bill asked. "The one you couldn't catch any fish with?"

"Same thing. She allas fish all right. Outta New Bedford."

At last we left the Mings'. We paid what they asked and then some. They seemed sorry to see us go. For us, money could never buy a night like that. Or pay for such human kindness.

Ellen went off to find a church somewhere. She felt a need to report in.

Betty and Bill and I took a long walk. Three miles or so, down the shore, searching for the dinghy. We had little hope of finding it. It would have been smashed on the rocks or stove in.

We came to a seawall. On it, upside down, was a dinghy. Of course, it couldn't be ours. But it was. Without a scratch on it. There was a house nearby. A man came out of it grinning.

"I saw you looking at the dinghy," he said. "Yours?" He was a sculptor. He had seen the dinghy being swept toward shore. He knew it would be pounded to shreds, so he ran down and wrestled it in, then dragged it up onto the seawall. He figured someone would be searching for it. The oars were in his house.

"Now," he offered, "I've got a station wagon. We'll just haul the dinghy aboard and I'll drive you to wherever you need to go." Sculptor, you are a kind man. Wherever you are. He did what he said he would do.

Betty went in search of Ellen. Bill and I rowed out to *Old Squaw*. The chaos in the cabin was awesome. It was as though a maniac had raged through the boat. Everything we owned, it seemed, had been torn from its place and flung onto the cabin sole.

Bill and I sat and stared at it all. Where to start? There was no beginning. No end. Well, start somewhere. We toiled. Sorting, sifting, carrying, heaving. When at last I rowed ashore to pick up the women, *Old Squaw* was presentable again. We glanced over at the destruction *322* had wrought the night before. But just glanced at it. We really didn't want to see it. We knew it all too well.

At one point Mings had said, "That Lieutenant Hiller, he is one good man. He keep at it. Some men, mebbe they quit. He try. He do the best anybody can do." We saluted that.

Betty had bought flounder filets, fresh corn, peaches, thick cream. It was Ellen and Bill's last night aboard.

Later, we sat in the cockpit.

"Do you think *Old Squaw* is a jinx?" Ellen asked.

Betty was sorry she had brought it up. "Oh," she said, "I don't know. But we've had so many things go wrong. Like the engine quitting in the canal. And this hurricane or whatever it was."

"Do you believe in such things?" I asked Bill.

"Well, in a way, I guess. Like Mings. I've had cars that seemed jinxed. Things happening to them for no good reason."

We talked about it for a while. Talked about the storm. The Coast Guard disaster. But it was such a beautiful night. Venus was a baleful eye on the western horizon. Somewhat higher was a circlet of diamond chips, the Corona Borealis, Ariadne's crown. Little waves gurgled and chuckled past the hull. *Old Squaw* tossed her head occasionally in her sleep. The air was soft and cool.

"Jinx or no jinx, I wouldn't have missed these days for the world," Ellen said. She sighed deeply, contentedly.

"Think how dull it would have been if the engine hadn't failed in the canal," Bill added. "And if we hadn't gone through the storm. As it is, I'll be talking about this when I'm eighty."

We agreed it had been memorable. Unforgettable. The talk came in small starts. Somebody would say something. Someone would answer—or not. It was time. The last word had been said. Unforgettable. We knew Lieutenant Hiller would agree.

The next morning I rowed Ellen and Bill and their luggage in to the wharf. They had brought light and gaiety into these past days. It was hard to see them go. Betty's mood was dark, apprehensive. I knew she'd have liked to take the bus with them. I understood how she felt, the question in her mind: What has *Old Squaw* got planned for our sail back home? She was sitting in the cockpit with a book in her lap. But the book was unnoticed. Her gaze and her thoughts were somewhere off in the distance.

"If we leave by six tomorrow morning, we can make it across the bay and through the canal with the tide," I said. Betty brought her mind back from some distant, blue heaven.

"That will give us plenty of leeway? Time for engine failures and shark attacks?"

We joked a little, or tried to. But the gloom was pervasive. A heavy fog bank wandered slowly but purposefully over the land spit to starboard. Well, why not? Come and join the fun. Join your cold, clammy hand with ours.

In the afternoon we went ashore, wandering all over Provincetown killing time, killing time, waiting for tomorrow and the shark attacks. The word "jinx" continually ran through my mind. Was *Old Squaw* the wrong boat for us? Like some marriages that seem jinxed from nuptial day. People wrong for each other. Could people and boats be wrong for each other, as Mings had said?

When the day was used up we found a small restaurant and had dinner. Betty toyed with hers. "Ellen and Bill should be home by now," she said. I looked at her. Tan face, blue mood.

"Yes, but we're going to have a perfect sail home. Our luck is going to change. I can feel it."

She looked up. Then down. "We've said that before, I believe."

Betty is not by nature an unhappy person. But she is her own kind of pragmatist. She believes that, if you have a bad situation, it will continue to be bad until you change it. Sailing *Old Squaw* home wasn't changing anything. Ergo, more bad luck. As simple as that.

I awakened to a bright sun beaming through the portholes. Little waves tapped their dance against the flanks of the boat. No sooner had my feet touched the cabin sole than Betty was awake. "It's a beautiful day," I said. "Sun's bright. All's well with the world. And it's 20 of six."

Betty rolled out of her bunk without a word. Let's get this show on the road, her manner said.

I went up on deck. Oh, oh. Breeze from the southeast, where stormy weather comes from. But the sky was already turning blue. We'd have a fine morning, anyway. We'd even make Onset, with a little luck.

While Betty turned to, preparing breakfast, I went forward and heaved the storm anchor aboard. If it hadn't gotten itself so muddy, I would have kissed it. It, with the Danforth, had held *Old Squaw* in the worst blow we would ever know. I hoped.

Start the engine to see if it still functioned. Surprise. It did. No doubt the sediment would lie in wait. To catch us at some crucial time. *Old Squaw* stepped smartly toward the harbor entrance, then rolled and frolicked through the bay. She was so *good.* So *innocent.* Betty and I were unmoved. You'll wait until our very lives are on the line to play your tricks. You're sly. Methinks you are evil.

Betty went below and got her knitting, then returned to the cockpit and went at it. Later, she said she dropped so many stitches it would be the world's first see-through sweater. The miles passed.

We approached the canal at the top of the tide.

"What would the Coast Guard do if we sailed through?" Betty wondered.

"Probably take our boat away from us."

For the first time in two days she showed some animation. "Hot spit," she said. "Let's keep those sails up."

We dropped them. The engine and the tide took over. That day I held my breath for one hour! We passed all three bridges and never saw one of them. We don't remember anything except the sound of the engine. Putt putt putt. And the tide kept right on running just like it was supposed to. It didn't reverse even once.

We had traveled the better part of a day and nothing happened.

"Where would you like to put in for the night?" I asked my rose petal.

"White Plains," she replied.

"If we can't make White Plains?"

"Not Onset."

"Why?"

"If we go in there, it'll probably run dry or something."

She bent over the chart. "What about this place?" She put her finger on a spot. The name sounded like a plant you give somebody at Christmas.

"Mattapoisett?"

"Why not?" Betty asked.

She went below and returned with the cruising guide. "The book says it's a big harbor, wide open to the southeast."

I looked at the chart again. "Sure is. With a southeast breeze we'll roll and pitch all night. Let's look for another harbor."

"Listen," my tulip said firmly, "we've *got* to have some bad luck. So instead of the boat or the weather choosing it, let's us. Let's us make a few of the decisions around here."

Did that make sense? I pondered it. I didn't think so, but her spirits were brighter. I didn't want to spoil that.

Mattapoisett was an easy harbor to enter. We made our way in and anchored. It took a bit of doing. It is a large harbor, but large harbors, it seems, breed large boats in copious numbers. We did, however, find ourselves an anchorage.

The water was restless from the all-day breeze. *Old Squaw* tossed and jiggled around for a while. But she must have discovered that we were prepared for a rough night, so that took all the fun out of it. In an hour she settled down. The harbor became calm.

We went over the side and bathed, then topped it off with a freshwater sponge. We even changed clothes. This looked like a rather ritzy area and we wanted to be dressed properly in case we were invited to a couple of dinner parties.

The sun dropped down toward the horizon. It was a red ball. Small gray and yellow and blue clouds gathered around it. One passed over its face, blurring it. Bruised-looking. It reminded me of a black eye Michael once got.

"That's a mean-looking sky," Betty remarked, ominously.

"Naw. Red sky at night—" I started.

"That's not going to work. We've had a southeast wind all day. You know what that means. Bad weather!"

"Not necessarily."

"*Old Squaw* is just lulling you into a false sense of security. We're going to catch it. And soon. *Then* you'll be sorry."

I looked at her in wonderment. Then *I'll* be sorry? Wouldn't she? No, I guessed not. She wanted vindication. She wanted typhoon Sally, or an earthquake. Perhaps she didn't want them. But she expected them.

The sun had been up long enough. It took a sudden dive and was gone. We sat back and listened to voices of people on other boats. Peace. Deep-throated music boomed from the stereo in the bowels of a 70- or 80-foot yacht anchored nearby. It was beautiful. Classical. It was the kind of music our little transistor wouldn't pick up. All it got was weather reports. Their machine was playing Mozart's *Symphony #40 in G Minor*. How did I know that? A woman on the yacht hollered over the music at a guy.

"What's the name of that?"

"That's *Mozart's Symphony #40 in G Minor!*" he hollered back.

"Well, shut it off! It stinks!" the lady shouted.

Gulls tried out their evening voices. We had supper, then

loafed on deck again. *Old Squaw* must have found rock to rest on. She was perfectly still.

Suddenly Betty sat up. "Lightning." She sounded triumphant.

"Couldn't be."

"But it is. I saw it, over there behind you."

"Naw. Somebody just set off a bomb in Roxbury. You saw the flash."

A searchlight of sun streamed through a porthole. It beamed on the blanket at the foot of my bunk, then moved on as *Old Squaw* swung to a gentle breeze. I looked over at Betty's bunk. Empty. So! She'd gotten up before the sun, packed her belongings and was hitchhiking home.

On deck I found my apple blossom, mopping the decks.

"Beautiful morning," I announced.

"Yep, and the wind's still out of the southeast. I don't understand why it isn't raining."

"*Old Squaw*'s bringing us good luck for the run home."

Swish, swish went the mop.

The day ended as it started. A fresh breeze and blue skies. Betty had a point. A breeze like this is a weather breeder. But why wonder? Accept it. The sail was a frolic. The Atlantic heaved great rollers at us and small whitecaps topped them off. Dabs of cream on blueberries.

The jinx was gone. The final evening we ducked in behind Sheffield Island. We could have made it home to Mamaroneck, but we needed just one more night aboard. The cruise was behind us. Just a few short days ago we ached to be home. Now we sat and watched a lone small boat with a huge outboard tow a water-skier.

It was a soft evening. In a few weeks the leaves on the maples would be turning to gold. Except for some diehards reluctant to have their boats hauled for the winter, the Sound would be empty. Abandoned to the tugs towing barges loaded with sand and gravel.

"The weather held, didn't it." It was a statement, not a question.

"Yes." Betty's gaze was off there somewhere. "A southeast wind all the way, and hardly a cloud in the sky." I knew that her orderly mind found it difficult to accept this breakdown in nature's laws. "And *Old Squaw's* a fine boat," she added at last.

The next day it rained. Poured. The tree tops swayed and thrashed in the heavy southeast wind. Rain dashed against the windows and gutters ran full. But we were home. The timing was perfect. It wasn't our timing. It was somebody else's. *Old Squaw's*? Was she making it all up to us? Silly, silly. But what then? No thrashing to windward, no heavy, frothing seas, no driving rain. No engine trouble! We wondered about it all, could find no reason, and finally ceased to try. The cruise had ended in glory.

fifteen

the bird of hope

It was a Sunday morning in early February. Snow had fallen all the previous day and into the night. Now gray clouds scudded over the chimney tops before a heavy wind. The day before, I had purchased linoleum to lay on the galley counters. I paced the house, wondering whether to go over to the yard and do the job. The boatyard would be deep in snow, lonely, silent.

Betty said stay home. There are little things you can find to do around the house. But I had done "little things" yesterday. I was restless, restless with the weariness of a winter that already seemed endless. Perhaps working on the boat would hasten spring; at least, it might conjure up visions of blue skies, blue waters, and a fair breeze.

I wanted to go. Betty said all right, then I'll go over with you. If you must go, you shouldn't be alone. She seemed concerned. But why? Here the temperature was below freezing. Over in the boatyard the winds of the Sound would only make it worse. No, Betty, I'll go over alone. I shouldn't be gone more than two hours.

I assembled some things, an electric heater, the roll of linoleum, a half-gallon can of adhesive, some tools, and a long coil of electric cord to plug into a yard outlet for light and the heater.

Betty walked me to the door. She *was* concerned. "Are you sure you don't want me to go? I could hold the linoleum, or spread the glue."

"No, I feel a need to do something. But there's no use in both of us freezing." I turned away, then came back a step. "What's bothering you?"

"Nothing, nothing. I just—" It was so tentative.

"Is it that 'jinx' business still?"

"No. Of course not. The sail home convinced me. It's just that—" When Betty couldn't finish sentences, I knew she was upset.

It was about 9:30 when I turned down the steep, short hill to the boatyard in Mamaroneck. A few people were scurrying about, most of them in Sunday clothes. As I unloaded the car the bells in a church tower down the street pealed. It was the only sound except for wind, which rustled loose-fitting canvas that shrouded the boats. Ahead, a cat hurried about her business. She needed a mouse. She and I made the only tracks through the deep snow.

I plugged in the power line and led it through the canvas under which *Old Squaw* huddled. I hooked up a light and the heater. It seemed 20 degrees colder in the cabin. Another day would have been better. But I was here now. The old, crumbling linoleum came up quickly. Cutting the new material to fit properly took much longer. Despite the electric coil, my fingers were almost numb. My feet, too. Once the knife slipped and I nicked my thumb, even through a glove. It bled some and smeared the ivory-colored linoleum. Finally it was cut. It fit all the angles and corners. Not bad.

I read the instructions on the adhesive container. Spread thin, evenly, wait a few moments before applying the covering material. There was a warning. This adhesive should not be exposed to open flames or excessive heat. No flames here. Only excessive cold. I had the heater on the counter three or four feet from the work surface. Everything felt frigid to the touch.

The work went well. I'd be home in another hour. I had spread the adhesive over perhaps half of the surface. Then it happened. WHOOM. Fire exploded in my face. In a flash the surface of the counter was a mass of flame. Something knocked the half-gallon container over. It spilled over more counter surface, dribbled down onto the sole, and caught fire. Now the entire cabin was a roaring inferno. I dove for the companionway ladder, burst out into the cockpit. I threw open the flap in the canvas cover and started down the ladder to the ground, a distance of nine or ten feet. I would race to the nearest house, telephone a fire alarm. But with this wind the whole yard would be aflame in minutes. Flame would leap from canvas cover to cover. The nearest house? Minutes away. And would anyone be home? The Orienta Yacht Club was barred and shuttered for the winter. Phone service would have been canceled. The yard office was tightly secured. No hope there. Where to go, where to go? God! There was a fire extinguisher aboard *Old Squaw*. A large one, just inside the entrance to the cabin. Hanging in a bracket on the wall.

I dashed up the ladder again and in under the canvas cover. Flames and smoke were billowing out of the cabin. In a moment the canvas could burst into flame. The smoke was impenetrable, burning, acrid. Gasping for air, I reached in, yanked the extinguisher off the wall. There was a little wire lock affair on the handle. I wrenched it off and turned the powder substance into the cabin. In moments the fire was out. It was no act of heroism. I just didn't want to have to tell people, "Yes, I burned out the boatyard. A million dollars' worth of boats went up in flames. I'm the fellow who started it all."

Insurance would have covered most of the loss, but there would have been little sailing the next summer for many boating people. Yeah, McCracken. He's the boob who caused it all.

I stood for a moment as the fumes and gases continued to roll out of the cabin. Choking, tears streaming from my eyes. My face felt hot and stiff. But it wasn't quite over yet. The right sleeve and side of my heavy work coat was afire. Flames had caught it as I reached in with the extinguisher. Once again a mad dash for the ladder. Halfway down my foot slipped on a snowy rung and I fell, half standing, to the ground. My ankle hurt as I rolled in the snow. At last the flames were extinguished and I lay there, gasping and choking. There was no question now about that jinx.

Betty had known, or felt, something. A premonition. I rolled over and started to get up, but my ankle hurt. I was sick at my stomach. My lungs hurt. Coughs wrenched early-morning food into the snow. I heard a church bell again, tolling, tolling. Epiphany. Consciousness seemed to take its leave.

Later, I tried to tell Betty about it. Was I awake? Was I dreaming? Conscious? The sun was warm, hot in fact. My face was burned. A story came to mind. Another fire. This time it wasn't a boat burning. There was nothing but sand. A desert?

The flames of the fire climbed into the sky. They burned, then subsided. At last there were only ashes left. Then a beautiful white bird rose from the ashes, rose and circled slowly, gracefully. It was the Phoenix. A bird in a tale out of Egyptian mythology. The Phoenix was said to live 500 years. Then it died in flames, and rose from its ashes.

In my dream, the Phoenix, as it circled lazily in the sky, took the form of a boat. A sloop with white topsides and sails as pristine and pure as the soul of a saint. I propped myself up against a timber, one of the supports for *Old Squaw*'s cradle. We'd sail the sloop, Betty and I would, to Cuttyhunk, Martha's Vineyard, Casco Bay. We'd round Cape Small, sail past Seguin, Damariscove, and bleak Monhegan. Yes, we could find our wings in another sloop, a boat like *Hornpipe*, but without the crippled stem.

I shivered. It was cold there in the snow. But the fire was out. My ankle hurt, but not much. The skin on my face felt tight, stiff. There was nothing now in *Old Squaw*'s cabin worth taking home. The insurance company would do what had to be done. I would call Fred Gade tomorrow. *Old Squaw* belonged in other, more compatible hands.

But now I wanted to go home. Home to my life, my love, my Betty.

Somehow I managed it. I stumbled into the house and flopped in a living-room chair. Betty was doing the *Times* crossword puzzle. She looked up, stared.

"Either you made a fast trip to Florida to pick up a sunburn, or you've been drinking. Your face is scarlet!" She came over and looked closely. "What did you do with your eyebrows? You're burned!"

I was glad she had narrowed it down.

She anointed my face with unguents. While she clucked, I told her about the fire. She thought I was a hero. I told her about the Phoenix. She thought I was hallucinating.

The day passed. We agreed that we should sell *Old Squaw*. We read, listened to music, talked about many things. Neither of us mentioned a jinx. It was too real. We agreed I was lucky to have only superficial burns. Early in the evening the telephone rang. It was Sterling. Could he and Connie drop in?

He thought we might be interested in something he had heard. We were delighted. We needed company, particularly that company.

Betty said she thought it would be better if I didn't mention that odd dream I had about that bird.

I opened the front door. Connie made a motion to kiss me, then backed off. Sterling stuck out his hand. "I heard some news . . . *what happened to you*! You look like a face painted on a red balloon."

I got them drinks and told the long tale of the morning. Amazing. Astonishing. You were lucky. Lucky you didn't burn down the whole boatyard. Good thing you got it out.

"You intend to sell *Old Squaw*?" Sterling asked. We told him we did.

"Good."

Good?

"Right. I know just the boat for you."

We looked at each other. At Connie. At Sterling, who was grinning.

"Yes, the perfect boat." He was looking at the black fireplace. Betty had wanted me to build a fire before they arrived. Nothing doing, I said. One blaze a day was enough.

"She's down in City Island. Belongs to a friend of mine, and he wants to sell her. She's sloop-rigged." He went on to describe her. A 30-footer. New Dacron sails. Mahogany-planked on oak ribs. New engine! Now I wished I had built a fire. It would be nice to look into it and dream.

"She has the same clean lines as *Hornpipe*," Sterling went on. "I've sailed aboard her a couple of times. She's fast and handles beautifully. There's not a soft piece of wood in her."

I could see the New England coast in Betty's eyes. Oh, the compensatory reserves of human nature. The bad times were only a dim memory. The good times, the long days of warm summer, were a knight in shining armor. We talked long into the evening. At last it was time for them to go.

"She's got an odd name," Sterling said, "with a story." He was standing. Now he sat down. Connie knew Sterling. She hadn't even gotten up.

Odd name?

"She's called *The Phoenix*."

"I can see your tonsils, Jim," Connie smiled.

I swallowed and brought my jaw back up from my lap.

"This friend of mine, Bob Emery, wanted a strong name for the boat. He told me *The Phoenix* was a bird of hope and good fortune. It was pure white, like a sloop, I guess." And Sterling sat back and told the myth of the Phoenix.

"Pretty name for a boat, don't you think?" he said at last, then added, "Of course, you can change it if you don't like it."

Betty and I smiled at each other, sharing a secret. We allowed as how it was a beautiful name for a boat. We knew it would be wrong to change it.